Canterbury and Rome: Sister Churches

CANTERBURY AND ROME: SISTER CHURCHES

A Roman Catholic Monk Reflects upon Reunion in Diversity

Robert Hale

Foreword by Alan C. Clark, Bishop of East Anglia

Afterword by A. M. Allchin,
Canon Residentiary of Canterbury Cathedral

Darton, Longman and Todd
London

First published in Great Britain in 1982
by Darton, Longman & Todd Ltd
89 Lillie Road, London SW6 1UD

© Robert Hale 1982

ISBN 0 232 51555 7

British Library Cataloguing in Publication Data

Hale, Robert
   Canterbury and Rome.
   1. Christian union
   I. Title
   262'.72   BX8.2

ISBN 0–232–51555–7

Phototypeset by Input Typesetting Ltd, London SW19 8DR
Printed in Great Britain by
The Anchor Press Ltd
and bound by Wm. Brendon & Son Ltd
both of Tiptree, Essex

To my Camaldolese Benedictine Order, and to the
(Anglican) Order of the Holy Cross,
two sister monastic communities bound together in
covenant;
and to the (Anglican) Church Divinity School of the
Pacific,
and to the Jesuit School of Theology at Berkeley,
two sister academic communities bound together in
the Graduate Theological Union;
and to my Anglican and Roman Catholic friends
and family members.

'Greetings from the children of your elect sister'

(2 John 13)

Contents

Foreword by Bishop Alan C. Clark, Bishop of East Anglia   ix

Acknowledgements   xi

Introduction   1

1 Sister Churches:
The Affirmation of a Model   12

2 A First Response to the Model:
Conversion and Commitment   54

3 Discovering Consanguinity:
The Monastic-Benedictine Spirit of Anglicanism   80

4 A Second Dimension of Consanguinity:
The Lay-Prophetic Current of Anglicanism   105

5 What Then are We to Do?
Some Practical Ways to Live the Model of Sister Churches   145

Conclusion   172

Afterword by Canon A. M. Allchin
Canon Residentiary of Canterbury Cathedral   180

Select Bibliography   182

Index   184

Foreword

From time to time religious leaders seem inspired to say in a few words something the truth of which cannot be either proved or gainsaid. Such words, in the author's judgement, were spoken by Pope Paul VI, on the occasion of the Canonization of the Forty Martyrs of England and Wales, when he said movingly:–

> There will be no seeking to lessen the legitimate prestige and worthy patrimony of piety and usage proper to the Anglican Church when the Roman Catholic Church – this humble 'Servant of the servants of God' – is able to embrace her ever beloved sister in the one authentic Communion of the family of Christ.

The theme of this present book is to unravel the meaning of words formerly reserved to the Orthodox Churches and their relationship with the Roman Catholic Church and now, for the first time, applied to the Anglican Communion. What was Pope Paul VI saying? Was he speaking prophetically, discerning a relationship that had grown out of past divisions and had now reached 'family proportions'? Were they merely loving words of longing – that this would be where our years of healing would lead us at some time in the future?

The answer, in Father Robert Hale's discernment, is that the 'model' of the Church suggested by these words, if strenuously explored, discloses an existing relationship with sometimes startling consequences. Even though estranged, the 'sisters' are intimately united in one family; and the patient investigation of their differences and oppositions is even now opening up the way to a reconciliation in these present times.

Critics may not be slow to question whether one 'model' of the Church is being asked to bear more than it can carry. Analogies can offer so much and no more – and even blind one to the realities of the situation. Nevertheless, this essay is provocative in its conviction that we should interpret the Pope's words as a discernment of the present rather than the future.

The author has ransacked his ecumenical resources, and, in the course of his argument, provides almost a primer in ecumenism by his appeal to the writings and statements of well-known figures in the field of Christian unity. There is an urgency in his effort to bring the reader along with him in building up his conclusion that *now* is the time for reconciliation because of the existing family relationship.

Whether one is convinced by the argument he uses or whether one feels that more is demanded than a sapiential, contemplative approach (such as he advocates), there can be no doubt that he has pointed to valuable and necessary indicators of where we, Anglican and Roman Catholic, now stand. When all the theological homework has been done, the inspiration hidden in his running commentary will be a support of substance to the act of faith that will be demanded when we face one another in an act of enduring reconciliation.

+ Alan C. Clark
Bishop of East Anglia

Acknowledgements

Chapter 3 of this book appeared in a shorter form in the USA in the *American Benedictine Review*, in England in *Christian*, in Italy in *Humanitas* and in Canada in the *Little Paper*.

Biblical quotations made by the author are taken from the Jerusalem Bible, published and © 1966, 1967 and 1968 by Darton, Longman & Todd Ltd, and Doubleday & Co. Inc.

The author wishes to thank particularly Prof. Samuel Garrett for his helpful suggestions, and Bro. Thomas Gower, O.H.C., and Fr. Roy Parker, O.H.C. for proof-reading and helping with the index.

Introduction

What is the real relationship, theologically, between the Roman Catholic Church and the Anglican Communion? Or to express the issue much more concretely: how should the Roman Catholic look upon the Anglican parish church down the road? Is it simply a centre of perhaps well-intentioned but misguided confusion, an unsatisfactory and incomplete attempt at being a real church such as one's own, and so to be studiously avoided? Or is it to be seen as not so well-intentioned, but rather, quite frankly as a fraudulent counterfeit, to be directly opposed insofar as it is seducing people away from the one true (Roman Catholic) Church? Perhaps, with either of these models, it will be looked upon as a reservoir of potential converts, who may (should) be individually approached and proselytized. Or maybe whole groups (the 'high church people') can be convinced to break away and 'come over'. In any case, clearly the question about how that Anglican parish is to be understood by the Roman Catholic is very directly linked up with the way in which that Roman Catholic will behave towards that parish and its members. The theological is tied directly into the pastoral, and vice versa.

There remains at least one other major option, beyond those noted above, regarding how that parish is to be understood: maybe it could be seen as a fellow Christian community (whatever real difficulties remain between the two Churches), an ally and friend in the faith (friends don't always agree on everything), helping in the very urgent business of nourishing Christians spiritually and proclaiming the salvific Word to non-Christians. This is at least

1

logically another possibility, however little this model has been used theologically and pastorally in the last, turbulent four centuries. Perhaps the Anglican parish down the road, and the Roman Catholic church round the corner, are in fact sister churches. In a family there can be an older sister and a younger sister, each with her special role and contribution to make.

But unfortunately sisters can fall out, can come to disagree on the terms of their relationship and on many other things. But sisters do remain sisters, and there is the common flesh and blood, the family life and heritage, which is constantly pulling them back together despite themselves. And indeed the primary step in the reconciliation process will be to remember and acknowledge reciprocally that the two are in fact sisters, that they should begin behaving again as sisters, and not as strangers, or worse, as adversaries.

But is it true that these two parishes are sister churches, not strangers, rivals or adversaries? This basic issue is, of course, quite as real for the Anglican as for the Roman Catholic; how is the 'C of E' member to regard that 'Roman' church two blocks away? The same series of options, however reformulated and renuanced, confront the Anglican.

This basic issue reaches beyond the two parishes in the local community to involve all members of both world-wide communions. It is as much a dilemma and a challenge in Montreal and all of Canada, in Boston and all of the United States, in Melbourne and all of Australia, in Burundi and all of Africa. In fact, the local issue inevitably extends into the universal: what is the real relationship between the Anglican Communion and the Roman Catholic Church as such?

It is to be noted that the issue can no longer be the Roman Catholic attitude just towards *individual* Anglicans (and, vice versa, the Anglican attitude towards individual Roman Catholics). The Roman Catholic, even many years ago, might have been prepared to acknowledge the sincerity, and indeed the deep sanctity, of a George Herbert, for instance; but he might have believed that this sanctity had been attained independent of the fact – or indeed despite the fact – of Herbert's being an Anglican, as an astonishing example of the miraculous efficaciousness of Roman Catholic grace, operative somehow even beyond the visible boundaries of the true

2

Church. But this individualistic approach to the challenge of the obvious virtue and sanctity of separated brethren is seen as no longer satisfactory; if George Herbert was anything, he was Anglican, baptized into Christ by that Church, illumined in the Word by that Church, nourished into the fullness of Christ by that Church. Outside the visible limits of the Roman Catholic Church it is not just individuals but entire 'Churches and Communities' that are given by Christ's Spirit 'significance and importance in the mystery of salvation'[1] as Vatican II already acknowledged years ago. It is these ecclesial communities that 'the Spirit of Christ has not refrained from using as means of salvation,[2] even if Roman Catholics have respectfully to argue a lack of definitive plenitude in the life of these Churches and Communions, until such time as reunion in diversity is achieved (and Roman Catholic theologians will acknowledge a lack of definitive plenitude in their own Church until all Churches are completed by each other through reunion, and by Christ in his Kingdom).[3]

What, then, is the Anglican to think, not just of individual Roman Catholics, but of the Roman Catholic Church as such? And how are Roman Catholics in their turn to view the Anglican Communion? This is not just a kind of 'churchy' concern to fill up the time and attention of people who spend much of their lives in sacristies and at parish teas, and have to talk about something after all. If we take at all seriously the international economic crisis and the widespread misery it is generating, the terrifying proximity of war and nuclear disaster, the 'zero hour' almost upon us, then it becomes very important to know if the two Churches, in their mission to a desperate humanity, can finally work together as sisters, and not just separately (and to that extent, ineffectively), as rivals. Beyond the hunger for a bread that perishes, a world-wide spiritual famine is at its most destructive precisely in our own 'traditionally Christian' Western nations, where neo-paganism, secularism and nihilism seem to be expanding in our own back yards. How will our two Churches preach the Christ who reconciles, if they themselves remain enemies? If they could embrace each other after centuries of rancour, would not that itself bear potent witness to the saving gospel that heals and is able to 'gather together in unity the scattered children of God' (John 11:52)? Roman Catholics and Anglicans alike should ask whether our two

3

Communions are not called to embrace each other again as sister Churches, not because it is a trendy topic for churchy people, but in order 'that the world may believe' (John 17:21).

In his address to the General Synod of the Church of England in 1978, Cardinal Hume affirmed:

> A divided Christianity is a scandal. Our divisions are a stumbling block and diminish the credibility of Christ's message to the world. They impede the spreading of the good news. And there is an urgency about the present situation today. In Britain there is an increased urgency. For here we see in a special manner both man's need for God and society's need for a Christian witness, a prophetic voice that is clear, consistent and courageous.[4]

Quite apart from our mission to others, reunion in diversity is needed urgently for our own salvation. Dr Harry Smythe, former Director of the Anglican Centre in Rome, underlines the great progress made through the official Anglican–Roman Catholic dialogues, and the concomitant obligation of all of us to respond in our lives:

> Issue after issue has been clarified regarding the three major theological problems (Eucharist, ministry, and authority), and the identity of the faith of the two Churches has been acknowledged, in the diversity of forms; but the fundamental problem – to incite a will to unity – remains. No international commission, however eminent its members, can resolve this issue, because it is tied into the problem of sin. Every division is a sin against love, and constitutes the worst of all sins for Christians, for the Love whom they serve has the name of a Person, and He himself has made the mission of his Church depend upon the unity of love of his people. We are called to a spiritual resurrection.[5]

This essay, then, will presuppose, in the words of one Anglican–Roman Catholic Consultation, 'the Gospel priority, injunction, and urgency of ecumenism'.[6] As a specific proposal for the reconciliation of the two Churches, it will argue that the biblical, patristic and medieval model of 'sister Churches' clarifies and illumines important dimensions of the Anglican–Roman Catholic (hereafter 'A/RC') relationship. This model certainly does not exhaust every facet of that relationship; Churches are transcendent mysteries and their profound identities and deep relationships cannot be spelled out by any one model, or indeed any series of models. But it will be argued that, to the extent that the mystery of the A/RC relationship can be articulated theologically in the venture of 'faith seeking understanding', the model of 'sister Churches' remains particularly apt.

This essay, then, is an attempt at an ecumenical theology of the Church, or rather of the Churches (the plural form is the more congenial to the New Testament ecclesiologies, and to much of patristic theology, however strange we find it). Any theology, we recognize with particular clarity today, is going to be conditioned by its method and language.

The scholastic and neo-scholastic approaches, with their Aristotelian categories, their *quaestiones* and *ad primum* dialectic, as well as their endeavour to achieve *summa* exhaustiveness, constituted a certain way of doing theology; a few years ago some Roman Catholics felt that it was the only way. But, after all, Catholic theology had been done before the thirteenth century and its scholastic innovations. Benedictine scholars such as Leclercq and Vagaggini have noted that there is a distinctively pre-scholastic way, which, with Vatican II, has been rediscovered and reaffirmed in the Roman Catholic Church. This method, which Leclercq would term 'monastic' in its specific medieval expression, moves forward 'through the reading of the Bible and the Fathers within the liturgical framework'.[7] And in a particular patristic-medieval development of this method the important word is no longer *quaeritur* but *desideratur*.[8] Its aim, as Vagaggini notes, is not just 'conceptual knowledge' but 'a whole commitment, involving affections, will, intuition, and eventually, very concrete attitudes, methods of acting' in this 'wisdom model' of 'biblical-patristic-medieval theology.'[9] The result is an experiential knowledge which ideally flows into spirituality and religion, and directly calls out 'purification, both preparatory and concomitant', leading on to 'calm, harmony and thanksgiving'.[10] This biblical-patristic-medieval approach will find concrete models of more help than abstract categories for penetrating into a deeper, more religious understanding.[11] Vatican II, with its insistence on the centrality of liturgy, the importance

5

of the Word of God as 'the soul of sacred theology',[12] has renewed this general theological approach in the Roman Catholic Church.

A similar approach has always marked Anglican theology. Dr Michael Ramsey, in an early essay on 'What is Anglican Theology?', written while he was still Professor of Divinity in the University of Durham, sketches an Anglican method of theologizing that quite resembles what Vagaggini and Leclercq are describing. Ramsey also rejects any scholastic pretensions to monopolize the theological venture (the neo-Thomist revival was in full swing in the Roman Catholic Church of the time), and this in the name of the scriptural foundations of theology:

> The *bona fide* Anglican can never suffer the Latin scholastics to dominate the theology of his Church. This refusal need not involve a deprecation of what the scholastics can do in the field of Christian philosophy. But the refusal must be made, because the scholastic would substitute other categories than those of the Bible at the very heart of theology, where the Anglican believes that only the Biblical categories can rule.[13]

In the name of Anglicanism Ramsey rejects, however, any fundamentalism or biblicism that would isolate the Scripture, treating it 'as a self-contained law'; rather, 'Scripture needs interpreting with the aid of the tradition of the Church as the witness and keeper of holy writ.'[14] 'The study of the ancient Fathers'[15] is therefore important, to be done like all theology within 'the living tradition of the Church'.[16] The privileged moment of this living context is that of worship: 'Though the form without the Spirit is dead, it is through His use of the form – in creed, sacrament, order, liturgy – that the Spirit preserves the true salt of Christian life in its union with the objectivity of Gospel and Church.[17] This biblical-liturgical-patristic theology will also want to 'appeal to Christian experience. This appeal will put the utmost emphasis upon the inward experience of Christians and its moral fruits.'[18]

This 'mode and spirit'[19] of doing theology, 'neither a system nor a confession . . . but a method, a use and a direction',[20] is both traditional and prophetic. Furthermore, it is virtually interchangeable, at least in its broad strokes, with what Leclercq and Vagaggini have sketched as a biblical-patristic-medieval method in the Roman Catholic tradition. Such a startling convergence opens up new possibilities for dialogue; for if we are finally 'speaking the same language', that of the sources we share, our conclusions will very possibly not be too discordant. If the ARCIC consultations have borne such fruit in the agreed statements, surely much of the credit goes to the initial methodology; Pope Paul VI and Archbishop Ramsey, in their Common Declaration of March 1966, announced the establishment of the Consultation 'founded on the gospels and on the ancient common traditions'.[21] The very first paragraph of the Agreed Statement on Eucharistic Doctrine affirms the members' endeavour to understand the eucharist in a manner 'which is consonant with biblical teaching and with the tradition of our common inheritance'.[22] This approach constituted a kind of Copernican revolution ecumenically; for, as a member of the Consultation has noted, previously 'both Communions developed an understanding of these points of their faith in contradistinction to each other and formulated their understanding, at times in polemical terms aimed against the position which the other espoused'.[23] But the new dialogue 'is based on the tradition which both the Roman and Anglican communions share';[24] certainly we must seek to assimilate 'the insights and concerns of the sixteenth century' and later developments of the separated Churches, and we must avoid a mere 'exercise in archaic theology'.[25] But it is the rediscovery of our common biblical-liturgical-patristic-monastic heritage that can render our new dialogue 'so contemporary'.[26]

It is characteristic of medieval, patristic and especially biblical theology, as we have noted, to use not just abstract, technical terms, but 'all kinds of pictures, images, metaphors, models',[27] categories directly linked 'to the world of experience'.[28] There is a special propensity to affirm God and his Church 'in terms of phrases which spread from, and presuppose a family model'.[29] Thus God is described by concrete family models such as father (cf. Jer. 3:19, etc.), but also as mother (Deut. 32:18; Isa. 66:13, etc.), as well as bridegroom and husband (Hos. 2:16, etc.).[30] There is something about the depth and the primordial intensity of interpersonal family relations that particularly recommends that cluster of models to biblical-patristic-monastic theology. The model of *sister* Churches to be analysed in this essay presupposes an entire context of familial theology and spirituality.

If such models drawn from the family are charged with a profound and illuminating vitality absent from abstract, metaphysical categories, they work according to their own special logic, which is neither Aristotelian nor mathematical. As Ian Ramsey emphatically insisted, disclosure models are not photographs reproducing to scale every aspect of the reality they illumine; thus they are not to be forced in a literalistic or anthropomorphic way beyond the strict limits of their intentions. The Scriptures want us to affirm God as our Father; but we are not then to ask whom God married, when and where, who our grandparents are, and other such related issues that the 'father' model would normally open up to enquiry. The model in religious language does not deal with such matters, but points rather to something mysteriously true about God: that in a profound way to which abstract terms cannot do justice, he is life-giver, nurturer and protector. God can be father and also mother and bridegroom, precisely because the three models are pointing to transcendent dimensions of the divine mystery quite beyond the earthly level where a father cannot be a mother. Models point beyond themselves to Mystery, and if they illumine some little aspect of the ineffable, they also remind us of their own built-in limits of articulation; abstract categories are not always as obvious regarding their own limits, and so can be more misleading.

Any treatment of Anglicanism should be aware of the centrality of Mystery to that ecclesial experience. In his essay on 'The Spirit of Anglicanism' Paul Elmer More affirms that, 'if there is any outstanding note of the English temper it is a humility and awe before the divine mysteries of faith and a recognition of the incompetence of language to define the ultimate paradox of experience'.[31] Thus if we treat here of the two Churches as 'sisters', it is not to offer the definitive and exhaustive articulation of the relationship, but to remind ourselves of the depths of the mystery, of how much else has to be said, and how much can never be said. Canon Allchin refers to a basic theme which runs through his writings: 'that sense of the mystery of things' which requires 'an attitude of humility and respect' before 'the deep things of man', and the complementary 'attitude of humility and worship before the deep things of God'.[32] The human person and his relationships are mysteries, and they are the deepest image of the mystery of the Triune God.[33]

If the model method underlines Mystery, it must also favour pluralism; one model is never enough to exhaust the transcendent,

8

so that it inevitably evokes other, complementary models. Having said that Christ is king, we hasten to add that he is suffering servant; describing him as shepherd, we add that he is lamb. So also in the area of ecclesiology, the Scriptures and Fathers amass a great variety of images: flock, temple, bride, body, vine, friend, etc. When therefore in this essay we take sisterhood as the key model in ecumenical ecclesiology, we do not suppose that it will say everything about the A/RC relationship. Fortunately there is no presumption to say everything here; the ARCIC Agreed Statements, the body of A/RC documents of the British, US and other national consultations, a whole series of doctrinal, theological and historical studies have already explored many facets and aspects of the A/RC relationship. So, with gratitude for the work already undertaken, we shall seek to focus on the one relational model of sisterhood which seems to us particularly fecund.

That model of itself proposes the theme of unity, but at the same time insists on diversity: sisters are bound by consanguinity into one family experience, but on the other hand sisters are rarely identical twins. Indeed, precisely to the extent that her love is authentic, a sister will glory in the uniqueness and difference of the other. That interpersonal relationship is one in which union differentiates. All this is of critical importance, for as John Macquarrie has noted, true ecumenism is quite as committed to furthering authentic diversity as it is to promoting true unity, because 'only unity and diversity together can be useful'.[34] Paul VI, in making his own the prophetic formula of Dom Beauduin at Malines – 'reunion, not absorption' – has formally affirmed the same principle regarding Anglican/Roman Catholic reunion.[35] This book, in proposing the theme of sister Churches, seeks to affirm and explore in a concrete way that unity in diversity which our two Churches are seeking, in response to Christ's prayer for unity and his commandment to love.

Notes

1 Vatican II, Decree on Ecumenism, I, n.3.
2 ibid.
3 See Avery Dulles, S. J., *Models of the Church* (Image Books, New York, 1978), pp. 156, 165: 'Let it be granted, then, that non-Roman

Catholic churches are imperfect realizations of the sacrament of the Church. . . . But the Roman Catholic who makes this statement must be on his guard against assuming too hastily that his own church is in all respects perfect. . . . The Roman Catholic Church, like other communions, is always subject to improvement as a symbolic embodiment of the Church of Christ . . . no empirical church can absolutely identify itself with the Church of Christ . . . the Church will attain its full perfection only in the glory of heaven.'

4 Cardinal Hume, Address to the General Synod of the Church of England, February 1, 1978; the entire text is given in *Documents on Anglican/Roman Catholic Relations*, IV (United States Catholic Conference, Washington, 1979), pp. 85–94; for an Anglican commentary on the Archbishop's comments, see the *Church Times* (February 3, 1978),pp. 1, 5.

5 Dr Harry Smythe, 'Il dialogo Anglicano-Cattolico Romano: tre importanti accordi', in *La Comunione Anglicana* (Camaldoli: Quaderni di Camaldoli n. 17, 1978), pp. 33–4.

6 'The Ecumenical Vocation of Religious in Sister Churches: Agreed Statement of the Anglican/Roman Catholic Consultation on the Religious Life' (New York, March 1981), p. 1 n. 3.

7 Jean Leclercq, O.S.B., *The Love of Learning and the Desire for God: A Study of Monastic Culture* (Fordham University Press, New York, 1974), p. 3.

8 Cyprian Vagaggini, O.S.B., 'Teologia' in *Nuovo Dizionario di Teologia* (Edizioni Paoline, Rome, 1977), p. 1609. Vagaggini, member of the International Theological Commission, and formerly Rector of the Pontifical Benedictine College, is a Camaldolese monk; this essay on theology, 117 pages long, documents the rich diversity in theological forms and methods.

9 ibid.

10 ibid., p. 1610. Its suitability for ecumenical reflection is therefore evident.

11 See Ian T. Ramsey, 'The Logical Structure of Religious Language: Models and Disclosures' in Ian T. Ramsey, ed., *Words about God* (SCM Press, London, 1971),pp. 203–23. See also Robert Hale, O.S.B., 'Religious Symbols as Evocative of Insight' in *Symbolisme et Théologie, Sacramentum* 2 (Studia Anselmiana, Rome, 1974), pp. 71–90.

12 Vatican II, Dogmatic Constitution on Divine Revelation, VI, n. 24.

13 A. M. Ramsey, 'What is Anglican Theology?' in *Theology* 48 (Jan. 1945), p. 5.

14 ibid., pp. 2–3.

15 ibid., p. 3.

16 ibid., p. 5.

17 ibid., pp. 5–6.

18 ibid., p. 5.

19 ibid.

20 ibid., p. 2.

21 Pope Paul VI and Archbishop Ramsey, Common Declaration, March

24, 1966; the complete text is given in Alan C. Clark and Colin Davey, ed., *Anglican/Roman Catholic Dialogue: The Work of the Preparatory Commission* (Oxford University Press 1974),pp. 1–4.

22 *Agreed Statement on Eucharistic Doctrine*, September 1971, n. 1.

23 Herbert J. Ryan, S. J., 'Commentary on the Anglican-Roman Catholic Agreed Statement on Eucharistic Doctrine' in *Documents on Anglican/ Roman Catholic Relations*, II (United States Catholic Conference, Washington, 1973),p. 2.

24 ibid.

25 ibid.

26 ibid.

27 Ian T. Ramsey, op. cit., p. 202.

28 ibid., p. 205.

29 ibid., p. 203.

30 ibid.

31 Paul Elmer More, 'The Spirit of Anglicanism' in *Anglicanism: The Thought and Practice of the Church of England, Illustrated from the Religious Literature of the Seventeenth Century* (SPCK 1962),p. xxxvii.

32 A. M. Allchin, *The World is a Wedding: Explorations in Christian Spirituality* (Darton, Longman and Todd 1978), p. 13.

33 Thus personal finite transcendence is the supreme model of divine personal transcendence, and human interpersonal love the chief icon of inter-Trinitarian love; see Gordon Kaufman, 'Two Models of Transcendence: An Inquiry into the Problems of Theological Meaning', in *The Heritage of Christian Thought: Essays in Honour of Robert L. Calhoun* (Harper, New York, 1965), pp. 182–96. See also Ewert Cousins, 'A Theology of Interpersonal Relations: Richard of St Victor' in *Thought* 176 (Spring 1970),pp. 56–82.

34 John Macquarrie, *Christian Unity and Christian Diversity* (Westminster Press, Philadelphia, 1975), p. 7.

35 See Paul VI, Discourse to Archbishop Coggan, April 29, 1977, in *L'Osservatore Romano* (April 29, 1977), p. 1: 'The history of relations between the Catholic Church and the Anglican Communion has been marked by the staunch witness of such men as Charles Brent, Lord Halifax, William Temple and George Bell among the Anglicans; and Abbé Portal, Dom Lambert Beauduin, Cardinal Mercier and Cardinal Bea among the Roman Catholics. The pace of this movement has quickened marvellously in recent years, so that these words of hope, "the Anglican Church united not absorbed" are no longer a mere dream.' For the history of the phrase itself, see S. A. Quitslund, 'United not Absorbed' in *Journal of Ecumenical Studies* 8 (Spring 1971), pp. 255–85.

Sister Churches: The Affirmation of a Model

Pope Paul VI

The words and actions of Pope Paul VI in relation to the Anglican Communion remain of particular significance, for he was the most informed Pope in history in the area of Anglicanism. The Rev Owen Chadwick, Anglican ecumenist and Professor of Ecclesiastical History at Cambridge, has written of a very early initiative of Archbishop Fisher in sending Leonard Prestige, shortly to be Canon of St Paul's Cathedral, to Rome in 1949 to explore the ecumenical climate. Prestige's friend Gregory Dix, the famous liturgist and Anglican Benedictine monk of Nashdom, 'greatly admired the pro-secretary of state, Monsignor Montini, partly because he believed him to be a very holy and good person . . . and partly because he knew him to have a real understanding of the Church of England. He advised Prestige that he must see Montini.'[1] Thus Montini was known to be informed on the subject of Anglicanism in 1949, fourteen years before his accession to the Papacy. Prestige had prepared a memorandum suggesting a dialogue; Chadwick notes his programme:

1. to use every opportunity of promoting friendly relations;
2. to encourage full co-operation between scholars;
3. to promote conferences for the exchange of information;
4. to attempt to find a common policy on practical issues;
5. to discourage by authority all expressions of ill-will.[2]

If we recall the attack on the early ecumenical movement by Pius XI in his encyclical *Mortalium animos* (1927), we can understand how Prestige's memorandum, which seems so moderate in its proposals today, appeared rather radical and dangerous to Roman circles of his time. 'This memorandum', Chadwick notes, 'he gave to Monsignor Montini, whom he saw for twenty minutes, and with whom he was profoundly impressed.'[3] Bernard and Margaret Pawley, in their important history of Anglican/Roman Catholic relations, note that 'Prestige records that Montini was clearly anxious for contacts on these lines to begin and to continue.'[4] Montini was thus already at work in 1949 for the reversal of four centuries of hostilities between the two Churches.

Montini was made Archbishop of Milan, and in 1955 received a visit from the great Anglican ecumenist, Bishop George Bell; the Pawleys note that 'each took an immediate liking to the other'.[5] They also record Bell's reflections on the meeting: 'I was never more impressed, even by my friends among catholic bishops in the north of Europe, than by that man's desire to learn.'[6] The opportunity for a more ample exchange of information was soon to be provided. In the following year (1956) 'Archbishop Montini received at Milan a delegation (arranged by Bishop Bell) of four Anglican priests and a layman who stayed with him some ten days.'[7] Finally, a real contact had been made at a high level between the two Churches in Italy itself, and the occasion was not just a formality: 'The object . . . was the exchange of basic information. The group showed books and photographs and answered endless questions. The Archbishop was clearly trying to build up for himself a picture of other Christians on a basis of what they said about themselves.'[8] Chadwick writes of the intensity of this encounter, and of the depth of the understanding of Anglicanism which they initiated:

> Pope Paul VI, during the years when he was Monsignor Montini, had taken a close interest in the Anglicans. He was learned in the study of St Anselm of Canterbury, and felt devotion towards that archbishop. In 1956 . . . he asked Bishop George Bell to send him some Anglicans . . . [they] accompanied him on his daily work. When he visited or confirmed, he would ask, how do Anglican bishops do this? What is the custom in the Church

13

of England? It is an understatement to say that this Pope knew more than any other Pope about the Church of England. He was the only Pope who had given the necessary time and trouble to understanding the Church of England.[9]

These encounters offer the context for understanding the Pope's later commitment to ecumenism in general, and to the Anglican Communion in particular. It would be beyond the scope of this study to note the Pope's role in the Council, in its ecumenically significant work, and especially in the formulation of the Decree on Ecumenism.[10] But this very significant background must be borne in mind as we consider the key affirmations of the Pope in 1970 at the Canonization of the Forty Martyrs of England and Wales.

The immediate occasion did not augur well; it had been under an Anglican English sovereign that the saints had been martyred, and so the ceremony might have assumed, explicitly or implicitly, quite an anti-Anglican thrust. In the past, how many similar commemorations in Great Britain and on the continent, whether of Roman Catholics or Anglicans or Protestants, had inflamed the spirit of Christian rancour and intolerance? How amazing then that precisely within the context of such a celebration, some of the most fruitful affirmations for western ecumenism yet expressed were authoritatively pronounced.

In the course of his address the Pope welcomed the Anglican representatives, official and unofficial, present at the Canonization:

While we are particularly pleased to note the presence of the official representative of the Archbishop of Canterbury, the Rev Dr Harry Smythe, we also extend our respectful and affectionate greeting to all members of the Anglican Church who have likewise come to take part in this ceremony. We indeed feel very close to them. We would like them to read in our heart the humility, gratitude and hope with which we welcome them.[11]

These words cut through the splendour of the setting and occasion (for pomp there is nothing quite like a Canonization liturgy in St Peter's) and establish an evangelical spirit of humility, hospitality and love. The tragic context of the deaths of the forty martyrs would have proved, for any other spirit, an insuperable obstacle

14

for ecumenical encounter; but this Pope committed their very deaths to the cause of Anglican-Roman Catholic reconciliation in a startling Gospel-like reversal of the logic of the world:

> May the blood of these martyrs be able to heal the great wound inflicted upon God's Church by reason of the separation of the Anglican Church from the Catholic Church. . . . Is it not one – these martyrs say to us – the Church founded by Christ? Is not this their witness? Their devotion to their nation gives us the assurance that on the day when – God willing – the unity of the faith and of Christian life is restored, no offence will be inflicted on the honour or the sovereignty of a great country such as England.[12]

The Pope wished to stress that these martyrs were models also because of their 'loyal respect for the sovereignty of civil society'.[13] In the complicated tangle of causes of the separation of the two Churches, the political component loomed very large; English sovereigns had been combatting what they felt to be an unjust political interference by the Papacy into sovereign affairs (certainly not the first time such a complaint was heard emanating from a European royal palace). Thus a very substantial part of the 'Elizabethan Settlement' was constituted by the 'Act of Supremacy' which abolished the political jurisdiction in England of any 'foreign prince, person, prelate, state or potentate, spiritual or temporal', and imposed an oath upon all officials acknowledging Elizabeth 'not as "supreme head" but as "supreme governor" of both Church and State'.[14] It was to this whole knot of issues that Pope Paul VI spoke in his address, not in terms of hurling excommunications at sovereigns and fulminating about the supreme authority of the Pope, but rather in a spirit of 'loyal respect for the sovereignty of civil society' with gentle assurances that when the two Churches were reunited 'no offence will be inflicted on the honour or the sovereignty' of England. Here is consummate ecumenism, which confronts directly a thorny issue of division, but in such a Christianly irenic manner as to disarm it of its destructive explosiveness. The state visit of Queen Elizabeth II to Pope John Paul II and the Vatican in October 1980 was an outgrowth of this reconciling gesture of Paul VI, and carried it forward even further.[15]

But if Pope Paul VI dealt directly with the 'political' component of the separation, it was especially the spiritual and ecclesial which he wished to address; and his bold and assuring words certainly constituted a turning point for the two Communions:

> There will be no seeking to lessen the legitimate prestige and the worthy patrimony of piety and usage proper to the Anglican Church when the Roman Catholic Church – this humble 'Servant of the servants of God' – is able to embrace her ever beloved sister in the one authentic Communion of the family of Christ: a communion of origin and of faith, a communion of priesthood and of rule, a communion of the saints in the freedom of love of the spirit of Jesus. Perhaps we shall have to go on, waiting and watching in prayer, in order to deserve that blessed day. But already we are strengthened in this hope by the heavenly friend- ship of the forty martyrs of England and Wales who are can- onized today.[16]

The passage deserves to be analysed clause by clause; although space does not allow the exhaustive study that would be desirable, we should certainly note some principal affirmations of the state- ment. The Pope, with over two decades of first-hand experience of Anglicanism, and all the labours of Vatican II behind him, knew very well what he was saying and why he wanted to say it. We should note in particular how explicitly he acknowledged the 'legit- imate prestige and the worthy patrimony of piety and usage' of the Anglican Communion as such (and not just of individual Angli- cans). Such a distinct identity and heritage constitute a Church, and also ground its right to a distinctive place in the eventual communion of Churches which is the objective of the ecumenical movement; 'reunion, not absorption' must be the operative formula towards historical Churches possessed of their own 'worthy patri- mony of piety and usage'.

It is also notable that Paul VI explicitly invoked Gregory the Great's splendid title for the Roman Pontiff: 'servant of the ser- vants', a title which can only be understood in the context of Gregory's quarrel over the title of 'oecumenical' or 'universal' which the Patriarch of Constantinope wished to assume. The great medieval scholar Paul Meyvaert notes in connection with Gregory's understanding of Rome and the other Churches:

The fundamental motive in Gregory's attitude . . . can be summarized thus: no one except Christ and the Church has the right to be called Universal, because all bishops are equal having the same power of orders and because if one of them is called 'universal', the *raison d'être* of all the others would cease to exist. . . . Thus the Catholic Universal Church consisted of a plurality or diversity of Churches, none of which could lay claim to a monopoly. . . To understand Gregory's views on the nature of [the Pope's] primacy, it is essential to bear in mind his concept of authority. . . . Authority always lay heavily on his shoulders . . . how well he realized the dangers inherent in wielding authority . . . the temptations to pride, to thinking oneself above others. This only served to make him more keenly aware of the need for humility. It also pushed him to develop the whole concept of authority in terms of 'service'. When viewed thus authority became acceptable to him because it fitted within the framework of unifying charity.[17]

Paul VI's reference to 'this humble "Servant of the servants of God" ' thus sets his own role in the context of Gregory's 'diversity within unity' ecclesiology which affirms 'a multiplicity of churches, distributed like the *regiones terrae* over the face of the earth, all united together in the bond of a common faith and charity'.[18] This vision of unity in diversity and of authority as service of Gregory, who certainly has a special significance for the Church in England,[19] creates a particularly fruitful context for the Anglican/Roman Catholic dialogue. It is in that spirit that Paul VI continued, speaking of that awaited moment when the Roman Church will be 'able to embrace her ever beloved sister'; this was an historic utterance and an ecumenical breakthrough. For it was the first time, certainly since the Reformation, that the Roman Church at such an authoritative level had applied the 'sister' model to another Church in the West, reserved up to that time to the Eastern Churches. It cast an entirely fresh light on the relationship of the Anglican and Roman Catholic Communions. Both Churches are still working out its implications.

There was, however, in the Pope's remarks, a 'not yet' dimension: the embrace of final reconciliation has not yet come; the full 'communion of origin and of faith . . . of priesthood and of rule' has not yet been achieved. Paul VI was not papering over the real problems that remained, nor minimizing the tremendous work that still needed to be done. And yet there was also an 'already' dimension to his words: 'Already we are strengthened in this hope' he affirmed. He specified too that key title of 'sister' with the decisive qualifier of 'ever beloved': 'When the Roman Catholic Church . . . is able to embrace her *ever beloved sister*. . .'. Ian Ramsey, in his analysis of models in religious and theological discourse, has noted the key importance of 'qualifiers'; God is not just Father but *eternal and loving* Father; reception of the eucharistic gifts is *holy* communion; the word preached is a *saving* and *efficacious* word. So the Anglican Communion is for the Roman Catholic Church '*her ever beloved* sister'. Each qualifier needs to be pondered here in its full significance: '*her* sister', for there can be a kind of abstract brotherhood or sisterhood that remains merely rhetorical. Or someone can be a sister of an enemy or a stranger, and the significance of that to oneself is negligible or even negative. But to say, 'You are my sister' is to make an existential commitment of the deepest sort. A sister can be hated or ignored, but we know that sisters should not be treated thus, that there is but one true human and Christian attitude towards a sister, and Paul VI committed himself to it in his words, '*beloved* sister'. This profound relationship is not to come into being in some uncertain future, if and when various conditions are met; Paul VI courageously affirmed, and with obvious joy and thankfulness, the 'already' and 'given' nature of the relationship in his words '*ever* beloved sister'.

In the light of this key affirmation of the two Churches, it would be fruitful to reconsider the various statements of Paul VI in his important encounter with Archbishop Ramsey, in March of 1966, and with Archbishop Coggan, in April of 1978. These important statements have been extensively analysed in church reviews and theological journals, but two sets of *gestures* or *symbolic actions* have not received the attention they deserve. This is no doubt because written texts and spoken addresses are more readily analysed by journalists and theologians, who are more at home with words. But the deepest roots of our faith are implanted in sacred *actions*: incarnation, crucifixion, resurrection. Some of the key moments of Scripture (the embrace of father and prodigal son, Christ's washing of the disciples' feet) go quite beyond the merely verbal, as do key moments of liturgy, of pastoral work, of human and Christian love. Thus, in considering the theme of sister Churches which Pope Paul VI affirmed, we must look not only at what he said, but at what he *did*.

It is important to see a symbolic gesture in its context, if we are to understand its full significance. So in what capacity was Archbishop Ramsey welcomed to the Vatican? Certainly not just as a private individual. The official publication of the Jesuits in Italy, *La Civiltà Cattolica*, known to be very close indeed to the mind of the Vatican, stressed the significance of the visit in the following words:

> The first point to be underlined is that Dr Ramsey has come not only as the Primate of the Church of England, but also as president of the Lambeth Conference, which every ten years gathers all the bishops of the Anglican Communion . . . in the intervals between one Conference and another, work is carried on by a committee composed of the Archbishop of Canterbury and of the Primates. . . . This Conference is the concrete expression of the solidarity and the unity of the Anglican Communion, disseminated today into all continents. . . . Archbishop Ramsey, moreover, has come to Rome not just as the most eminent personage of the Church of England . . . he has visited the Pope also as president of the worldwide anglican Communion. This particular fact is important not only for understanding the significance of the visit in itself but also for grasping the effects that the conversations between the Pope and the Archbishop will be able to have on the relations of Christians in various parts of the world. Wherever Catholics and Anglicans live side by side, a new thrust will be able to be given to their action of mutual comprehension and co-operation.[20]

This official interpretation of the significance of the Archbishop's visit provides the context for understanding the importance of Paul VI's symbolic gestures on the last day of the visit. It should also be noted that the article was published *after* the visit, thus validating and confirming everything that did in fact happen; there were no 'second thoughts' afterwards.

On the morning of March 24, in the Basilica of St Paul outside the Walls (where John XXIII had announced the Council), the

Pope and the Archbishop took part in an ecumenical service of worship at which large numbers of the faithful from the various Roman Catholic parishes, and from the two Anglican parishes in Rome, took part. Their Common Declaration was read; and, as the Roman Catholic ecumenical journal *One in Christ* reports, 'also noteworthy is the fact that the Pope invited the Archbishop to give a blessing with him after the reading of the Common Declaration.'[21] The Archbishop did, in fact, humbly decline, but the invitation had been made, and it serves as a significant precedent for future joint blessings.

Outside the Basilica, 'in one of those significant gestures of his'[22] the Pope did something which astonished the Archbishop and those in the immediate vicinity aware of it. The gesture might have been hushed up afterwards, to remain a personal but confidential tribute of the Pope to Archbishop Ramsey, but the Pope willed it to be a public action, and the official press declared it openly. We may follow the *Civiltà Cattolica* account, itself quoting the official Vatican paper, to understand the remarkable spirit and significance of the gesture:

At the end of the reading of the Common Declaration, the Pope and the Archbishop embraced, exchanging the parchments just signed. At the doors of the basilica they were very warmly applauded by the congregation and by the crowd gathered outside. The two were about to depart when there occurred an episode which *L'Osservatore Romano* thus described: 'At the doors of the basilica, before descending, the Supreme Pontiff did something that was unforeseen and of highest significance *[di altissimo significato]*: he took his ring off his ring finger and placed it himself on the finger of His Grace Archbishop Ramsey. It is a personal precious ring, of particular significance to the Holy Father, which he wished to give to the Archbishop at the conclusion of the community celebration, as a lofty and symbolic remembrance of his visit and as a sign of the esteem and friendship felt for the distinguished Anglican prelate. This friendly gesture of Paul VI was not lost upon those who in that moment were surrounding the two protagonists of the memorable celebration, so that a true ovation arose from those present.'[23]

The ring was, in fact, given the Pope 'by the people of Milan when he was Archbishop there, and a treasured personal possession'.[24]

What is the significance of this concrete and simple, yet very moving, symbolic gesture? Such actions communicate at a level deeper than words; we can only try to articulate some aspects of the event. First, it should be noted that the gesture takes the form of a *gift*, a personal gift that cost the Pope something. The action is thus not merely formal in character, but specifically interpersonal, human and Christian – for Christianity has to do with self-giving. Then, the recipient: it was the man who received the ring, but not as a mere individual. The Archbishop was there as head of the Church of England, head of the Lambeth Conference, head of the Anglican Communion. The gift was made at a great moment in ecumenical history, for the Common Declaration had just been signed and solemnly read:

> In this city of Rome, from which St Augustine was sent by St Gregory to England and there founded the cathedral of Canterbury, towards which the eyes of all Anglicans now turn as the centre of their Christian Communion, His Holiness Pope Paul VI and His Grace Michael Ramsey, Archbishop of Canterbury, representing the Anglican Communion, have met to exchange fraternal greetings . . . they declare that, with His help, they wish to leave in the hands of the God of mercy all that in the past has been opposed to this precept of charity . . . and 'reaching forth unto those things which are before. . .'[25]

The context was thus an intensively moving historical moment, and was also a liturgical one. The gift itself, an archepiscopal ring, placed by the Pope on the Archbishop's finger, has its own obvious significance. The episcopal ring has a tradition of at least ten centuries, and in the Roman Catholic Church only a Bishop, Archbishop, Cardinal or Pope may wear it at all functions, liturgical or otherwise.[26] This gesture was thus indeed of 'highest significance'; Rome had publicly given to Canterbury an archiepiscopal ring, certainly a most profound way of affirming the Anglican Communion as 'ever beloved sister'.

Another significant form of religious symbolism inserted by Paul VI into the A/RC relationship was that of the joint blessing. What is the significance of the blessing in the life of the Church? J. R.

21

Quinn, a Roman Catholic liturgical theologian, notes that, 'the chief sacramental actions of the Church next to the sacraments themselves are the blessings'.[27] Blessings are closely related to the central moment of Christian existence: 'As sacramentals they are sacred signs that, through her impetration, dispose men for the grace of the Sacraments and render holy various occasions in life.'[28] We have noted how Pope Paul invited Archbishop Ramsey to bestow with him the solemn blessing at the conclusion of the ecumenical liturgy in St Paul's. It is of particular significance that the Common Declaration, which had just been read, concludes with a joint blessing and invocation of reconciliation for the Churches, and peace for all of humanity. The text deserves attention:

> His Holiness the Pope and His Grace the Archbishop . . . are of one mind in their determination to promote responsible contacts between their Communions in all those spheres of Church life where collaboration is likely to lead to a greater understanding and a deeper charity, and to strive in common to find solutions for all the great problems that face those who believe in Christ in the world of today. Through such collaboration, by the grace of God the Father and in the light of the Holy Spirit, may the prayer of Our Lord Jesus Christ for unity among His disciples be brought nearer to fulfilment, and with progress towards unity may there be a strengthening of peace in the world, the peace that only He can grant Who gives 'the peace that passeth all understanding', together with the blessing of Almighty God, Father, Son and Holy Spirit, that it may abide with all men for ever.

> +Michael Cantuariensis   Paulus PP. VI[29]

It is often stressed by ecumenical theologians that the reunion of the Churches will not be achieved primarily by human negotiations and cleverness, but will happen as the mysterious gift implored from and bestowed by the Father in the reconciling Spirit of His Son; ecumenical efforts should therefore always terminate in worship, imploration, and invocation of His blessing. But who is to invoke the blessing? The Churches through their leaders. When they are able to do this together in solemn ecumenical commitment,

22

it is a sacramental sign that the unity in diversity of sister Churches which is being prayed for in fulness has already been achieved to a significant extent.

This sacramental sign of joint blessing found fuller expression during the visit, some eleven years later, of Archbishop Coggan to Paul VI. The ecumenical liturgy was celebrated in the Sistine Chapel, which, as site of the solemn election of the Popes, holds a particular significance for the Roman Communion. Michelangelo's ceiling panels of salvation history, and his dramatic giant fresco of the Last Judgement which dominates the front altar, provide a particularly intense and profound context. The *Civiltà Cattolica* briefly but effectively recalls the ecumenical liturgy:

> At 11 a.m. on April 29, in the presence of 29 cardinals, a dozen archbishops and bishops, the diplomatic corps accredited to the Holy See, and numerous other guests, a solemn celebration of the Word was held in the Sistine Chapel, with chants in English and Latin (the *Veni Sancte Spiritus*; the *Credo*; the *Pater noster*; the *Sanctus*), and prayers. The service culminated in the embrace of peace between the Pope and Archbishop Coggan and in the solemn blessing bestowed together upon those present.[30]

The chronicle of the journal goes on to cite the addresses of the Pope and Archbishop at the liturgy, making no further comment about the joint blessing, as though it were now the most natural thing in the world for an Anglican prelate to offer a blessing in the Sistine Chapel to 29 Cardinals, numerous Roman Catholic Archbishops and Bishops, and other guests. Such a liturgical event would have been absolutely unthinkable a few decades earlier. It is helpful to remember the extraordinary conditions prescribed for the first visit of an Anglican Archbishop, that of Dr Geoffrey Fisher, to Pope John XXIII in 1959. That visit was considered then an extraordinary ecumenical breakthrough, although there were no public and solemn joint blessings of Cardinals and Archbishops:

> Cardinal Tardini had laid down four conditions for the Archbishop's visit and sent them to HM Minister to the Holy See, Sir Peter Scarlett. They were that there should be no photographs of the Archbishop with the Pope, that the Archbishop was not to see Cardinal Bea, that there was to be no press release after

the visit, and that the Minister was not to invite any Vatican official to meet the Archbishop at his house.[31]

It is remarkable that just eighteen years later Archbishop Coggan was publicly celebrating an ecumenical liturgy in Rome, not just as guest in the Vatican, but also as host, in St Paul's Episcopal Church on the Via Nazionale. At a Festival Evensong, the splendidly sculpted Doors for Christian Unity were solemnly dedicated; there was a joint blessing of all present by Archbishop Coggan and Cardinal Willebrands, head of the Secretariat for Christian Unity. The *Osservatore Romano* itself, official paper of the Vatican, gave ample coverage, with pictures, of this 'moving encounter of prayer participated in by numerous faithful of both confessions' at which a Cardinal was 'significantly'[32] presiding with the Anglican Archbishop.

It was at this liturgy that Dr Coggan, in his homily, urged immediate intercommunion, because the two Churches had drawn so close. This homily raised some eyebrows. Vatican officials, and others, evidently felt the proposal was somewhat precipitate, and even ill-advised in its timing and manner of presentation. The press naturally seized upon the incident as a sign of the problematic nature of the A/RC dialogue. But surely the problem is symptomatic of the amazing progress made. Archbishop Fisher would not have dreamed of proposing such a thing in an ecumenical liturgy in Rome just eighteen years earlier. Seen in a truly historical perspective, the two Churches appear to be fairly rushing towards each other in reconciliation. And of course 'churchy' things such as ecumenical liturgies and joint blessings tend to be lost upon the press, as of no real journalistic interest. Though we shall want to thank God that this is true in the sense that they are no longer exceptional, their significance nevertheless should not be lost upon us. Joint blessings are sacramental signs that the two Churches are worshipping and invoking their one Father in the Spirit of their one Lord, and precisely as sister Churches.

Cardinal Hume

The Roman Catholic Church expresses itself not just through the Pope to the universal communion, but also through national

Church leaders to the specific Church. Vatican II, through its theology of the local church and of collegiality, has stressed this important and living dimension of 'being Church'.[33] The English hierarchy of the Roman Catholic Church have in fact played a key role in the A/RC dialogue, influencing it significantly in critical moments. The role they have played has certainly been controversial at times, such as during the consideration of Anglican orders, and the period of the Malines Conversations. It is particularly significant, therefore, that the contribution of Cardinal Hume seems appreciated on both sides as informed, constructive, and indeed inspired. If the remarkable progress of the A/RC dialogue can be tangibly measured over the last few decades in Rome, this is also the case in London. Since the life of the Churches is lived out at the local level of diocese and parish, it is particularly important that they be sisters at this level, which can only be achieved if they are recognized and affirmed as such, not only in Rome but also in London.

On the very day of his installation as Archbishop of Westminster, Basil Hume, in an unprecedented and extraordinary gesture, travelled the short distance from the Roman Catholic Cathedral to Westminster Abbey, to meet the Anglican community in prayer. The Anglican Dean of Westminster Abbey, in welcoming the Benedictine Cardinal, stressed the 'Benedictine centuries' as a common, uniting heritage of the two Churches, and welcomed the visiting monks of Archbishop Hume's community: 'For over five centuries Benedictine monks sang in this choir and served this church . . . we are glad to have with us the Ampleforth community with whom, at the Abbey, we have a unique and intimate connection. It is good that they should be here.'[34] We shall deal more fully in a later chapter of this book with the ecumenical significance of our common, Benedictine heritage; suffice it to note here that the fact that Cardinal Hume is a Benedictine is surely not coincidental to his understanding and appreciation of the Anglican Communion. There is between his own living religious formation and the Anglican experience 'a unique and intimate connection' that is particularly providential for his ministry as head of the Roman Catholic Church in England.

In his reply to the Dean's welcome, the Archbishop himself began by referring to this common heritage, and by placing his

25

own visit in a liturgical context, that of the monastic *opus Dei*, the sung vespers service:

> It is always good to be with one's monastic brethren to sing the praises of God. How grateful we all are to you and to the chapter for making it possible for us to sing vespers with you. Thank you. You invited us because you appreciate our English monastic heritage. Westminster is an important part of the monastic history of these islands, and of very special significance for the English Benedictine Congregation.[35]

The Archbishop thus created an ecumenical bond with Anglicanism through its monastic heritage. In his reference to the participation of Anglican Benedictines in the vespers service, he suggested that the real bond is created by the life of prayer of the two Churches, which is simply participation in the one prayer of our common Intercessor and High Priest:

> We have also shared these vespers with our Anglican Benedictine brothers from the community of Nashdom. We have been at prayer together, and when two or three are gathered in his name there He is in our midst. His prayer is, surely, at this moment 'that we may all be one, that they too may be one in us, as thou Father art in me and I in thee; so that the world may come to believe that it is thou who hast sent me' (John 17:21–3).[36]

There are problems in the relationship, and Cardinal Hume, like Pope Paul VI, tends to confront them head on, frankly but with great gentleness. A basic problem for the rapport of the two Churches in England seems to be a long history, which is heavy and tragic in some respects. These tragic moments act like wounds and scars within the relationship of the two Churches: 'Wounds heal only with time and patience. The same is true of communities and institutions. They too can be wounded by their past and the scars take a long time to disappear. Our two Churches give proof of this. Our wounds are ancient; the healing is slow.'[37] The image is a vivid one, and evangelical in its profundity. Christ assures us that he has come not for the healthy but for the sick, and that he himself is our physician. But we need to recognize and acknowledge our own unhealthy state. If we of both Churches could see our own past not just as a series of heroic events, demonstrating that our side is right and those others have always been wrong in every century and every confrontation, if we could recognize clear symptoms that we have been sick and are still wounded (for should Christians have ever comported themselves as we did?), then we would recognize the seriousness of the wounds of our division and the need for patience for their healing, after some four centuries of festering.

The Archbishop suddenly changed images in his next sentence, and at the risk of seeming to mix his metaphors, he moved with eagerness into what was to be the dominant model of his address, that of sister Churches: 'We have been, I think, like two sisters, estranged, not on speaking terms, quarrelsome, misunderstanding each other.'[37a] The Archbishop was applying the concrete image in a vivid way to highlight the gravity of our past as adversaries; yet already he was recognizing an implicit hope: sisters can fight ferociously, and yet they remain sisters. He then made a vivid, concrete application of the model in this two-fold sense, and its effect is very moving:

There are many tombs in this abbey, but there is one which speaks, if we would listen, with a poignant, indeed tragic eloquence. It is the tomb which contains the remains of two sisters, Elizabeth and Mary. Read there the inscription: 'Consorts both in throne and grave, here we rest, two sisters, Elizabeth and Mary, in the hope of one resurrection.' Think of them as you will, judge them as you will, but pass on in your mind to the last phrase, 'in the hope of one resurrection'. New life springs up out of death.[38]

An Anglican who was present at this service told me that this reference had a very profound effect upon the whole congregation. Social psychologists would counsel us against repressing our collective pasts, and would stress that ecumenism must come to terms with our violent and divisive histories; but we must do this in a Christian perspective, which means a Paschal one. Ecumenism itself, and the affirmation of the two communions as sister Churches, can be the particular expression in our own times of our Paschal hope: 'The sister Churches can now look back on a past that is dead and buried. We can look forward to new life, to new hope and in God's time to the goal of Christian unity. Already in the

27

last decade we have seen much achieved to reunite the two sister Churches.'[39]

The Archbishop then quotes the full passage of Pope Paul VI's address concerning the Anglican Communion, concluding: ' "When the Roman Catholic Church . . . is able to embrace her ever beloved sister in the one authentic communion of the family of Christ." '[40]

Cardinal Hume began his ecumenical ministry in England with the affirmation of a basic interpretive model of sister Churches. He has said and done many things since in this area, and they all can, and should, be understood in the light of this primary affirmation.

Canon A. M. Allchin and the Anglican Ecumenical Heritage

We have been dedicating most of our attention in this chapter so far to what Roman Catholic leaders have said and done. Even in the case of the visits of the three Archbishops of Canterbury to the Vatican, we have focused on the response of the Popes, not upon the initiative, which required real courage, of the Archbishops in going, nor upon their significant statements and actions during and after the visits. This omission is not intended as a slight; it is just that we have come to presuppose that Anglicanism is more than carrying its weight at any particular phase of the ecumenical venture. We have come to expect from Canterbury (at least from the time of William Temple) from Lambeth, and from Anglican bishops, clergy and laity (at least from the time of the Lambeth Quadrilateral) real courage, creative initiative and generous support of the ecumenical task, and of the dialogue with Roman Catholicism in particular.

But what of the sister Church model and Anglicanism? It is our thesis here that Anglican ecumenism, at least from the last century (though in many cases for much longer), and in terms of the Roman Catholic Church and the Orthodox Churches, has presupposed the sister Churches model and the concomitant theology of unity in diversity as its basic working principle. In his 'Conference with Mr Fisher the Jesuit' William Laud was already articulating in the seventeenth century an ecclesiology of several Churches gathered, even if bickeringly, into the universal Christian communion:

28

'The Church' may import in our language 'the only true Church' . . . and this I never did grant of the Roman Church, nor ever mean to do. But 'a Church' can imply no more than that it is a member of the whole. And this I never did nor ever will deny, if it fall not absolutely away from Christ. That it is a 'true Church' I granted also. . . .[41]

Archbishop Bramhall, in the same century, sketched a similar theology of sister Churches, although granting a seniority to the Roman See that is surprising in such a defender of 'the English Church . . . against the RC Church':[42]

Let him [St Peter] be 'first, chief, or prince of the Apostles' in that sense wherein the ancient Fathers styled him so. Let him be the 'first' ministerial 'mover'. And why should not the Church have recourse to a prime Apostle or Apostolical Church in doubtful cases. . . . But yet we dare not rob the rest of the Apostles to clothe St Peter. We say clearly with St Cyprian, 'The rest of the Apostles were even the same thing that Peter was, endowed with an equal fellowship both of honour and power; but the beginning cometh from unity, the primacy is given to Peter, to signify one Church and one Chair.' It is well known that St Cyprian made all the Bishoprics in the world to be but one mass. . . . All that he attributeth to St Peter is this 'beginning of unity', this primacy of order, this pre-eminence to be the chief of Bishops, to be Bishop of 'the principal Church from whence Sacerdotal unity did spring'. . . . This primacy neither the ancients nor we do deny to St Peter – of order, of place, of pre-eminence. If this 'first movership' would serve his turn, this controversy were at an end for our parts. But this primacy is over lean. . . . This was that which made the breach, not the innocent primacy of St Peter.[43]

Our elder sister was and remains our elder sister, Archbishop Bramhall seems to be saying; if only she wouldn't behave as a tyrant. If only she would give just breathing room to her other sisters. One hopes that Vatican II and its affirmation of collegiality and the local church, and the pastoral approaches of John XXIII and his successors, have offered fresh reassurances that a Petrine ministry to the various Churches need not oppress them, but might more fully guarantee their own heritage and contribution.

It has not always appeared like this to our Anglican brethren, yet there has not ceased to be a love, even in the most difficult moments, for that problematical Roman sister. One of John Keble's more obscure poems, entitled significantly 'Gunpowder Treason', concludes thus:

> And O! by all the pangs and fears
> Fraternal spirits know
> When for an elder's shame the tears
> Of wakeful anguish flow.
>
> Speak gently of our sister's fall
> Who knows but gentle love
> May win her at our patient call
> The surer way to prove?[44]

Canon Allchin has been speaking 'gently' about sister Rome more recently, and not so much about her fall as about the notable opportunities opened up through her ecumenical commitment in Vatican II. He has been engaged for many years in the Anglican/Orthodox dialogue, and in a significant paper read at the International Ecumenical Colloquium held at the Pontifical Benedictine College in Rome in 1974, the Canon urged that the Roman Catholic Church give top priority to the dialogue with the Orthodox Church: 'The division between that Church and the Church of Rome is, I believe, more fundamental than that between our separated Western confessions. It is a division whose healing is vital to any genuine renewal of Christian vision, to any real liberation of new powers of Christian action.'[45] There has been a remarkably selfless spirit to Anglican ecumenism from the beginning. The recommendation from a Canterbury Canon that Rome give priority, not to the dialogue with the Anglican Communion but rather with Orthodoxy, is an example of ecumenism acting not with political tactics and strategy, but rather as a reconciling ministry within the Christian family of Churches. The Canon goes on to recommend the sister Churches theology as most fecund for Rome's approach to the Eastern as well as the Western Churches:

These factors incline us to favour very strongly the recovery of the old vision of sister Churches within a single family. We rejoice at all the signs here in Rome that the vision is coming to new life, as heads of various Churches come to visit and confer with the Bishop of this city. But we believe that this line of thought can fruitfully be developed, only on condition first that the specific character of the 'great' Church of the East be recognised, and secondly that the concept of sister Churches be extended, with due modifications to the various ecclesial communities of the West.[46]

The Canon amended his paper, for its later published form, with an 'Additional Note' that was particularly positive in spirit. In it he was able to point out developments that corresponded to hopes he had expressed in the body of his paper:

Since 1974 two developments in ecumenical relations have taken place which have particular significance in relation to this paper. At the international level there is the decision to inaugurate an official Roman Catholic-Orthodox theological dialogue. In the British Isles, there are the terms in which the new Archbishop of Westminster spoke in his address at the end of the Vespers celebrated in Westminster Abbey. . . . Taking up and commenting on the words used by Pope Paul . . . the Archbishop spoke clearly and cogently of the relations between 'the sister Churches' which have long been estranged but are now seeking reconciliation.[47]

The Official Anglican/Roman Catholic Consultations

If the sister Churches model, with its theology of unity in diversity, has been affirmed by Church leaders and theologians on both sides of the dialogue, what about the dialogue itself? At its reunion in Venice in 1970, the Anglican/Roman Catholic International Commission decided to focus specifically on the Eucharist as the focal point of the Christian faith and the central moment in the life of the two Churches. From that issue the theme of the minister of the Eucharist suggested itself, and from that topic the question 'by what authority does the minister celebrate' raised the issue of Church authority. The amazing degree to which substantial agree-

31

ment was discovered in these various areas is well known, and documents the fecundity of this theological approach of focusing on key issues within ecclesiology, rather than on the underlying general models of ecclesiology. We propose here the thesis that the method used, and the remarkable results achieved, presuppose the sister Churches model with its affirmation of unity in diversity. The first Agreed Statement, for example, affirms: 'The result [of the two years consultation] has been a conviction among members of the Commission that we have reached agreement on essential points of eucharistic doctrine . . . nothing essential has been omitted . . . we believe that we have reached substantial agreement on the doctrine of the Eucharist.'[48] This affirmation of unity in essentials is complemented by a stress on diversity within specific ecclesial heritages: 'In the course of the Church's history several traditions have developed in expressing Christian understanding of the Eucharist. . . . We are all conditioned by the traditional ways in which we have expressed and practised our eucharistic faith. . . . We acknowledge a variety of theological approaches within both our communions.'[49]

National commissions have been set up alongside the International Commission. Among the oldest and most active is 'ARC-USA', initiated in 1965, and which met in November 1981 for its twenty-fifth session. The Commission is an official ecumenical consultation, the group of representatives being named by the Roman Catholic Bishops' Committee for Ecumenical and Inter–religious Affairs, and by the Joint Commission on Ecumenical Relations of the Episcopal Church in the USA.

In 1977 this official Consultation published its 'Twelve Year Report: Where We Are: A Challenge to the Future'.[50] After much hard work, the Consultation had come to some very positive conclusions: 'Having met nineteen times over a twelve-year period, the national consultation . . . believes it has discovered a significant and substantial unity of faith between the two Churches, a unity which demands visible expression and testimony now.'[51] In the nineteen joint sessions the Commission had studied a wide range of themes, from the sacraments of Christian initiation to the Eucharist, from priestly ministry to methodological considerations and agreed responses to the ARCIC statements.[52] What were the basic conclusions, after twelve years, from this broad and intensive review of A/RC relations? Certainly problem areas continue to exist: 'The Consultation honestly recognizes differences which continue to separate the two churches.'[53] But the Consultation had discovered significant areas of convergence: 'After twelve years of study ARC contends that the Episcopal Church and the Roman Catholic Church agree at the level of faith on such topics as the Holy Eucharist, priesthood and ordination, and the nature and mission of the Church.'[54] These and other significant areas of accord[55] encouraged ARC-USA to affirm the two Communions to be sister Churches. The statement is remarkable for its emphatic explicitness: 'ARC finds after nineteen joint consultations that the Episcopal and Roman Catholic Churches share so profound an agreement on the level of faith that these Churches are in fact "sister Churches" in the one *communio* which is the Church of Christ.'[56]

A parallel ecumenical body, the Anglican/Roman Catholic Consultation on the Religious Life, made up of major superiors from both Churches, officially reaffirmed this statement of ARC-USA and added 'that we mutually recognize the authenticity of our vows as religious of sister Churches'.[57]

And the official 'Conference of Episcopal and Roman Catholic Leaders in the US', meeting in June of 1981, made the 'sister Churches' image the key model of their final document. Archbishop John Roach, President of the US Catholic Conference and the National Conference of Catholic Bishops, together with thirteen Roman Catholic church leaders (diocesan bishops, national lay leaders, representatives of religious orders) met with the Presiding Bishop of the Episcopal Church and a comparable group of thirteen Episcopal church leaders for four days of consultations. In their final, official document, the first paragraph begins by affirming: 'United as sister Churches in the one authentic communion of the family of Christ, we rejoice in the gifts bestowed on us during our days of prayer, reflection and study together.'[57a] A following paragraph reads: 'We recommend improved communication between our sister Churches at all levels. . .'[57b] And another begins: 'So that we may give witness as sister Churches to our common mission in social justice, we recommend that a joint task force be established. . .'[57c]

Besides Archbishop Roach, Roman Catholic participants included Archbishop John L. May, Bishop James Malone, Vice-

33

President of the National Conference of Catholic Bishops, Bishop Raymond W. Lessard, Co-Chairman of ARC-USA, Alan McCoy, O.F.M., President of the Conference of Major Religious Superiors of Men's Institutes, Fr Alex J. Brunett, President of the National Association of Diocesan Ecumenical Officers, Fr Herbert J. Ryan, S.J., Member of ARCIC and ARC-USA, and other bishops, ecumenists and lay leaders.

Besides the Presiding Bishop, other US Anglican participants included Bishop Arthur A. Vogel, Member of ARCIC and Co-Chairman of ARC-USA, Fr J. Robert Wright, Member of ARC-USA, Fr William B. Lawson, President of the Episcopal Diocesan Ecumenical Officers, Charles Lawrence, President of the House of Deputies of the General Convention, and other Anglican Bishops, ecumenists and lay leaders.[57d]

Two very distinguished and representative church groups thus concluded days of consultations with a series of concrete recommendations emerging from the central experience of being 'sister Churches'.

Biblical and Patristic Roots of the 'Sister Church' Model

It is important to note that the image of 'sister Churches', and its related theme of unity in diversity, are not recent, modish innovations; rather, they trace back to the earliest Christian ecclesial experiences. In 2 John explicit use of the model is made in verse 13: 'Greetings to you from the children of your sister. . .'. Exegetes are in general agreement with R. R. Williams (the former Bishop of Leicester) that, 'clearly we are dealing with a letter to a church, from a writer who is situated, either permanently or temporarily, in another church.'[58] *The Jerusalem Bible* note interprets 'your sister' as 'the church (perhaps Ephesus) from which the letter is being written'.[59] Neil Alexander observes that the Church in question is obviously, 'not the whole catholic Church, since (as Dodd remarks) it has no "sister".'[60] Rather it will be 'another local congregation in . . . the Asian diocese'.[61] Alexander goes on to note that: 'Female personification of a community was common enough. Israel, for example, was "daughter of Zion".'[62] Bultmann argues that the 'sister' model not only connotes plurality of churches, but stresses their close relationship: 'The bond uniting the two congregations is expressed by the fact that the congregation addressed is designated as the *adelphé* ("sister") of the congregation writing.'[63] Alexander notes the parallel with 1 Peter 5:13: ' "She in Babylon called together with you", i.e. your sister-Church in Rome.'[64] The Jerusalem Bible goes as far as to translate 'the co-chosen (*suneklektè*)' as 'your sister in Babylon'[65] observing in the note that 'co-chosen (feminine)' is equivalent to 'the co-chosen church', that is, 'the church at Rome'.[66] Joseph Fitzmyer, S. J., notes that 'she' in the first letter of Peter is 'the local church of Rome'.[67]

These texts and exegetical comments serve to remind us how strongly the consciousness of the local Church was to the early Christians. And a local Church was always seen in relation to other local 'sister' Churches. Later ecclesiology so insists on the *one*, *universal* Church, on its characteristics and dignity, that we find it difficult to recover today this theology (let alone experience) of Christian Churches. But only such a theology of Churches can open the way to resolving our ecumenical problems. Such a theology presupposes the other, universalistic ecclesiology and is complementary to it – but it should not simply be absorbed by it.

There is a 'lively discussion . . . not yet fully solved'[68] among exegetes as to whether, in the earliest Christian community:

> . . . the idea of the Church as the totality of all Christians forms the starting point of the consideration: and thus whether the single community is fundamentally only the 'appearance of the whole in the part'; or whether the consideration proceeds first from the single community and develops from this point to the formulation of the idea of the unified body of Christ – the Church.[69]

This subtle issue need not delay us here, for however it might eventually be settled, the fact remains that St Paul almost always uses 'church' (*ekklesia*) in the sense not of the universal community of all Christians, but rather of the local gathering of the faithful. As Cerfaux notes:

> As an apostle of the local church at Antioch, he naturally gave the name of 'churches' to the foundations which he made. This is certainly the principal use of the word in his epistles. The

singular refers to a local church, while the use of the plural form in addressing the collectivity of Churches is very common. But the meaning of the word is identical, whether it is used in the singular or in the plural.[70]

Fitzmyer notes that in his early letters Paul uses *ekklesia* 'in two senses . . . it either denotes the local congregation of believers dwelling in Thessalonica – a unity developed from their community in belief and worship – or it is a title of predilection for Judean communities (cf. 1 Thess. 2:14).'[71] Fitzmyer observes that, 'when we move to the *Great Letters*, we find the same two senses again'.[72] Paul applies the term *ekklesia* here to the local churches of Galatia, Judea, Macedonia and Cenchreae. The special title 'church of God' is conferred in honour on the Judean Churches, but now also applied to the Church of Corinth. According to Cerfaux and Fitzmyer, 'This title does not designate the universal Church as manifested at Corinth, but is a Pauline way of flattering a church with which he has had rather stormy relations. He accords the title otherwise reserved for the mother churches of Palestine.'[72] In parenthesis we might note the model of 'mother churches' here, which will require more attention below. We might observe too that Paul's tactic of flattering a particular Church by giving it a grander title than usual will be used again, and not infrequently, in the history of the Eastern and Western Churches. Having once received such a title (either from another Church or from its own leaders), a Church has often proved unwilling to let it go. Such 'developments' do not make the task of ecumenical dialogue any easier. In such matters also a return to the sources opens up fresh possibilities, casting a different light on some later developments.

But in Paul's use of the term *ekklesia* perhaps the chief 'observation worthy of note is the plural "churches".'[73] This use, as the exegete John Murray observes, heightens the Pauline significance of the particular church, and bestows upon it full ecclesial weight:

We may not tone down the unity of the church. This comes to expression repeatedly in Paul. . . But Paul is also jealous to maintain that in every instance where the saints are gathered together in Christ's name in accordance with his institution, there the Church of Christ is.[74]

D. E. H. Whiteley sums up an exegetical consensus on this important point when he affirms that: 'Cerfaux does not go beyond the evidence when he quotes with approval the words of Fridrichsen: "Each community represents on the spot the one and indivisible church." '[75] And, 'in a similar vein, Schmidt declares that "each community, however small, represents the universal community, the church".'[76] To what extent, we might ask in parenthesis, has Roman Catholicism maintained a consciousness, especially after Trent, of the real plurality of Churches, and of the full ecclesial significance of each? Vatican II does represent a significant rediscovery of the Churches,[77] but we should note how central this consciousness has been for Anglican ecclesiology since the Reform. The great seventeenth-century Anglican divine John Pearson, an attentive scholar of Scripture as well as an important patrologist,[78] observed in his key work that in the New Testament the word *ekklesia* has a double use:

> Sometimes it admitteth of distinction and plurality; sometimes it reduceth all into conjunction and unity. Sometimes the Churches of God are diversified as many; sometimes, as many as they are, they are all comprehended in one. . . . When the Scripture speaketh of any country where the Gospel had been preached, it nameth always by way of plurality the Churches of that country, as the Churches of Judaea, of Samaria, and Galilee, the Churches of Syria and Cilicia, the Churches of Galatia . . . yet the Scriptures always speak of such Congregations in the notion of one Church.[79]

D. E. H. Whiteley spells out in three points the significance of the particular Churches for Paul:

- First, as we have just remarked, the whole power of Christ is available to every local congregation.
- Secondly, each congregation has a function to perform in its own area analogous to that of the universal Church in the world as a whole. . .
- Thirdly, the local congregation is no mere isolated group: it is in a state of 'solidarity' with Christ and with the Church as a whole.[80]

It is the function of ecumenism today, of course, to recover that 'solidarity' between Churches, and with the Church as a whole. The reaffirmation of the ancient 'sister Churches' model is an expression of that endeavour. Banks has noted how central family imagery is in Paul's theology of Christian community, and how this imagery is founded in Paul's most basic theology:

> All Paul's 'family' terminology has its basis in the relationship that exists between Christ, and as a corollary the Christian, and God. Christians are to see themselves as members of a divine family; already in his earliest letters Paul regards the head of the family as being God the Father. In a unique sense Jesus is his Son, and it is only through his identification with men, and actions on their behalf, that they are able to 'receive adoption as sons'. . . . As a result, says Paul in Galatians, 'God has sent the Spirit of his Son into our hearts' so that along with Jesus we are able to address him in the most intimate terms as 'Abba! Father!'. . . This privilege, he adds in Romans, confirms to our own spirit the fact that we are indeed 'children of God, and if children, then heirs, heirs of God and fellow heirs with Christ'. . . . Paul sees implications from this for the life of the local communities. Those who belong to them should see one another primarily as members of a common family. So in Galatians Paul encourages both himself and his readers, as they have opportunity, 'to do good to all men, and especially to those who are of the household of faith'. . . . Both the local gathering and the heavenly 'assembly' are to be regarded as nothing less than God's family.[81]

This long quotation reminds us of the broader familial context, of its richness and fundamental importance for the 'sister Churches' model. Banks notes that, 'Although in recent years Paul's metaphors for community have been subjected to quite intense study, especially his description of it as a "body", his application to it of "household" or "family" terminology has all too often been overlooked or only mentioned in passing.'[82]

But Paul's interpretation of his churches in terms of family themes takes a particular twist that most modern readers would not expect. Because of his special esteem for 'the Jerusalem Christian community in serving as the source from which the gospel was disseminated',[83] he tends to look upon that community as a *mother*

38

community for his own Gentile Churches, although he never uses the term explicitly. According to Cerfaux, Fitzmyer and others, Paul normally reserved the title 'Church of God' . . . for the mother Churches of Palestine'.[84] He gave so much to this group, Schnackenburg notes, because: 'He wished to demonstrate the unity between his gentile Christian Churches and the Jewish mother Church. In this way, brotherly love becomes a more profoundly comprehended unity, that of all the "churches of Christ" (Rom. 16:16).'[85] The evolution of the use of the term *ekklesia* reflects this maternal function of Jerusalem, argues Cerfaux, for, 'the word "church" meant first the primitive community at Jerusalem and then the local communities which were the offspring of the mother church.'[86] It seems paradoxical that it was the Apostle to the Gentiles, who, having stressed that his own authority did not derive from the authorities in Jerusalem but from on high (see Gal. 1:17), and having stressed the superiority of the new dispensation over the law and circumcision, should look with such reverence to Jerusalem as the mother Church. But that same salvific dispensation had come through the Jerusalem community of believers; thus Cerfaux notes:

> In spite of proclaiming his independence, Paul's gaze was fixed unswervingly on the community of the holy city. He thought of his approval by the apostles as an indispensable condition for his work to have any value or efficacy in the eyes of God (Gal. 2:2). And he believed that the church of Jerusalem had communicated to the churches of the Gentiles the spiritual gifts which she held (Rom. 15:27; see 9:4). . . . The Supper had to be celebrated according to the customary rite of Jerusalem, and the same customs had to be observed in all the gatherings. . . . When he had completed the task of founding the churches of Galatia, Macedonia, Achaia and Asia, he desired that they should recognize the supremacy of the church of Jerusalem in the form of a great collection to be taken from them all.[87]

Paul's wishes that the Gentile sister Churches founded by him look to the Jerusalem Church as their mother community can be linked with the position of Rome and Canterbury today. For we are also Gentile Churches and should, as sisters, look to the early Jerusalem Church as our mother. The concept might strike us as being remote from any familiar ecclesiology, indeed possibly bordering on the bizarre, but these feelings might be symptomatic of our problem, of the limits of our ecclesiologies. The Jerusalem Church, under the pressures of the fall of Jerusalem in 70 AD and of resurgent Jewish nationalism, faded from history, and the Gentile Churches dominated the scene thereafter.[88] Thus much of the Semitic spiritual, theological and liturgical profundity of the Church was lost upon the other Churches, which became increasingly dependent upon Greco-Roman categories and approaches. But if we are to understand Paul, Matthew and John, and particularly Jesus and his deep roots in Israel, we must attempt to recover the experience of the mother Jerusalem Church. Only by doing so will we recover the Old Testament, the Jewish covenant, torah, liturgy, mysticism and eschatological hope that is the living context for the first and generative Christian experience. Louis Bouyer begins his important *History of Christian Spirituality* with the chapter on 'The Legacy of Judaism' in which he observes: 'The celebrated phrase of Pius XI: "Spiritually we are all Semites" is the best introduction to any history of Christian spirituality. We cannot enter upon such a study by any way other than that of Judaism as it was at the origins of Christianity.'[89]

If Rome and Canterbury are able to rediscover their common maternal heritage (looking for a moment beyond subsequent ecclesial development) their awareness of how profoundly bound together they are as sisters, will be considerably deepened.

Our reflection on the role of the Jerusalem Church as mother provides the necessary backdrop to a query that is bound to arise in connection with the relationship between Rome and Canterbury. Should not Rome be described as Canterbury's *mother* rather than *sister*? Wouldn't the maternal model do more justice to the key role of Pope Gregory the Great in founding, through Augustine, the British Church? Wouldn't it be more theologically and historically accurate if Anglicanism were affirmed the *daughter* of Rome rather than her sister? In fact many Anglicans will, in certain moments of deference, have recourse to this kind of thinking. Macquarrie writes for example, 'The separated churches of the West are the estranged daughters (or, in some cases, grand-daughters) of Rome. The Roman Catholic Church is, for us in the West, the bearer in a special way of the Catholic substance and is for this reason at the centre of the movement towards unity.' Macquarrie adds: 'Of course, this does not necessarily mean a privileged position for Rome – it could mean equally well a special role of responsibility.'[90] So, is Rome to be seen as Canterbury's mother or sister? The first point we need to make is that the two models are not mutually exclusive, given the curious logic of models. Rome might be *both* mother and sister to Canterbury, so we then need to know which model, if either, should *predominate*. Mary, for instance, is described by the Fathers (and by Dante) as both mother and daughter of Christ; Christ is described by Christian mystics as our father, mother and brother.[91] One model illumines one dimension of the mystery, another illumines another: none exhausts the possibilities or excludes the others.

One problem with claiming motherhood for Rome on the basis of Gregory the Great is that Christianity existed in England well before the Gregorian mission. As Neill notes:

> No man knows when the Gospel of Jesus Christ was first preached in the British Isles; but there is reason to think that no long period elapsed between the Resurrection and the origins of a Church in England. Tertullian at the beginning of the third century claimed that parts of Britain unreached by the Romans had become subject to the law of Christ . . . there is no reason to doubt that [his statement] is substantially correct.[92]

Anglicans have always been aware of the importance of Celtic Christianity within their heritage. The pre-Gregorian roots of that current are now lost in the mist of time, but to the extent that they are related to Gallic monasticism, they might be ultimately and equally rooted in an Eastern Christian experience (one thinks of an Irenaeus, or of a Cassian). Even figures after Gregory and Augustine of Canterbury, such as the very influential Theodore, brought at least as much Eastern Christianity to England as Roman. Thus it becomes difficult to ascribe to Rome in any unqualified way the model of 'mother' in relation to Canterbury.

Moreover, if the model is applied precisely, it draws forth the need for the 'sister Church' model, as we note below in chapter 3. For if Roman Catholics are to take at all seriously the pluralism of national Churches within the one Roman obedience (so that, for example, the Scottish Roman Catholic Church is distinct in many ways from the Nigerian Roman Catholic Church), then it must be recognized that the English and Scottish Roman Catholic Churches are as much daughters of Rome as the Church of England or the Episcopal Church in Scotland, and as daughters of the same mother, they inevitably become sisters one to another. Thus the only Anglican Churches directly in contact with their 'mother', rather than their Roman Catholic 'sister', would be the two Anglican parishes in the city of Rome (All Saints and St Paul's).

One positive thing to be said in favour of the 'mother' model, is that it at least opens up space explicitly for *other Churches*, even if they be seen in the subordinate position of daughters. The problem with a former Roman Catholic ecclesiology, still widespread among clergy and faithful despite Vatican II and all that has come afterwards, was that it made the One True Church correspond exactly in its boundaries with the Roman Catholic Church; so non-Roman Catholic communities could not by definition be Churches. They were necessarily frauds, it was often thought, and nothing more. Such an exclusivistic and ultramontane ecclesiology cannot be squared with Vatican II's Constitution on the Church, or with its Decree on Ecumenism or more recent official ecumenical statements.[93] But it cannot even admit that Rome could be a mother Church to other daughter Churches. Once familial models are introduced at all, the way is at least re-opened to the early patristic and biblical ecclesiology of a plurality of Churches.

Another problem, however, with the mother-daughter model is that it remains ambiguous on a decisive point: does the relationship betoken an *infant* daughter, dependent upon and obedient to the mother in perhaps everything, or an *adult* daughter, fully mature, and so possessing her own way of doing things, her own autonomy and responsibility to care for, counsel, perhaps even correct her mother? Anglicans would take it that, if the mother-daughter model is used, it is with the sense of the grown-up daughter; for it must be assumed that Christianity in Britain has, after some seventeen hundred years, reached an age of maturity. Mothers might not always like the particular ways their daughters have developed since childhood, but they have to 'let go' at a certain point and acknowledge the right of daughters to 'go their own way'.

If the mother-daughter model is used in this way, it does not illumine a great deal in terms of the present relationship of the two

Churches, for the roles in such a case are notoriously unclear. The model only succeeds in illuminating the past, the fact that the one comes from the other, as a daughter comes from a mother. If in the case of the Rome-Anglicanism rapport this particular point needs significant qualifications (because of the whole pre-Gregorian Christian presence, etc.), then the model can become more problematical than illuminating.

The main problem in insisting on the priority of the Rome-as-mother model over the Rome-as-sister one is that such a stress draws us all further away from the truly normative experience of the New Testament Churches, for whom the Jerusalem community was the mother Church and the Gentile Churches her daughters and hence sisters among themselves. Another distinct biblical theme, that of the 'Jerusalem above [which] is free and is our mother', (Gal. 4:26), is lost contact with, if other subsequent mothers are stressed. The underlying biblical affirmation of the unique paternity of God the Father is certainly blurred when later ecclesiastical developments are stressed to interpret a 'daughter' model. To speak of Rome and Canterbury as 'sisters', on the other hand, safeguards these three biblical currents of familial theology, and draws us closer to the mind and spirit of Scripture, the very 'soul of sacred theology'.[94] There need be no interdict on the model of Rome-as-mother, but the image needs to be understood in the light of the more fundamental biblical affirmation that all Christian Churches are daughters of the Jerusalem community, daughters of the Jerusalem on high and daughters of our one Father. Pope Paul VI, Cardinal Hume, Canon Allchin and others are therefore correct in giving the clear priority to the affirmation of Rome and Canterbury as 'sister Churches'.

If space permitted, we could usefully probe at length the ecclesiology of Luke and Acts, with its creative tension between 'to all the nations' and 'beginning from Jerusalem' (Luke 24:47). We could also usefully see how Luke situates the founding of the Gentile Churches within the thrust of salvation history itself, and how he theologizes ecclesial pluralism with his Pentecost narrative.[95] Indeed all the other books of the New Testament could be studied in terms of our theme.

We could analyse the writings of the apostolic fathers, with their fresh, springtime spirit and zeal for the Churches. The fraternal

43

solicitude of Clement, writing to the Church of Corinth should be carefully studied, for its note both of authority and of gentle persuasion:

> But if there are any who refuse to heed the declarations He has made through our lips, let them not doubt the gravity of the guilt and the peril in which they involve themselves.[96]

> So you will afford us great joy and happiness if you will lay to heart what we have written through the Holy Spirit, and will respond to the appeal for peace and harmony which we have made in this letter, by putting an end once and for all to the rancours of an impious rivalry.[97]

The marvellous letters of Ignatius to his six sister Churches and to his beloved Polycarp could also be analysed. They are a canticle to ecclesial love: 'I sing songs of praise to the churches, and I pray for their corporate as well as their spiritual unity – for both of these are the gifts of Jesus Christ, our never-failing Life.'[98] The Anglican patrologist Staniforth notes how this fraternal love between the Churches was expressed through self-sacrifice and commitment:

> During his stay at Troas, news had reached [Ignatius] that the persecution of Christians in his own city of Antioch had now died down. He therefore suggests that the Philadelphians should follow the example of other churches and send one of their deacons to Antioch with a message of congratulation. The length of such a journey and its arduous nature make this a striking instance of the brotherly feelings which linked the Christian churches of the period.[99]

Another patrologist, Cyril C. Richardson, notes this same bond of love between the Churches as evidenced in these priceless letters of Ignatius:

> Nothing is more touching in his correspondence than the sense of Christian fellowship which the various Churches enjoyed with one another. His letters to Asia Minor are written to thank the Churches for the expression of their Christian friendship in sending delegates to meet him in Smyrna. In these representatives he sees, as it were, the whole congregation of each church, and he

rejoices in their brotherly love . . . thus binding together the Churches in a wide fellowship of love.[100]

In the context of this communion of sister Churches, Ignatius offers the first, and most evangelical and ecumenically fertile, patristic formulation of Rome's primacy: 'Yes, you rank first in love.'[101] The phrase has been extensively discussed,[102] but however it is to be interpreted, clearly that primacy of love does not eliminate the other Churches but rather presupposes them and seeks to minister to their unity in diversity; Christian *agape* can mean nothing else. Irenaeus should also be examined carefully for his ecclesiology of the several sister Churches and the special role in their midst of 'the very great, very ancient, and universally known Church founded in Rome by the two most glorious apostles, Peter and Paul.'[103] One could study Tertullian's ecclesiology, and in a special way his splendid hymn to all the Churches as apostolic, all the Churches as primitive:

And after first bearing witness to the faith in Jesus Christ throughout Judaea, and founding churches there, the apostles next went forth into the world . . . founding churches in every city, from which all the other churches one after another, derived the heritage of the faith, and the seeds of doctrine, and are every day receiving them. . . . Therefore the churches, although they are so many and so great, comprise but the one primitive Church, founded by the apostles, from which they all spring. In this way all are primitive and all are apostolic *[sic omnes primae et omnes apostolicae]*, expressing all unity in their communion of peace and title of brotherhood *[et appellatio fraternitatis]*.[104]

The real goal of modern ecumenism is to restore that 'title of brotherhood' between the Churches.

A study of the later Fathers would also be useful, and especially of Gregory the Great. Augustine of Canterbury had been under Gregory's monastic authority in their community in Rome, and it was Gregory who had sent Augustine to England; yet with what careful attention does Gregory respect the letter and spirit of that 'title of brotherhood' between the Churches as he addressed a letter to Augustine telling him that he has dispatched the pallium to him: 'To our most reverend and holy brother and fellow-bishop Augustine: Gregory, servant of the servants of God. . . .'[105] We will refer in chapter 3 to Gregory's extraordinary awareness of the special gifts of the various Churches, but one passage deserves to be repeated; he counsels a perplexed Augustine about the diversity of ecclesial customs encountered in Gaul and Britain:

> My brother, you are familiar with the usages of the Roman Church in which you were brought up. But if you have found customs, whether in the Church of Rome or of Gaul or of any other that may be more acceptable to God, I wish you to make a careful selection of them, and teach the Church of the English whatever you have been able to learn with profit from the various Churches.[106]

Paul Meyvaert has noted how 'diversity within unity' is a central Gregorian theme:

> A first point that needs stressing is the very concrete view which Gregory has of the Church: it is both one and many. The *sancta universalis Ecclesia* for him means a multiplicity of churches, distributed . . . over the face of the earth, all united together in the bond of a common faith and charity.[107]

A fuller study of these Fathers would probe also the profound relationship often existing between the 'sister-Church' model and an ecclesiology of *communio* according to which the universal Church is present in each local Church gathered round its bishop. This rich experience of the dialectic Church-Churches, already present in New Testament times, challenges us today and has been re-affirmed by Vatican II in the Dogmatic Constitution on the Church (paragraph 26 etc.)

For a full study of the theme of sister Churches, particularly as it relates to Rome and Canterbury, that Archbishopric would need to be studied throughout the Middle Ages, with reference to its role in England and its prestige on the continent.[108] One thinks of an Anselm of Canterbury (himself originally from Italy) and of the remarkable invitation of Urban II at the Council of Bari to the Archbishop to take a seat of honour beside him: 'Let him be a part of our circle, he who is in some way pope of the other part of the globe *[includamus hunc in orbe nostro quasi alterius orbis papam]*.'[109]

46

Any such extended study of these points is quite beyond the scope of this single volume. But we must at least refer briefly to this whole range of material, to note the very broad and rich theological heritage of ecclesial pluralism within which the 'sister-Churches' image is to be understood. Particularly after the Counter-Reformation (though also before) we Roman Catholics often slipped implicitly into a kind of ecclesiological unitarianism with a pronounced pyramidical 'shape'. The damage done is not restricted to ecclesiology. Awareness of the pluralism-in-unity of the Churches within which we live deepens our experience of the primordial and marvellous pluralism-in-unity of the Divine Persons; but the Western stress on the unity of God, sometimes to the detriment of an affirmation, and experience, of the plurality of the Divine Persons, can impoverish every aspect of our spiritual life.[110]

Seen in this broader context, the affirmation by Paul VI of the Eastern Churches and the Anglican Communion as sister Churches goes far beyond mere ecclesiastical courtesy in its implications. It opens up to us again the marvellous variety of Christian heritages, the splendid complementarity of ecclesial gifts, and the biblical and patristic experience of sister Churches. But because of the hostility and suspicions and divisions that still remain, it also confronts us not just as consolation but also as challenge: and that first of all to Christian conversion.

Notes

1 Owen Chadwick, 'The Church of England and the Church of Rome from the Beginning of the Nineteenth Century to the Present Day' in *Anglican Initiatives in Christian Unity: Lectures Delivered in Lambeth Palace Library 1966* (SPCK 1967), p. 95.
2 ibid.
3 ibid., pp. 95–6.
4 Bernard and Margaret Pawley, *Rome and Canterbury through Four Centuries: A Study of the Relations between the Church of Rome and the Anglican Churches 1530–1973* (Mowbrays 1974), p. 322.
5 ibid., p. 327.
6 ibid.
7 ibid. The Anglican priests were J. C. Dickinson, C. C. W. James, C. L. Gage-Brown, and B. Pawley; the Anglican layman was C. J. A. Hickling.

47

8 ibid., pp. 327–8.

9 Owen Chadwick, op. cit., p. 104.

10 See Werner Becker, 'Decree on Ecumenism: History of the Decree' in Herbert Vorgrimler, ed., *Commentary on the Documents of Vatican II* (Herder, New York, 1968), vol. ii, pp. 1–57 especially pp. 2, 3, 22, 37, 48, 49, 50, 54–6, 58. It must be remembered that not all the Council Fathers were equally enthusiastic about the notion of ecumenism; Cardinal de Arriba y Castro, Archbishop of Tarragona, for instance, affirmed to the assembly: 'Let us beware of the dangers and always strictly respect the laws of the Church, such as the Index, which prohibits books favouring heresy. It is inopportune to speak of ecumenism in a council. This will scandalize the faithful of little education, who will be confused and put all churches on the same level. Proselytizing is increasing. Let us ask our separated brethren to renounce all proselytizing among Catholics. But the Church's right to preach the Gospel everywhere must be recognized. . . . This scheme [on ecumenism] does not please me. It is very badly done. It is better to avoid such a subject altogether.' Quoted in Henri Fesquet, *The Drama of Vatican II: The Ecumenical Council June 1962–December 1965* (Random House, New York, 1967), p. 239; see also the cautions of Cardinal Ruffini and His Beatitude Stephanos I Sidarouss, pp. 238–9.

11 Pope Paul VI, Address at the Canonization of the Forty Martyrs of England and Wales, St Peter's Basilica, October 25, 1970; for the full text see *Acta Apostolicae Sedis* 62 (1970), p. 753. For the passages of the Address relative to the Anglican Communion see *Documents on Anglican/Roman Catholic Relations*, I (United States Catholic Conference, Washington, 1972), pp. 42–3. See ibid., p. 44 for Archbishop Ramsey's response to Pope Paul VI's statement: 'I welcome gratefully the words used by His Holiness the Pope on October 25: "There will be no seeking to lessen the legitimate prestige . . . when the Roman Catholic Church . . . is able to embrace her ever beloved sister. . ." Responding to the warmth of these words I said in my Christmas letter to the Pope: "I read with happiness the words which Your Holiness spoke of warm and friendly feeling towards the Anglican Communion . . . and you can be sure that your warmth of feeling to us Anglicans is reciprocated. . .".'

12 Pope Paul VI, Address at the Canonization of the Forty Martyrs.

13 ibid.

14 J. R. H. Moorman, *A History of the Church in England* (Adam and Charles Black 1976), p. 200.

15 In her speech the Queen affirmed: 'We support the growing movement of unity between the Christian Churches throughout the world, and we pray that your Holiness's visit to Britain may enable us all to see more clearly those truths which both unite and divide us in a new and constructive light.' She also referred to 'the Roman Catholic community in Great Britain, where some four million of my people are

members of the Roman Catholic Church'. See *The Times* (October 18, 1980), p. 1.

16 Pope Paul VI, loc. cit.

17 Paul Meyvaert, *Benedict, Gregory, Bede and Others* (Variorum 1977), pp. 155–6; see the whole of his chapter 6: 'Diversity within Unity, A Gregorian Theme.' The work of Meyvaert demonstrates how fertile these early founts of our common heritage can be for our dialogue today, and how the 'biblical-patristic-medieval' approach can cast new light on ecumenical problems.

18 Paul Meyvaert, ibid., p. 154.

19 An authorized liturgical book of the Episcopal Church in the USA affirms, 'The Venerable Bede justly called Gregory the Apostle of the English.' *The Proper for the Lesser Feasts and Fasts, together with The Fixed Holy Days* (Church Hymnal Corporation, New York, 1980), p. 164.

20 John F. Long, S. J., 'Il significato della visita dell'Arcivescovo Ramsey' in *Civiltà Cattolica* 117(1966), p. 110.

21 'Ecumenical Notes and Documentation: The Meeting of the Pope and the Archbishop of Canterbury' in *One in Christ* 2(1966), p. 273.

22 ibid.

23 'Cronaca Contemporanea: Visita ufficiale del Primate Anglicano al Papa' in *Civiltà Cattolica* 117(1966), p. 190.

24 'Ecumenical Notes. . .' in *One in Christ*, op. cit., p. 273.

25 'The Common Declaration by Pope Paul VI and the Archbishop of Canterbury', Rome, 24 March 1966; in Clark and Davey, op. cit., p. 1.

26 See J. Nabuco, 'Rings, Ecclesiastical Use' in *New Catholic Encyclopedia* (McGraw Hill, New York, 1967), vol. xii, pp. 506–7.

27 J. R. Quinn, 'Blessings' in *New Catholic Encyclopedia* (McGraw Hill, New York, 1967), vol. ii pp. 163–14.

28 ibid. See also Vatican II, Constitution on the Sacred Liturgy, n. 60: 'Holy Mother Church has, moreover, instituted sacramentals. These are sacred signs which bear a resemblance to the sacraments: they signify effects, particularly of a spiritual kind, which are obtained through the Church's intercession. By them men are disposed to receive the chief effect of the sacraments, and various occasions in life are rendered holy.'

29 'The Common Declaration'; in Clark and Davey, op. cit., p. 2.

30 'Cronaca Contemporanea: Visita ufficiale del Primate Anglicano al Papa' in *Civiltà Cattolica* 128(1977), pp. 381–2.

31 Bernard and Margaret Pawley, op. cit., p. 335. The Pawleys note (ibid.) that in fact Cardinal Bea was able to meet the Archbishop, and that many positive ecumenical developments resulted from this first visit.

32 'La cerimonia della dedicazione delle porte: alla Chiesa Episcopaliana di San Paolo in Via Nazionale' in *L'Osservatore Romano* (April 30 1977), p. 5.

33 Vatican II, Dogmatic Constitution on the Church, nn. 26–7, etc.

34 The full text of the Dean's welcome address and of the Archbishop's address is given in *The Tablet*, 230(April 3, 1976), pp. 348–9.
35 ibid., p. 349.
36 ibid.
37 ibid.
37a ibid.
38 ibid.
39 ibid.
40 ibid.
41 William Laud, 'A Relation of the Conference between William Laud and Mr Fisher the Jesuit', n. 20; in Paul Elmer More and Frank Leslie Cross, *Anglicanism*, op. cit., pp. 56–7.
42 'Bramhall, John' in *The Concise Oxford Dictionary of the Christian Church* (Oxford University Press 1977), p. 73.
43 John Bramhall, 'Schism Guarded', I, i; in More and Cross, *Anglicanism*, op. cit., pp. 65–6.
44 John Keble, 'Gunpowder Treason' in his *Christian Year* (1827). I am grateful for this reference to Dr Samuel Garrett, Professor of Church History at the Church Divinity School of the Pacific, California.
45 A. M. Allchin, 'The Nature of Catholicity: an Anglican Approach' in Gerard Békés and Vilmos Vajta, ed., *Unitatis Redintegratio, 1964– 1974: The Impact of the Decree on Ecumenism* (Editrice Anselmiana, Rome, 1977), p. 113.
46 ibid., p. 114.
47 ibid., p. 118.
48 Anglican/Roman Catholic International Commission, *Agreed Statement on Eucharistic Doctrine*, September, 1971, preface, conclusion.
49 ibid., n. 1, conclusion.
50 The full text may be found in *Documents on Anglican/Roman Catholic Relations*, IV, op. cit., pp. 31–48.
51 'Twelve Year Report', preface; in *Documents*, p. 31.
52 See the various reports and statements of ARC-USA in *Documents on Anglican/Roman Catholic Relations*, I–IV, op. cit.
53 'Twelve Year Report', preface; in *Documents*, p. 31.
54 ibid., introduction; in *Documents*, p. 32.
55 For other areas of agreement see the 'Malta Report', n. 3; in Clark and Davey, op. cit., p. 108: 'We record with great thankfulness our common faith in God our Father, in our Lord Jesus Christ, and in the Holy Spirit; our common baptism in the one Church of God; our sharing of the holy Scriptures, of the Apostles' and Nicene Creeds, the Chalcedonian definition, and the teaching of the Fathers; our common Christian inheritance for many centuries with its living traditions of liturgy, theology, spirituality, Church order, and mission.'
56 'Twelve Year Report', introduction; in *Documents*, p. 32.
57 Anglican/Roman Catholic Consultation on the Religious Life, 'The Ecumenical Vocation of Religious in Sister Churches', (New York, 1981), nn. 1, 2.
57a 'Recommendations from the Anglican-Roman Catholic Leaders Con-

ference, June 12, 1981; the entire document is reprinted in *Cross and Dove*, 3 (1981), pp. 4, 8.

57b ibid.

57c ibid.

57d For the complete list of participants, see for instance *Ecumenical Bulletin*, 48 (1981), p. 3.

58 R. R. Williams, *The Letters of John and James* (Cambridge University Press 1965), p. 63.

59 *The Jerusalem Bible*, (Darton, Longman and Todd), 2 John 13, note.

60 Neil Alexander, *The Epistles of John: Introduction and Commentary* (SCM Press 1962), p. 146.

61 ibid.

62 ibid., pp. 146–7.

63 Rudolph Bultmann, *The Johannine Epistles* (Fortress Press, Philadelphia, 1973), p. 115.

64 Alexander, op. cit., p. 147.

65 *The Jerusalem Bible*, I Peter 5:13.

66 ibid., I Peter 5:13 note.

67 Joseph A. Fitzmyer, S. J., 'The First Epistle of Peter' in *The Jerome Biblical Commentary* (Geoffrey Chapman 1969), p. 368.

68 Johannes Weill, *Earliest Christianity: A History of the Period A.D. 30–150* (Harper, New York, 1965), p. 615.

69 ibid., pp. 615–16.

70 Lucien Cerfaux, *The Church in the Theology of St Paul* (Herder and Herder, New York, 1959), p. 189.

71 Joseph A. Fitzmyer, S. J., *Pauline Theology* (Prentice-Hall, New Jersey, 1967), p. 76.

72 ibid.

73 John Murray, *The Epistle to the Romans* (Eerdmans, Michigan, 1965), p. 233.

74 ibid.

75 D. E. H. Whiteley, *The Theology of St Paul* (Blackwell 1964), p. 189.

76 ibid.

77 See Vatican II, Dogmatic Constitution on the Church, especially nn. 26, 27.

78 Pearson defended the authenticity of the Epistles of St Ignatius of Antioch against the attacks of J. Daillé, for example.

79 John Pearson, *An Exposition of the Creed* (Clarendon Press 1890), pp. 597–8.

80 Whiteley, op. cit., p. 190.

81 Robert Banks, *Paul's Idea of Community* (Paternoster Press 1980), p. 54.

82 ibid., p. 53.

83 Keith F. Nickle, *The Collection: A Study in Paul's Strategy* (Allenson, Illinois, Studies in Biblical Theology, 1966), p. 120.

84 Fitzmyer, *Pauline Theology*, op. cit., 76.

85 Rudolf Schnackenburg, *The Church in the New Testament* (Herder and Herder, New York, 1965), p. 129. See also G. Bornkamm, *Paul*

(Harper and Row, New York, 1969), p. 40: 'It was aid to be given by the Gentile Christian churches specifically to the mother church in Jerusalem.'

86 Cerfaux, op. cit., p. 188.

87 ibid., p. 260.

88 See Jean Daniélou and Henri Marrou, *The Christian Centuries: The First Six Hundred Years* (Darton, Longman and Todd 1964), ch. 3 'The Crisis of Judaeo-Christianity', pp. 29–38.

89 Louis Bouyer, *A History of Christian Spirituality: The Spirituality of the New Testament and the Fathers* (Seabury, New York, 1963), p. 3.

90 John Macquarrie, *Christian Unity and Christian Diversity* (Westminster Press, Philadelphia, 1975), p. 50. King James I referred to the Church of Rome as 'our mother church.' See Moorman, op. cit., p. 222.

91 See Dante, Paradiso, Canto XXXIII, 1: 'Virgin mother, daughter of your son' ['Vergine madre, figlia del tuo figlio']. It is interesting how religious poetry, utilizing the model method in a most free manner and full of every sort of logical surprise, penetrates to such a depth the area of faith and spiritual experience. For the image of Christ as mother, see St Anselm, *Prayers and Meditations* (Penguin 1973), 'Prayer to St Paul', pp. 153–4: 'And you, Jesus, are you not also a mother? Are you not the mother who, like a hen, gathers her chickens under her wings? Truly, Lord, you are a mother; for both they who are in labour and they who are brought forth are accepted by you. . . . So you, Lord God, are the great mother.' See also Julian of Norwich, *Showings* (Paulist Press, New York, 1978), ch. 59 (long text), p. 295: 'So Jesus Christ, who opposes good to evil, is our true Mother. We have our being from him, where the foundation of motherhood begins, with all the sweet protection of love which endlessly follows.' It is interesting that the English heritage insists on this feminine dimension of Christ; the point is not without significance in its implication for the current question of the role of women in the two Churches.

92 Stephen Neill, *Anglicanism* (Mowbrays 1977), p. 9.

93 See Vatican II, Decree on Ecumenism, nn. 3, 13, 14, etc. Fr Herbert Ryan, S. J., who is a member both of ARCIC and of ARC-USA, notes the intentions of one of the official statements: 'When ARCIC set about to draft its Agreed Statement on Authority in the Church . . . ARCIC tried to express the faith of both the Anglican Communion and the Roman Catholic Church. The church which the Venice Statement describes is the whole Catholic Church in which both the Anglican Communion and the Roman Catholic Church subsist as "sister Churches" or *typoi*. The Venice Statement does not describe either of the "sister Churches" exclusively, but the whole Catholic Church.' Herbert J. Ryan, 'The Roman Catholic Vision of Visible Unity' in *A Communion of Communions: The Detroit Report and Papers of the Triennial Ecumenical Study of the Episcopal Church, 1976–1979*, J. Robert Wright ed. (Seabury, New York, 1979), p. 126.

94 Vatican II, Dogmatic Constitution on Divine Revelation, n. 24.

95 See Schnackenburg, op. cit., pp. 62–8. See also Jacques Dupont, O.S.B., *The Salvation of the Gentiles: Studies in the Acts of the Apostles* (Paulist Press, New York, 1979). pp. 11–60.

96 Clement of Rome, *Epistle to the Corinthians*, ch. 59.

97 ibid., ch. 63. This letter is moving not only for its sense of the solicitude of one Church for another, but also for its Christian experience of all Churches as marginal and transient in this world. His letter begins: 'The church of God living in exile in Rome, to the church of God, exiled in Corinth.' Every particular Church is, at some time or other, tempted to think of itself not only as the Universal Church but even as the Kingdom in its fulness. Such mistaken self-evaluation obviously constitutes a grave ecumenical obstacle for others, and also constitutes a spiritual hazard for the members of that Church itself.

98 Ignatius of Antioch, *Epistle to the Magnesians*, n. 1.

99 Maxwell Staniforth, ed., *Early Christian Writings: The Apostolic Fathers* (Penguin 1968), p. 110.

100 Cyril C. Richardson, 'The Church in Ignatius of Antioch' in *The Journal of Religion*, 17(October 1937), pp. 430–1.

101 Ignatius, *Epistle to the Romans*, introduction.

102 For the range of interpretations of the key phrase *prokathemene tes agapes* see Johannes Quasten, *Patrology* (Newman, Maryland, 1950), vol. i, pp. 68–70.

103 Irenaeus, *Against Heresies*, bk III, ch. 3, n. 2.

104 Tertullian, *Prescription against Heretics*, ch. 20.

105 Gregory the Great, Letter to Augustine, in Bede, *The Ecclesiastical History of the English People*, bk I, ch. 29.

106 ibid., bk I, ch. 27.

107 Paul Meyvaert, *Benedict, Gregory, Bede and Others* (Variorum 1977), p. 154. The whole of ch VI deserves to be studied carefully: 'Diversity within Unity, A Gregorian Theme.'

108 See Edward Carpenter, *Cantuar, The Archbishops in their Office*, (Cassell 1971).

109 Cited in Giovanni Domenico Mansi, *Sacrorum conciliorum nova, et amplissima collectio* (reprinted Paris: Welter, 1901–1927), vol. xx, p. 948.

110 For the consequences for liturgy and spirituality of the Western stress of the Divine Unity over the plurality of Persons, see Cyprian Vagaggini, O.S.B. Cam., *Theological Dimensions of the Liturgy* (Liturgical Press, Collegeville, 1976), pp. 193–4.

2

A First Response to the Model:
Conversion and Commitment

Church leaders and theologians have been urging that the Roman Catholic Church and the Anglican Communion are in fact *sister* Churches. The model is not new: it comes out of the biblical-patristic-medieval experience of Christian Churches. Yet it has more recently been neglected, which is perhaps why, once rediscovered, it strikes us as living and contemporary, capable of casting new light on a centuries-old problem. So what should be our response to the model?

Full Commitment

First of all, we should respond, and on a deep level. We might well decide against the model as a key to open up the true relationship between Anglican and Roman Catholic Churches. In that case we should be quite clear why we are against it, what our objections are, what we are going to say to Pope Paul VI, Cardinal Hume, Canon Allchin, ARC-USA and the others who have proposed it; or perhaps why we think this book has not accurately represented the real positions of these Church leaders. Rejection of the model must surely be based on reasons. A negative reaction based on habit or spontaneous emotions of inherited hostility is quite inadequate.

If, on the other hand, we feel we can give some kind of intellectual assent, what then? Bare intellectual assent alone is not enough. The challenge of this model must be answered at deeper levels of the personality also. A certain kind of theology perhaps can operate at the level of pure, abstract ideas; but the biblical-patristic-medieval manner of 'faith seeking understanding' engages the whole person, attains to the level of religious involvement. Joseph Butler, Anglican Bishop of Durham and theologian of the eighteenth century, argued that religion claims (a) a fuller discernment, to which we respond with (b) a total commitment; to have the discernment without the commitment is insincerity and laxity. The twentieth-century theologian Ian Ramsey, Butler's successor as Bishop of Durham, takes up this analysis and describes phenomenologically 'what kind of situations are religious'.[1] He argues that they are not so bizarre and irrational as sometimes thought, and are often parallel to empirical situations of everyday life, especially situations of interpersonal discovery, when the 'light dawns', the 'ice breaks', the 'penny drops . . . and so forth'.[2] He sketches with a whimsical touch such a possible incident:

> For our first example let us recall the setting of a High Court – all very impersonal, all very formal, quite lacking in 'depth' and 'vision'. The name of the judge is made as suitably abstract as possible – Mr Justice Brown. . . . Nor is the argument of the Court interested in persons. We have, instead, 'the Crown', 'the accused' and 'the prosecution'. Here is a situation as impersonal as may be. . . . Then, one morning, Mr Justice Brown enters the Court to see as the 'accused' the closest friend of his undergraduate days; or, if we may be more melodramatic, his long-lost wife. 'Eye meets eye'; astonishment; an odd word is uttered . . . the Court is 'electrified'. An impersonal situation has 'come alive'. . . . The situation has not 'come alive' merely by containing an unusually large range of facts; rather, in stretching to include these facts, the situation has taken on 'depth' as well.[3]

I find an analogy between this whimsical example and the present situation between Anglican and Roman Catholic. In the light of the 'sister Churches' model, that situation takes on depth, comes alive, opens our eyes to startlingly new possibilities. It was just twenty-two years ago that Archbishop Fisher thought he was being very optimistic when he affirmed in his sermon at the English Church in Rome: 'The period of the cold war between Churches is not altogether past. But it is passing.'[4] We have become accustomed to the cold war; each side has wanted to sit on the bench and declare the other guilty – of heresy, of schism, of anti-Christ blasphemies and of so much else. We can now live with the ebbing of the cold war, with a kind of polite, peaceful coexistence. We might even rule the defendant as innocent because of mitigating circumstances, invincible ignorance, etc. But to discover in that other a sister! Flesh of one's flesh, blood of one's blood! And this at the human level and also at the level of our faith! It is a breakthrough that really changes everything.

Commitment to Conversion

The radicalness of that change is perhaps best expressed in the key biblical category of *metanoia*: conversion, change of direction, change of heart. Certainly *metanoia* is at the very basis of Jesus' message: Jesus went into Galilee. There he proclaimed the Good News from God: ' "The time has come" he said, "and the Kingdom of God is close at hand. Repent, and believe the Good News" ' (Mark 1:15).

Two basic components of this *metanoia* are contrition for one's own sins, and forgiveness of others. The Gospels constantly pound away at these two sides. But could they be equally relevant, equally binding in the area of ecumenism?[5] Perhaps many of us have heard committed Christians suddenly shift into a violent, resentful, and acrimonious spirit as they bring up the topic of other Christian denominations. Maybe we ourselves are capable of this curious lapse. Certainly our two histories are full of tragic instances. Thus *metanoia*, at the heart of the Gospels, must also be at the heart of our dialogue. The Pawleys cite this 'memorable passage'[6] from Pope Paul VI's first allocution to the Council after his enthronement in which he speaks of:

the inexpressible consolation and reasonable hope that their presence [the observers'] stirs up within us, as well as because of the deep sadness we feel at their prolonged separation.

If we are in any way to blame for that separation, we humbly beg God's forgiveness and ask pardon too of our brethren who feel themselves to have been injured by us. For our part, we willingly forgive the injuries which the Catholic Church has suffered, and forget the grief endured during the long series of dissensions and separations.[7]

Commenting on this passage in the light of the four centuries of Anglican/Roman Catholic tensions which they themselves have objectively chronicled, the Pawleys of Canterbury note:

> Looking back over the sad centuries of quarrels recorded in this book, it will easily be appreciated how emotive these words were, when uttered for the first time by a Pope in Council. They laid a foundation on which could be built totally new relationships and which might make possible the progressive demolition of the old.[8]

If each of us wants to take at all seriously the sister Churches relationship and its challenge, we can lay no better foundation for our new commitment than that indicated both by the Pawleys and Paul VI: *metanoia*.

We really do not have a choice in that matter, if we are at all loyal to our Church leaders; in their Common Declaration Pope Paul VI and Archbishop Ramsey, in a text already cited, witnessed to their own *metanoia*, and enjoined upon all their faithful the same change of direction that *metanoia* entails:

> In willing obedience to the command of Christ Who bade His disciples love one another, they [the Pope and the Archbishop] declare that, with His help, they wish to leave in the hands of the God of mercy all that in the past has been opposed to this precept of charity, and that they make their own the mind of the Apostle which he expressed in these words: 'Forgetting those things which are behind, and reaching forth unto those things which are before, I press towards the mark for the prize of the high calling of God in Christ Jesus' (cf. Phil. 3:13–14).
>
> They affirm their desire that all those Christians who belong to these two Communions may be animated by these same sentiments of respect, esteem and fraternal love.[9]

As the Archbishop and Pope note, there are two key moments to *metanoia*: one is turning *away* from the past, insofar as it is dominated by sinfulness, and the other, more challenging moment is turning *to* the future which is recognized as God's future, full of new and saving possibilities. Both moments of the same movement are subtle, easier to describe than to bring about.

Commitment to Pardon

In our claims to turn away from the past, we often fudge a little, holding on to at least one or two favourite resentments, storing them up against possible future want. We *shall* forgive the Anglicans, but of course we are obliged to remember what they did to Thomas More and our other sixteenth-century martyrs. We have *quite* accepted the Romans, but it would be imprudent to lose sight of the Armada and Bloody Mary and that sort of thing. These events are part of our heritage, after all; and that is true enough, as is the Cross central to salvation history. In the same way we remember that we are all guilty of crucifying our Lord down through the ages; and that He from his cross has forgiven us. Ought we not then to forgive one another?

It is not a matter of repressing the past, of trying to cut ourselves off from our histories which give us our very identity. We must encourage our historians to work rigorously through every specific event in the relationship of the two Churches. But once that has been done, and it is an ongoing task, we must as Christians forgive and love. God knows a great deal about our pasts, individual and collective, and yet He forgives and He loves. That is the Good News.

Sometimes we don't so much hoard a few favourite resentments, but we clutch onto them all, even after conferring our own curious brand of lacquered 'forgiveness' upon them: 'I can forgive, but I can never forget', is the favourite formula in some circles. There is an element of truth to the formula, for the memory mechanism has its own autonomy and laws, quite apart from movements of the heart. But the way the formula is often pronounced, sometimes with an angry whine, tends to raise the suspicion that no real forgiveness has occurred at all, because the wrongs allegedly committed are so horrendous as to exclude a real cancelling of supposed debts. Our 'forgiveness' has just been a paternalistic recognition of the enormity of the wrongs committed against us by the other person; but such 'forgiveness' has not changed anything, only perhaps intensified the problems.

How different God's forgiveness is! It creates anew, transforms from within. In the vivid language of the prophets, God can restore sinful, adulterous Israel to her former virginity, 'to that joyful age of long ago when she was the virgin spouse of God'.[10] We Anglicans and Roman Catholics believe that this Old Testament forgiveness barely foreshadows the recreative power of Christ's redemptive death and resurrection. As the Paschal Exsultet (in the US *Book of Common Prayer* translation) affirms:

> How holy is this night, when wickedness is put to flight, and sin is washed away. It restores innocence to the fallen, and joy to those who mourn. It casts out pride and hatred, and brings peace and concord.[11]

It is at this depth of Paschal forgiveness that Anglicans and Roman Catholics must now encounter one another. Ecumenism should not consist of diplomatic negotiations; it must be Paschal proclamation.

At this depth we can really forget, not just 'forgive'; all the historical data will still be there, documented, on our shelves, but we will not need to dwell upon the instances of divisiveness and uncharity. A mystical classic that is a very important part of both the Anglican and Roman Catholic heritage, the fourteenth-century *Cloud of Unknowing*, speaks of the marvellous, ineffable mystery that is the locus of our encounter with God. But if we are to attain to this level, the anonymous author argues, we must fashion beneath us a 'cloud of forgetting' into which we trample down every disorderly thought, every unworthy attachment. This is particularly necessary in the case of past sins and unworthy actions:

> You are resolutely to step over them, because of your deep love for God; you must trample them down under foot. Try to cover them with the thick cloud of forgetting, as though they had never been committed, either by you or anyone else. And, indeed, as often as they come up, push them down. And if it is really hard work you can use every 'dodge', scheme and spiritual stratagem you can find to put them away.[12]

In another passage the author suggests that we should roll all specific sins and failures into a generic " 'lump', which one does not analyse, but knows to be himself".[13] Of course these are sugges-

59

tions in the context of contemplative, mystical prayer; but, at least from the time of the Fathers, such prayer and its laws have been considered generally relevant and instructive in an analogous sort of way for all serious Christians. Some of the loftiest teaching on mystical and contemplative prayer was given by Gregory the Great (whom we have seen to be such an influence in Anglican and Roman Catholic tradition) in homilies to all the faithful.[14]

We have stressed this theme of forgiveness, because it is evident, from speaking with many Roman Catholics and Anglicans, that the difficulty in forgiving all the horrendous things that have happened (or one thinks have happened) in the past often constitutes a major obstacle to a full commitment to the dialogue between the two Churches. Ecumenists speak of 'non-doctrinal and non-theological hindrances to reunion'. It has been discovered that these play a surprisingly large role in keeping us apart, and among them the difficulty of forgiving 'those others' is perhaps the principal hindrance.

Even if it be granted, for the sake of the argument, that 'all the horrendous things' were actually committed, and culpably so, by members of the other Church, how can living members today of that Church be rightfully blamed for things committed before their time? The Decree on Ecumenism of Vatican II makes the point quite explicitly that they should not be blamed:

> One cannot impute the sin of separation to those who at the present are born into these Communities and are instilled therein with Christ's faith. The Catholic Church accepts them with respect and affection as brothers.[15]

But if we are to embrace these others as kinsfolk in the one faith, if we are really to stop thinking of them as guilty for the past, what happens to the resentment obstacle to real ecumenical commitment? Doesn't it collapse? But what then are we to do with the past, with all those enormities committed by their predecessors? Surely we must do something with all that! We should roll it all into a huge lump, as the author of the *Cloud of Unknowing* has suggested, and offer it to Christ. It might be that the lump of that other Church is immense, cosmic in proportions, but Christ, who from the Cross forgave his crucifiers, has opened the floodgates of a redemptive pardon that is infinite in proportions. He is the one who 'takes away the sin of the world' (John 1:30). We have to believe this, simply in order to be Christians. Once again the ecumenical challenge commits us to stir up our elementary Christian faith and live it more seriously.

Let us also offer to Christ the little peccadillos of our own Church members in the past centuries; they also might have done some things they ought not to have done, and left undone those things which they ought to have done and specifically in relation to their own sister Church. All these little imperfections, gathered together into a second lump, might not mass up to the size of the pea. But we need to offer that lump to Christ also, especially when we remember that he came not for the just but for sinners. We will want to involve ourselves personally in this whole issue, and realize that we also have done some things better left undone, and failed to do some things better done, particularly in the area of unity of Christians. We will want to ask Christ's pardon for that little pea also, and remember that his forgiveness of those sins is bound up, and in some way preconditioned by, our forgiveness of others, for every day in the Lord's Prayer we are acknowledging that with Anglicans and Roman Catholics all over the world.

Commitment to Truth

But if *metanoia* requires a turning away from the past, it also entails a *turning to* the present and future possibilities of fuller reconciliation of the two Churches. A major issue that challenges us here is that of truth – dogmatic truth, theological truth, liturgical truth, spiritual truth. It is not enough just to forgive the faults of others, ask pardon for our own, and wish the best to everyone: Christ came to bring truth, and we must pursue it. Ecumenism without this commitment becomes pure sentimentality. Cardinal Hume concluded his 'sister Churches' address in Westminster Abbey with:

We must yield to the claims and demands made by the truth. Ours must not be the weak, helpless, indeed almost cynical response of Pontius Pilate: 'What is truth?' It must be a courageous, relentless and honest search for what is the truth about

God and his purposes for man, ultimately for Him who is the 'Way, the Truth and the Life'.[16]

The two principal commitments of ecumenism, to Christian love and to Christian truth, are not easily held together in happy balance in this complicated world where the several Churches still journey as pilgrims towards the Kingdom; only in that Kingdom will truth and love be manifestly and gloriously synonymous. Here we have still to exhort: truth, but also love; love, but also truth. It is part of our fallen state that we are capable of invoking the one in such a strident and partial way that we exclude the other. Sometimes in the past members of one Church have talked about their own commitment to the truth as though it were their property and they had a monopoly on it. The others, of course, were always in error, so there was no inclination for any sort of vague, woolly fellowship with those heretics. One's commitment to the truth was at the same time a commitment to battle against error, against that pack of heretics over there; and in the struggle all sorts of means could be used, since 'error can have no rights'.

We are a little slower today in hurling accusations such as 'heretic' at others, and at other Churches. Is it that we have gone soft in our commitment to truth? It may be that a degree of modern scepticism has crept into our Christian mentalities, making us flabby. But it is also the case that we are more aware of other dimensions of the truth, and of our commitment to it. The Decree on Ecumenism of Vatican II has affirmed our obligation to know more of the truth about other Christians and their denominations, about their opinions and values. It notes that face-to-face dialogue can be of immense help here:

We must come to understand the outlook of our separated brethren. Study is absolutely required for this, and should be pursued with fidelity to the truth and in a spirit of good will. When they are properly prepared for this study, Catholics need to acquire a more adequate understanding of the distinctive doctrines of our separated brethren, as well as of their history, their spiritual and liturgical life, their religious life and cultural background. Most valuable for this purpose are meetings between the two sides, especially for the discussion of theological problems, where each can treat with the other on an equal footing, provided that those who take part in them have the approval of authority and are truly competent.[17]

The Council goes on to note that as we grasp more truly the theological and spiritual positions of other Christians, we at the same time come to know more about ourselves, and present in a truer light the fullness and depth of Catholic theology and spirituality:

> From such dialogue will emerge still more clearly what the situation of the Catholic Church really is. In this way too the outlook of our separated brethren will be better understood, and our own belief more aptly explained.[18]

Full commitment to truth, then, is also a commitment to that truth which other Churches and Communities have discovered and lived, for they 'have been by no means deprived of significance and importance in the mystery of Salvation'.[19]

But if the dialogue that reveals such truth also requires competence and preparation, how many of us are really sufficiently qualified? If we draw back because we are not adequately prepared, does not the dialogue stall? Fortunately this dilemma is overcome in the case of the Anglican/Roman Catholic encounter. The national ARC, and especially the international ARCIC consultations, with their large number of highly qualified participants broadly representing the different tendencies in both Churches, have raised the dialogue to an official level and have borne remarkable fruit in the agreed statements. In terms of commitment to truth, these consultations have demonstrated the priority of this pledge for both sister Churches, and also its ecumenical fecundity. For the rigorous probings and studies that the consultations have entailed have revealed a remarkable convergence, in some cases undreamed of previously, in the faith and doctrine of the two Communions.

But how can the broad spectrum of the faithful (who constitute at least 99.9 per cent of both Churches), appropriate the fruit of ARCIC and ARC, so that such important work does not remain isolated and circumscribed in its results? Bishop Alan Clark, Roman Catholic Co-Chairman of ARCIC, stresses the urgency of this appropriation in his Address to the Anglican Synod:

> Agreements reached at commission level, however official the

commission, will have no value unless they are accepted by the Church at large. But by the nature of the case mere intellectual acceptance of our consensus has a way of being of little avail. No real commitment is involved, no real movement of persons towards one another need take place. It is only when our communities accept that the faith portrayed in our consensus documents is indeed their faith that something dramatic has occurred.[20]

What has been discovered and articulated by ARCIC and ARC is 'our consensus'. The path has now been charted for remarkable progress. It now behooves each one of us to travel along that path, become acquainted with it, make it ours; Bishop Clark, positive of the constructive results, urges that, 'our communities, using perhaps the statements as guide-lines, go through themselves exactly the same process as the members of the commission.'[21] ARCIC and ARC members are clearly not trying to hide anything from the faithful, producing some convenient compromise to mask the real problem. Rather, they are almost evangelical in their endeavour to make known their work and involve the faithful in its results and implications; Bishop Clark speaks of his 'own experience of hawking these [ARCIC] documents up and down the land'.[22] The results of ARCIC and ARC, with all their careful noting of problems that remain and work yet to be done, have been so positive that many of us have not been prepared for quite so much rapprochement between the two Christian Communions. We sometimes would prefer that the other Church keep its distance, that its doctrines and practices prove conveniently irreconcilable with the truth, that is, with our own doctrines and practices. Bishop Clark challenges us to move beyond this un-Christian separatism: 'We are all still victims of our past, which is inevitable. . . . It requires great faith and courage to accept the need to confront our habitual faith and to disentangle its constituent parts with a view to their re-ordering in deeper truth.'[23]

Commitment to Reunion by Stages

If two sisters, bitterly estranged for decades, were finally to discover themselves moving together again, and if each profoundly wished this reconciliation, they would be deeply grateful for every step that brought them together, and for those bonds of unity which had remained during the decades of hostility. Neither, if they were sincerely dedicated to re-establishing their original close relationship, would insist that suddenly every misunderstanding and difference of opinion be eliminated. Neither would force on the other a kind of 'all or nothing' ultimatum, to be met immediately, and without further discussion. The point is an obvious one, but in the dialogue between the two Churches, do not some of us in fact operate, even if perhaps only unconsciously, out of such presupposition? A Roman Catholic might reason: 'The Anglicans have not accepted Papal infallibility, they have not accepted as *de fide* the Marian doctrines of the Immaculate Conception and Assumption, moreover they differ with us on . . . [and here the list will be extended according to the perspective and theological understanding of that particular Roman Catholic]. We are therefore not united, and should note the differences and maintain our distance.' If one analyses the logic implicit in these reasonings, it seems to presuppose the 'all or nothing' postulate, which is very debatable indeed; yet how widespread this reasoning still seems to be.

J. M. R. Tillard, the Roman Catholic theologian and ecumenist and himself a member of ARCIC, has noted the danger in this mentality, urging us all to move beyond its immobilism:

> It would be a very grave mistake to think that the choice is between all or nothing. Communion has degrees. . . . It appears clearly to us that in fact from now on, if the two Churches take seriously the stages already passed, they can no longer, even in the difficult situation that the past has created in certain areas, be content merely to live side by side, showing only the ties of neighbourliness, politeness and Christian civility. The crisis through which the Gospel is passing with regard to the world obliges them to join forces and witness 'together' to the God of Jesus Christ. This is where their faithfulness to the Spirit is revealed. It is our firm hope that this 'togetherness' will take the form of true, organic unity, one which will shine forth when our work is done.[24]

Vatican II, in its Decree on Ecumenism, has officially sanctioned the theology of partial communion in tension towards ever fuller communion, and committed all loyal Roman Catholics to its positive perspective:

> Promoting the restoration of unity among all Christians is one of the chief concerns of the Second Vatican Council . . . among our separated brethren also there increases from day to day the movement which is termed 'ecumenical', and which is fostered by the grace of the Holy Spirit for the restoration of unity among all Christians . . . those who believe in Christ and have truly been baptized are in communion with the Catholic Church even though this communion is imperfect. The differences exist in varying degrees between the separated brethren and the Catholic Church, .whether in doctrine and sometimes in discipline, or concerning the structure of the Church. . . . The ecumenical movement is striving to overcome these obstacles. . . . This Sacred Council exhorts all the Catholic faithful to recognize the signs of the times and to take an active and intelligent part in the work of ecumenism.[25]

Simply in virtue of our one baptism, we are all engrafted into the one Christ, into his body. Ecumenical theology has still not probed the ultimate implications of that startling, primordial affirmation of faith; but it certainly at least indicates that the things that still separate us are far outweighed by the things that unite us, and most fundamentally, the very body of Christ. Beyond this basic and ultimate bond, the Anglican Communion and the Roman Catholic Church are tied together by a whole series of 'Catholic traditions and institutions' as well as doctrine, theology and spirituality, so that, in the famous words of Vatican II, among the Churches and ecclesial Communities of the West 'the Anglican Communion occupies a special place'.[26]

We have already noted how the Malta Report stresses the many fundamental doctrines of faith which bind the two Churches – 'our common faith in God our Father, in our Lord Jesus Christ, and in the Holy Spirit; our common baptism in the one Church of God; our sharing of the holy Scriptures, of the Apostles' and Nicene Creeds, the Chalcedonian definition, and the teaching of the Fathers. . .'[27] and so on. We very often take for granted this astonishingly significant and broad area of agreement, as we rush to focus on the differences that remain. But John XXIII's approach of 'stressing those things which unite rather than those that divide' reveals itself to be more than just an optimistic but somewhat arbitrary underlining of the positive; it is an emphasis imposed by the realities of our real, though imperfect, communion.

How united are we already? How quickly are we moving to overcome the differences that remain? Evaluations of the precise situation will differ widely, in both Churches, according to the particular theological outlook and enthusiasm for the dialogue of the evaluator. Thus disciples of Monsignor Lefebvre (whose disinclination to accept significant parts of Vatican II is well known) might judge Rome and Canterbury to be light years apart, and might also prefer to see them moving even farther apart daily. From the other side some Anglicans of a very emphatically 'evangelical' tendency might find themselves echoing this evaluation and hope. Indeed some Anglicans of a very different 'churchmanship' suggest that at least one aspect of this evaluation is true, though they acknowledge it more in sorrow than glee. They feel (and some Roman Catholics would agree with them) that the two Churches have actually crossed by in the night, and are now moving in opposite directions, Rome ever more Protestantward theologically, liturgically and spiritually, Canterbury ever more Catholicward. Stories abound of Roman Catholic priests sheepishly asking the local Anglo-Catholic parish if they might borrow a monstrance, thurible, dalmatic or tunicle, since these are now as rare in Roman Catholic circles as good Tridentine theology.

But, setting aside for a moment these more whimsical or militant evaluations, how close are the two Churches, what should they do about it, how fast are they moving together? Bishop Butler, Roman Catholic member of ARCIC wrote some fifteen years ago in a paper entitled 'Unity: An Approach by Stages?':

> It appears to us that a relatively large area of common action and common prayer is already theologically justifiable by the measure of doctrinal agreement which we gladly acknowledge . . . common action and prayer would appear to be desirable expressions of the amount of . . . 'communion' already existing between us. We would further emphasize that doctrinal agreement and prac-

tical joint action and prayer are likely to develop hand in hand and to exert a mutually beneficial influence.'[28]

These optimistic observations precede all the ARCIC joint agreed statements, and even the Malta Report itself, which went on to affirm the theology of 'our growing together' by stages.[29] The intervening fifteen years have brought astonishing, unexpected progress. Cardinal Suenens, himself very knowledgeable about ecumenism in general and the Anglican/Roman Catholic dialogue in particular, offered, some ten years ago, this evaluation:

> I have the impression that the Anglican world is very near to us. And I have met Anglicans of all different theological views. All the time you see something growing. We are growing together, and even if the Holy Spirit were not pushing us together, then the world would be doing so, because we are confronted by the same needs, we have to give answers to the same problems. Youth too are pushing, because youth are becoming so impatient.[30]

Does this very hopeful evaluation mean that in the relation between the two Churches things will become more facile, mellow, and rosy day by day? On the contrary, precisely because we have made such progress, we might be approaching a somewhat uncomfortable and demanding period. When two estranged sisters are finally talking again, discovering joyfully how much they share despite the long period of hostile separation, the moment finally comes when they have to bring up the thorniest of issues that have kept them apart; at that point, things become a little more intense. The present Archbishop of Canterbury, speaking in Westminster Abbey on March 11, 1981 on the theme of the Anglican/Roman Catholic dialogue, suggested that the two Churches have arrived at such a point. He declared that precisely because he was committed to reunion of the two Churches, 'deeply so, for both personal and theological reasons',[31] and because such 'substantial agreement' on so many 'key issues'[32] had already been attained, he felt the 'time is right to "get to grips" with the remaining obstacles that separate Anglicanism from Roman Catholicism.'[33]

If indeed things go forward according to the momentum built up in the last twenty years, the two Churches will soon be con-

confronting some difficult issues; there will be 'growing pains'. Of decisive importance will be the underlying bond and mutual commitment. Sisters, once they truly acknowledge each other again as sisters, can survive such periods, and can even come out on the other side more profoundly united than before. Indeed, once the familial bond is accepted, together with the idea of unity by stages, the challenge to go on discussing and debating becomes an ongoing one. There will never be a moment, at least on this side of the eschaton, when the two sisters are definitively, totally one in Christ. Or, to put the matter more positively, our relationship will always be able to go on growing. The commitment of Roman Catholics and Anglicans, therefore, to work for the unity in diversity of their two Churches is not confined to some temporary project of patching up basic problems; it is as permanent as our commitment to grow in truth and in love.

Commitment to Pluralism

Basic theological working principles of one Church may be expressed in language quite different from those of another. If the two Communities have been going their separate ways, it may easily be assumed that they are not only speaking different languages, but also articulating different, and irreconcilable theological principles. But should the two Churches turn about and start approaching each other again, even start dialoguing about their way of doing theology and understanding doctrine, they may be very pleasantly surprised to discover that those theological principles are really getting to much the same point. Such discoveries can constitute real ecumenical breakthroughs, and if two key and interrelated theological principles of one tradition are found to parallel two key and interrelated principles of another, the ecumenical possibilities opened up are even more hopeful and fecund.

Anglicans have, for example, long argued that the 'distinction between fundamentals and accessories, or, in the more usual language of the day [of Hooker] between things necessary for salvation and things convenient in practice,'[34] is basic to Anglican theology and spirit.[35] Such a key principle is tied in directly with another very characteristic Anglican value, that of 'comprehen-

69

siveness'. In one of the 1968 Lambeth Conference Reports, the connection is made explicit:

> Comprehensiveness demands agreement on fundamentals, while tolerating disagreement on matters in which Christians may differ without feeling the necessity of breaking communion. In the mind of an Anglican, comprehensiveness is not compromise. Nor is it to bargain one truth for another. It is not a sophisticated word for syncretism.[36]

Thus we have two characteristic and intimately related Anglican theological principles: the 'distinction between fundamentals and matters of secondary importance'[37] and 'comprehensiveness'. It can be argued that there is really nothing that new in all this, that it is virtually contained in the famous Augustinian programme of unity in essential things, diversity in debatable things, and love in all things. Indeed Anglicans tend to shun any idea of a private, Anglican reserve regarding theological principles, arguing that they are simply maintaining the ancient heritage. Archbishop McAdoo, Anglican Co-Chairman of ARCIC, relates this claim directly to the essentials/secondaries principle:

> The absence of an official theology in Anglicanism is something deliberate which belongs to its essential nature, for it has always regarded the teaching and practice of the undivided Church of the first five centuries as a criterion. This appeal to antiquity was closely involved with the distinction between fundamentals and matters of secondary importance.[38]

The Roman Catholic heritage, for its part, has always recognized the distinction between doctrinal certitude, theological unanimity, and 'disputed questions'. Some have thought that the full dimensions of this latter area, its own particular rules and requirements, have not always been fully respected in later Roman Catholicism. Certainly there has been a renewed insistence on this significant dimension of the theological venture; Pope John XXIII, for instance, insisted in his *Ad Petri Cathedram*:

> There are many points which the Church leaves to the discussion of the theologians, in that there is no absolute certainty about them. As the eminent Cardinal Newman remarked, such contro-

versies do not disrupt the Church's unity; rather they contribute greatly to a deeper and better understanding of her dogmas. These very differences shed in effect a new light on the Church's teaching, and pave and fortify the way to the attainment of unity.[39]

This principle is clearly related to the Vatican II teaching regarding 'hierarchy of truths', enunciated significantly in its Decree on Ecumenism. The context is that of dialogue with other Christians, and the clear implication is that theological differences between the Churches can actually enrich the penetration into Christian mystery:

> In ecumenical dialogue, Catholic theologians standing fast by the teaching of the Church and investigating the divine mysteries with the separated brethren must proceed with love for the truth, with charity, and with humility. When comparing doctrines with one another, they should remember that in Catholic doctrine there exists an order or 'hierarchy' of truths, since they vary in their relationship to the foundation of the Christian faith. Thus the way will be opened for this kind of fraternal rivalry to incite all to a deeper realization and a clearer presentation of the unfathomable riches of Christ (cf. Eph. 3:8).[40]

The references to 'fraternal rivalry' suggestively enriches the 'sister Churches' model: sisters do not have always have to echo and imitate each other, and indeed the family life is enriched by healthy sibling rivalry. The allusions to 'divine mysteries' and 'the unfathomable riches of Christ' indicate the ultimate ground and justification for theological pluralism. As Bishop Clark affirmed to the Anglican Synod: 'The Christian faith is one but also multiple. Because it exceeds the power of the human mind to comprehend, it must need to be expressed as a complex of mysteries.'[41] We have seen how decisive is the experience of Mystery for the pre-scholastic theological heritage, as well as for recent Roman Catholic theology. If, for nineteenth-century Roman Catholic thought, Mystery can sometimes appear as 'strictly speaking, merely provisional',[42] contemporary theologians such as Rahner will wish to stress Mystery's definitive character:

> What if we must take the mystery not as the provisional but as

the primordial and permanent, so much so that the absence or disregard of Mystery, preoccupation with the seemingly known and perspicuous proves to be the provisional, which dissolves before the gradual revelation of the abiding mystery. . . What if there be an 'unknowing', centred on itself and the unknown, which when compared with knowledge . . . is a positive characteristic of a relationship between one subject and another? What if it be essential and constitutive of true knowledge, of its growth, self-awareness and lucidity, to include precisely the unknown. . .?[43]

We have noted the centrality of Mystery for the Anglican spirit but could it be that this transcendent Mystery is now the common context which permits, indeed requires, the pluralism of theological, liturgical, and spiritual expressions which the two Churches represent? Perhaps we are finally coming to agree not primarily about this doctrine or that, but about the primordial nature of Mystery as such, as the horizon for the enunciation of any doctrine or theology or spirituality. It is indeed difficult for a rediscovery of Mystery not to go hand in hand with a new sense of the rightness of pluralism and of the ecumenical venture.

If Canterbury is affirming 'comprehensiveness' and the essential/secondary distinction, and Rome is noting with Vatican II the 'hierarchy of truths' and the value of theological pluralism, what is the relation between these various theological working principles? The Malta Report was already proposing in 1967–8:

> . . . particularly as matter for dialogue the following possible convergences of lines of thought: . . . between the Anglican distinction of fundamentals from non-fundamentals and the distinction implied by the Vatican Council's references to a 'hierarchy of truths' . . . to the difference between 'revealed truths' and 'the manner in which they are formulated' (Pastoral Constitution on the Church in the Modern World 62), and to diversities in theological tradition being often 'complementary rather than conflicting' (Decree on Ecumenism 17).[44]

The Archbishop of Canterbury, in his Westminster Abbey address on the Anglican/Roman Catholic dialogue in March 1981, expressed his own conviction that, 'comprehensiveness properly understood as the distinction between fundamentals and non-fundamentals will be seen not to be unrelated to the doctrine of the "hierarchy of truths" canonized by the Second Vatican Council, the implications of which have not yet been fully worked out.'[45]

In what area is authentic theological pluralism to be permitted? Is it simply that of certain 'disputed questions' that have never received one word of clarification from the highest magisterium? Or could even authoritatively pronounced definitions be partial, and therefore be open to fuller completion through the dialectics of pluralism? Bishop Clark opted for this second, much broader understanding, as he affirmed to the Anglican Synod:

> The faith we profess is a faith to be preached and proclaimed. It needs words to articulate it. Yet it is precisely in the arena of human words and argument that the faith can so easily be distorted. Particular words or expressions become signs of denominational identity, at times even shibboleths. The truth that even within the unity of one faith there can be different expressions of the same faith is not an abstract principle of semantics but the dynamic fact which admits the legitimacy of a certain pluralism even at the level of faith . . . it is evident that much of our doctrinal division requires our close attention in order to be sure that the divisions result from differing belief rather than from differing theology.[46]

The anti-ecumenical stance tends to be static and self-sufficient in its attitude: in its extreme form it maintains: 'We have the truth once and for all. They don't have it, never had, and never will, until such time as they disband and join us.' Vatican II sketched an entirely different understanding of the Church needing continual reformation, in its recognition that in its moral, spiritual, and even doctrinal life it may be lacking:

> Christ summons the Church, as she goes her pilgrim way, to that continual reformation of which she always has need, [*qua . . . perpetuo indiget*] insofar as she is an institution of men here on earth. Therefore, if the influence of events or of the times has led to deficiencies in conduct, in Church discipline, or even in the formulation of doctrine (which must be carefully distinguished from the deposit itself of faith), these should be appro-

73

priately rectified at the proper moment. Church renewal therefore has notable ecumenical importance.[47]

If no Church can pretend to be the definitive and perfect expression on earth of God's salvific truth, then obviously space is opened up for pluralism. And if this salvific truth is transcendent, ineffable Mystery, not destined to be 'resolved' and 'clarified', but ever deepened in its sublimity, then there is even more urgency for theological, liturgical and spiritual pluralism to point beyond any one human formulation to that absolute Mystery of which it is but sign and symbol. Moreover, if the ultimate ground of Mystery is not just monolithic, but in some way Triune, then pluralism is not just an earthly value, which will fade away as all merges into a neo-Platonic One. It is a definitive image, destined to endure also in the Kingdom, of definitive Triunity, just as union and communion between these pluralistic Christian families are destined to be eternal images of Divine Unity. The Anglican Communion and the Roman Catholic Church are thus seeking an organic bond that assures and deepens pluralism, for that is the ultimate structure of Reality. As John Macquarrie has argued:

> The divine Triunity represents the ultimate fulfilment of diversity-in-unity and unity-in-diversity . . . now . . . we have seen the theological background that points us to a form allowing for a maximum of diversity . . . taking as its ultimate model the Holy Triunity and one therefore in which there would be neither a dividing of the substance nor a confounding of enriching difference.[48]

Commitment to our Sister Church

What is to be our response to the affirmation of the other ecclesial body as 'sister Church'? We have mentioned the obligation to conversion and forgiveness, new attitudes that ought to affect each of us and our Church. But with these we are still focusing on ourselves, and the danger is that we will not move beyond our habitual self-centredness, even though we can enjoy more edifying collective dispositions. We shall focus on our own Church as converted and as forgiving, but we shall always be focusing on our own Church.

We have mentioned the response of commitment to truth, and to reunion by stages, and to diversity, but the danger with these undoubted values is that they can become mere abstractions. We can fix our attention on splendid abstractions – *our* abstractions, *our* concepts of what is truth, what is diversity, what is reunion by stages. Abstractions can always become 'ideology', and in the negative sense, rationalizations which divert and oppress.

The obvious primary response to the affirmation of the other community as 'sister Church' is to respond to *that community*: we must turn our attention out from ourselves and our collective ego, and move beyond abstract values to that concrete, living Church, confronting that Church as sister.

The personal model of 'sister' is particularly useful here, for it opens up to us all the insights of interpersonal experience, all the depths of personhood. A sister, if she really wants to be in communion with her fellow sister, cannot think of herself all the time; nor can she just ratiocinate about wonderful categories; she must open herself up to the living reality of her sister. This means not projecting her own stereotypes, or even idealizations onto the other, but acknowledging her as she is, in her concreteness and in her faults and limitations. These will illuminate her own faults and limitations, and above all open her to the living reality of the other *as other*.

Christian thought recognizes a mysterious 'absolute, infinite significance of the finite individual',[49] giving him an inalienable right to 'self-realization' through his own 'unique history of freedom for which no one else can deputize', because human personhood is posited as an image and likeness of Divine Personhood. The 'origin and goal' of human personhood is the 'free self-communication of God' which, 'as the free history of God himself, is also the ultimate ground and content of the history' of human personhood.[50] Such a theology of personhood needs to be applied, *mutatis mutandis*, to the relation of sister Churches. A Church cannot of course be a human person in a univocal, literalist sense, but a Church is in fact more than a human person, for she is a community of human persons, elevated to the level of member of the body of Christ, destined to be divinized.

Any Christian theology of personhood recognizes the dialectic of individuality-sociality: 'Inter-communication, self-realization and self-possession, grow in principle in like and not inverse proportion.'[51] This personalist principle alone is rife with implications for the ecumenical dialogue between the two Churches. Roman Catholics will yearn, for instance, to see the Anglican Communion in ever more committed dialogue with their own Church, and this for the good of both Churches; but they will be equally concerned lest the dialogue in some way infringe upon the authentic self-awareness and development of either Church. Of course in theory an authentic dialogue can only benefit the growth of both, but only now are we emerging from four hundred years of estrangement and separate development. At this point the efforts of one of the two Churches to 'help' the other might in fact pull the other away from its own heritage, not yet fully understood and appreciated by the 'helping sister'. On the other hand the self-development of each Church will certainly presuppose a flourishing exchange and communication with the other; if the risks of dialogue are significant, those of 'going it alone' are certainly more perilous. In any authentic interpersonal dialogue, one is not simply declaiming the 'truth' as one sees it to a passive, mute other; rather, one is attempting to understand the other in terms of the other's own self understanding; and of course the self-understanding of any Church is directed beyond itself to another Person, that of Christ, for 'We are those who have the mind of Christ' (1 Cor. 2:16). These are some of the 'personalist' dimensions that dialogue should assume between the two sister Churches. It is heartening to reflect, in the light of this, on a passage of Bishop Clark's address to the Anglican Synod in which he describes the spirit that has characterized the official ARCIC dialogues from the beginning:

> We began by asking what we, as representatives of our respective Churches, believed here and now to be Gospel truth. We began by speaking to each other in our own language, of course, but seeking to understand what each was saying. . . . Our dialogue was, and remains, an encounter of persons, persons in love with the same Lord and enjoying the love of the same Lord. This means that we did not seek to convince each other of the rightness of our own interpretations but rather, by reflecting *together* on the sources of the faith we professed, to reach a consensus of faith. . . . As Pope John pointed out some ten years ago, speak-

ing out of his generous vision of the redeemed community of our Lord and Saviour, all dialogue begins with a conversion of heart and mind.[52]

The ARCIC dialogue has certainly provided a splendid model for every local Anglican/Roman Catholic dialogue, for the present, and for the future. But what precise 'shape' do we want eventual organic reunion to take? We may have a specific juridical blueprint, and this can be helpful. But to the extent that we are truly committed to the other as sister Church because we are truly committed to Christ, we will always revert ultimately to the inspired principle of Abbé Paul Couturier: to will between the two Churches the unity Christ wills by the means that He wills.

Notes

1 Ian T. Ramsey, *Religious Language: An Empirical Placing of Theological Phrases* (Macmillan, New York, 1967), part I: 'What Kind of Situations Are Religious?', pp. 11–54. It is interesting that Ramsey, 'than whom no modern Christian philosopher is more remote from the schoolmen', participated at a very early date, in 1950, in a dialogue between Anglican and Roman Catholic theologians at Strasbourg; among the Roman Catholic representatives were de Lubac, Congar, Bouyer, Daniélou, all knowledgeable of the pre-scholastic Catholic theological tradition. See Owen Chadwick, 'The Church of England and the Church of Rome, from the Beginning of the Nineteenth Century to the Present Day', op. cit., pp. 97–8.
2 Ian T. Ramsey, ibid., p. 20.
3 ibid., pp. 20–1.
4 Archbishop Geoffrey Fisher, Sermon at the English Church in Rome, quoted in Owen Chadwick, op. cit., p. 104.
5 See Vatican II, Decree on Ecumenism, n. 7: 'There can be no ecumenism worthy of the name without a change of heart. For it is from newness of spirit through spiritual renewal (see Eph. 4:23) from self-denial and unstinted love, that yearnings for unity take their rise and grow toward maturity.'
6 Bernard and Margaret Pawley, op. cit., p. 347. See also Vatican II, Decree on Ecumenism, n. 7: 'St John has testified: "If we say that we have not sinned, we make him a liar, and his word is not in us" (1 John 1:10). This holds good for sins against unity. Thus, in humble prayer, we beg pardon of God and of our separated brethren, just as we forgive those who trespass against us.'
7 Paul VI, Allocution to the Second Vatican Council, quoted in Bernard and Margaret Pawley, op. cit., pp. 347–8.

8 Bernard and Margaret Pawley, ibid., p. 348.
9 The Common Declaration by Pope Paul VI and the Archbishop of Canterbury, Dr Michael Ramsey, Rome, 24 March, 1966; the full text of the Declaration is found in Alan C. Clark and Colin Davey, *Anglican/Roman Catholic Dialogue*, op. cit., pp. 2–4.
10 Carroll Stuhlmueller, C.P., 'Deutero-Isaiah' in *The Jerome Biblical Commentary* (Geoffrey Chapman 1970), p. 383; see Isa. 62:5; see also for similar ideas Isa. 65:19, Zeph. 3:17, etc.
11 *The Book of Common Prayer* (Church Hymnal Corporation, New York, 1977), p. 287.
12 *The Cloud of Unknowing*, Clifton Wolters (Penguin 1974), ch. 31, p. 90.
13 ibid., ch. 69, p. 136.
14 See, for instance, Cuthbert Butler, O.S.B., *Western Mysticism* (Constable 1951), p. 65.
15 Vatican II, Decree on Ecumenism, n. 3.
16 Archbishop Basil Hume, O.S.B., Address at Westminster Abbey, March 25, 1976; see *The Tablet* 230(April 3, 1976), p. 349.
17 Vatican II, Decree on Ecumenism, n. 9.
18 ibid.
19 ibid., n. 3.
20 Bishop Alan Clark, 'Where Anglicans and Roman Catholics Agree'. Address to the Anglican Synod, November 7, 1974; the text of the Address may be found in *Documents on Anglican/Roman Catholic Relations* 3 (United States Catholic Conference, Washington, 1976), pp. 59–69.
21 ibid.; in *Documents*, p. 68.
22 ibid.
23 ibid.
24 J. M. R. Tillard, O.P., 'The Deeper Implications of the Anglican-Roman Catholic Dialogue' in *One in Christ* 8(1972), p. 263.
25 Vatican II, Decree on Ecumenism, nn. 1, 3, 4.
26 ibid., n. 13.
27 The Malta Report, 1967–1968, n. 3; text in Clark and Davey, *Anglican/Roman Catholic Dialogue*, op. cit., pp. 107–15.
28 Bishop B. C. Butler, O.S.B., 'Unity: An Approach by Stages?' in Clark and Davey, op. cit., p. 103; see also the counterpart Anglican paper read at the same meeting: Bishop Henry R. McAdoo, 'Unity: An Approach by Stages?' in Clark and Davey, op. cit., pp. 84–100.
29 The Malta Report, n. 7; in Clark and Davey, p. 109.
30 Cardinal Leo Suenens, 'Visible Unity: An Interview' in *One in Christ* 4 (1972), p. 341.
31 Dr Runcie, Address in Westminster Abbey, March 11, 1981; quoted in Clifford Longley, 'New Runcie Initiative for Unity with Rome' in *The Times* (March 12, 1981), p. 4.
32 Clifford Longley, ibid.
33 ibid.

34 Paul Elmer More, 'The Spirit of Anglicanism' in *Anglicanism*, op. cit., p. xxiv.
35 See for instance Henry R. McAdoo, *The Spirit of Anglicanism: A Survey of Anglican Theological Method in the Seventeenth Century* (Scribner's, New York, 1965), *passim*; see also Paul Elmer More, op. cit., *passim*.
36 *The Lambeth Conference 1968* (London 1968), p. 140. Quoted in Stephen W. Sykes, *The Integrity of Anglicanism* (Mowbrays 1978), p. 9; Sykes illumines with rigorism the dangers and fuzzy ambiguities that 'comprehensiveness' can fall into, pp. 8-25. One would want to recall the basic ecclesiological principle of the medievals, and also of the seventeenth-century Anglican divines, that the abuse of a thing does not exclude the possibility of its proper use.
37 McAdoo, loc. cit., p. v.
38 ibid.
39 John XXIII, *Ad Petri Cathedram* 3; in *The Encyclicals and Other Messages of John XXIII* (TPS, Washington, 1964), p. 39.
40 Vatican II, Decree on Ecumenism, n. 11.
41 Bishop Alan Clark, 'Where Anglicans and Roman Catholics Agree', op. cit.; in *Documents on Anglican/Roman Catholic Relations*, op. cit., p. 63.
42 Karl Rahner, S. J., 'The Theology of Mystery and Symbol' in *Theological Investigations* (Darton, Longman and Todd 1974), vol. iv, pp. 40–41.
43 ibid.
44 The Malta Report, n. 6; in Clark and Davey, op. cit., p. 109.
45 Dr Runcie, Address in Westminster Abbey, March 11, 1981; quoted in *The Tablet* 235(March 21, 1981), p. 275; see *The Tablet* comment on the Archbishop's remarks, and upon the commentary of Clifford Longley in *The Times*, regarding which it suggests playfully '*The Times* almost becomes the Anglican Church in print when it turns to religious affairs.' *The Tablet* 235(March 21, 1981), p. 275: 'A Church United Not Absorbed.'
46 Bishop Alan Clark, op. cit.; in *Documents*, op. cit., p. 61.
47 Vatican II, Decree on Ecumenism, n. 6.
48 John Macquarrie, *Christian Unity and Christian Diversity*, op. cit., pp. 43, 47.
49 Max Muller and Alois Halder, 'Person' in *Sacramentum Mundi: An Encyclopedia of Theology*, Karl Rahner, S. J., ed. (Burns and Oates 1969), vol. iv, p. 405.
50 Karl Rahner, S. J. 'Person, Theological' in *Sacramentum Mundi*, ibid., vol. iv, pp. 417–19.
51 ibid., p. 418.
52 Bishop Alan Clark, 'Where Anglicans and Roman Catholics Agree', op. cit.; in *Documents on Anglican/Roman Catholic Relations*, op. cit., pp. 60–1.

Discovering Consanguinity: The Monastic-Benedictine Spirit of Anglicanism

The two Churches have been facing away from each other in hostility these last four centuries. Because we have now begun to turn towards each other in a mutual commitment of respect and love – ecumenical conversion – we will be discovering positive features in the other which had previously escaped our notice, even when we held them in common. They may indeed have been present throughout the last four hundred years, but our back-to-back posture and spirit of hostility will not have helped us to notice such things. So in our conversion towards each other, we should be prepared for some pleasant surprises.

To use another metaphor, it is as if we have been blind to the common elements we share, for hostility is blinding; but Christ's reconciling love heals our blindness, restores our sight. The process may be gradual, but Christ's light does bring back Christian perception:

> [Jesus] asked, 'Can you see anything?' The man, who was beginning to see, replied, 'I can see people; they look like trees to me, but they are walking about.' Then he laid his hands on the man's eyes again and he saw clearly; he was cured, and he could see everything plainly and distinctly (Mark 8:24–6).

What can Roman Catholics discover in the Anglican Communion once they turn to her as sister Church, face to face? Certainly there will be many defects, but we already knew that well, from our polemical literature. But if we start looking also for the best, and not just for the worst, and if we seek to penetrate to the deepest level of the Church's spiritual life, what might we discover?

Benedictine Spirit

It is impossible to set precise limits to the extension, influence and expressions of the Benedictine spirit. Benedictinism, as the abbots themselves have acknowledged, has expressed itself in 'great diversity . . . in a wide variety of forms.'[1] Downside is quite different from Pluscarden which differs notably from Prinknash, etc. Yet all these communities are Benedictine, as well as Nashdom, the Anglican abbey, in the fundamental sense that they all seek to follow the *Rule*, which in its flexibility and 'indetermination offers the possibility of many adaptations'.[2]

And in the broader sense of the *spirit* of the *Rule*, one can argue that the Benedictine ethos extends quite beyond cloister limits to inspire a variety of forms of Christian living. The Anglican spiritual theologian Martin Thornton, for instance, insists that 'the genius of St Benedict cannot be confined within the walls of Monte Cassino or any other monastery; the *Regula* is not only a system of monastic order, it is a system of ascetical theology, the basis of which is as applicable to modern England as it was to sixth century Italy.'[3]

Can the Benedictine spirit even inspire and characterize a Church as such, indeed an entire communion of Churches? Several Anglican theologians respond affirmatively in reference to their own Communion. This chapter proposes to examine this thesis and to offer some Roman Catholic reflections about its ecumenical implications, particularly for the affirmation of the Anglican Communion as our 'beloved sister'.

A Church of Continuities

Most Roman Catholics probably still think of the Anglican Church as arising in the sixteenth century and as a direct consequence of certain marital problems of Henry VIII. But Anglicans themselves resolutely propose another conception of their Church quite different from this simpler interpretative model. John Macquarrie, for instance, one of the most influential of living Anglican theologians, affirms: 'Anglicanism has never considered itself to be a sect or denomination originating in the sixteenth century. It continues without a break the *Ecclesia Anglicana* founded by St Augustine thirteen centuries and more ago. . . . Our present revered leader, Arthur Michael Ramsey, is reckoned the one hundredth Archbishop of Canterbury, in direct succession to Augustine himself.'[4]

In this view, then, the Anglican Church was founded by St Augustine of Canterbury (a *monk*, it might be noted here, sent to England by the great monastic Pope Gregory I).

The Anglican Bishop Stephen Neill insists in the same way as Macquarrie upon this continuity of Anglicanism with the pre-Reform Church in England, only he takes us back even further into the Celtic origins of Christianity in England; he writes: 'The [Anglican] has never imagined that the Reformation was anything other than a Reformation. It was in no sense a new beginning. The English Churchman regards himself as standing in the fullest fellowship and continuity with Augustine and Ninian and Patrick and Aiden and Cuthbert and perhaps most of all, that most typically Anglican of all ancient saints, the Venerable Bede.'[5]

Thus, the Anglican insists that if one wishes seriously to come to terms with Anglicanism, he is going to have to go back to its true roots and study Augustine, Ninian, Patrick, Aidan and Cuthbert (all of them monks), and especially that most Benedictine of these founding fathers, also 'that most typically Anglican of all ancient saints, the Venerable Bede'.

The Anglican theologian Anthony Hanson notes that there is nothing particularly new about this insistence on Anglican continuity with the pre-Reform Church: 'Anglican apologists in the sixteenth and seventeenth centuries constantly maintained that the Church of England was not a breakaway Church, like the Evangelical Church in Germany or the Reformed Church in France. It was the same continuous Catholic Church that had at the Reformation "washed its face".'[6] The Roman Catholic scholar of Anglicanism, George Tavard, citing Anglican theologians of the sixteenth century regarding the 'uninterrupted succession' of their sacraments, theology and faith, acknowledges that among the Anglican writers of that period 'this theme constantly recurs'.[7]

Thus, to the traditional polemical Roman Catholic query of 'Where was the Anglican Church before Henry VIII?' the Anglican pointedly responds: 'In England, where else?' And he proposes this response very sincerely, it should be noted, not as a rhetorical trick but as a true expression of his experience of the sacramental, liturgical, doctrinal, theological and devotional continuity of the post-Reform Anglican Church with the pre-Reform English Church.[8] The Roman Catholic may have some difficulties in accepting *tout court* and without qualification this Anglican thesis; but correct ecumenical method requires him to recognize that at least this is the way Anglicans ('high Church' *and* 'low', although emphasis might differ) sincerely experience their own Church life. It is primarily with this Anglican experience and self-identity that Roman Catholics must come to terms in a true ecumenical dialogue, and not just with their own conception of what Anglicans must be.[9]

This point is clearly decisive for the theme of this chapter, for if Anglicans understand their Church to be rooted in the early and medieval centuries of English Christianity, these centuries are characteristically *monastic*. They also constitute our own Roman Catholic heritage: thus *two* Churches, but within *one* family heritage.

Monastic Roots

The first chapters of a typical Anglican history of the English Church are filled with towering monastic figures of Celtic Christianity: St Ninian, who brought a missionary form of monasticism to England before the end of the fourth century.[10] St Germanus, who like Ninian was a disciple of the monasticism of St Martin of Tours, and who visited England in the fifth century: 'British Christianity, he found, was virtually indistinguishable from the fierce monasticism introduced from southern Gaul some time earlier.'[11] Thus English Christianity already had a monastic spirit in the fifth century. St Patrick, a British youth carried off into slavery in Ireland, escaped to France and there lived under Germanus in the monastery of Auxerre for more than a decade. 'Consequently, when in 432 Pope Celestine sent him to Ireland, the Christianity he brought was rather exclusively monastic.'[12] Thus Celtic Christianity, soon to spread to England in a very pronounced way, was essentially monastic, the abbot ruling supreme even over bishops. St Columba, who in the seventh century crossed from Ireland into western Scotland, carried with him the heritage of Celtic monastic Christianity. He founded the famous missionary monastery of Iona, and 'it was from this centre that most of the remaining districts of England were won to the Christian faith after the breakdown of Edwin's Christian kingdom in 632.'[13]

This Celtic form of Christianity failed, however, to have an evangelizing impact on the newly-arrived Anglo-Saxons. A new monastic missionary endeavour was called for, and with rare acumen Pope Gregory the Great responded. The Anglican Bishop Stephen Neill in his thoughtful *History of Christian Missions* notes that Gregory's endeavour, 'was fresh and remarkable since, in contrast to the haphazard way in which Churches had generally grown up, this was almost the first example since the days of Paul of a carefully planned and calculated mission.'[14] Bishop Neill also underlines the specifically *monastic* character of the mission since, 'Gregory, himself a monk, had seen the vital part that the monk could play in missionary work among the new nations.'[15]

Augustine not only brought the spiritual teachings of his monastic father to England[16] but also followed Gregory's pastoral directives after the first monks had settled in Canterbury. Gregory wrote to a perplexed Augustine who had asked what he should do about all the pagan usages of the Anglo-Saxons:

The temples of the idols among that people should on no account be destroyed . . . it is a good idea to detach them from the service of the devil, and dedicate them to the service of the true God. And since they have a custom of sacrificing many oxen to demons, let some other solemnity be substituted . . . so that they may learn to slay their cattle in honour of God and for their own feasting. . . . If they are allowed some worldly pleasures in this way, they are more likely to find their way to the true inner joys. For it is doubtless impossible to eradicate all errors at one stroke . . . just as the man who sets out to climb a high mountain does not advance by leaps and bounds, but goes upward step by step and pace by pace. It is in this way that the Lord revealed himself to the Israelite people.[17]

One wonders if the roots of the Anglican spirit of tolerance, reasonableness and comprehensiveness cannot already be detected here. These are monastic virtues also, it might be noted. Gregory in his *Vita Benedicti* (written just two years before the mission of Augustine) praises St Benedict's *Rule* for its balance and lucidity,[18] two qualities that characterize his own pastoral and spiritual theology.

Augustine had also written to Rome about his perplexity at the variety of liturgical forms and customs: 'Since we hold the same faith, why do customs vary in different Churches, why does the method of saying Mass differ in the holy Roman Church and in the Churches of Gaul?'[19] Gregory's response, not what one might expect from Rome, is almost Anglican in its serene insistence on ecclesial pluralism:

My brother, you are familiar with the usage of the Roman Church in which you were brought up. But if you have found customs, whether in the Church of Rome or of Gaul or of any other that may be more acceptable to God, I wish you to make a careful selection of them, and teach the Church of the English whatever you have been able to learn with profit from the various Churches. . . For things should not be loved for the sake of places, but places for the sake of good things.'[20]

Anglican ecclesiology, with its biblical and patristic cast, and nourished by its own experience as an international communion of autonomous Churches, tends 'to favour very strongly the recovery of the old vision of sister Churches within a single family.'[21] If there is such a thing as a characteristically monastic ecclesiology, it certainly tends in a similar way to stress the importance of local and regional Churches.[22] The above text of the monk and pope who was so little concerned with centralization and *Romanitas* reflects this monastic-Anglican ecclesial perspective.[23]

Augustine and his fellow missionary monks, following the directives of Gregory, not only founded monasteries and schools, but established parishes, dioceses and provinces, laying the very foundations of the *Ecclesia Anglicana* of the Middle Ages and of the following centuries.[24]

Thus Gregory's monks evangelized the newly-arrived Anglo-Saxon peoples as the Celtic monks had evangelized their predecessors, so that these two fundamental roots of the English Church and nation both bear a clearly monastic stamp.

But one might pose the objection that if the specific topic of this chapter is the *Benedictine* spirit of Anglicanism, Celtic monasticism is not Benedictine, nor (as some scholars insist) is Gregorian monasticism.[25] But it has been pointed out that the problem is somewhat anachronistic, since monasticism did not tend to accept a single rule as binding until the Carolingian reform, and the category 'Benedictine' appeared only many centuries after St Benedict and the *Rule*.[26] St Columba and St Augustine would not have thought of themselves as 'Benedictine', it is true, but neither would St Bede, St Dunstan or St Anselm. They were simply monks seeking to live faithfully their particular monastic calling, in a spirit of kinship with their fellow monks who had preceded them. Such a sense of continuity and kinship, characteristic in general of monasticism, had a particularly solid 'objective' basis in the case of English monasticism, because Celtic and Gregorian monasticism were assimilated into later English 'Benedictine' experience through the synthesizing genius of the Venerable Bede.

Venerable Bede and After

The Anglican historian Bishop J. Moorman notes that Bede 'has rightly been called the "Father of English History" ' and that his *History of the English Church and People* still remains the basis of modern knowledge of the English Church in the early period.[27] It was almost exclusively through Bede that the English Church of the Middle Ages and of the Reform had access to its origins.

St Benedict Biscop, the learned monastic founder of Wearmouth and Jarrow, the two abbeys in which Bede lived his entire monastic life, decided that these two houses should follow an amalgam of several rules, including probably the *Rule of St Benedict*. Consequently, according to our modern religious categories, this monastic life was probably 'Benedictine' in some sense, but never in the exclusive sense, for 'it came to combine all that was best in the Benedictine and Celtic ideas of monasticism.'[28]

Bede himself, in his *History*, enthusiastically championed the monastic and ecclesial forms brought to England by the monks of Pope Gregory, whom he venerated as the 'apostle' of the English Church. In parenthesis, we might note that Bede's esteem is shared by Anglicans; Patterson, for instance, affirms that, 'it is . . . to the great Pope Gregory that we must look as our apostolic father.'[29] Certainly English Roman Catholics look to Pope Gregory as their 'apostolic father'. Both Churches thus esteem Gregory as their father, a rather significant indication that they are indeed 'sister Churches'. It would be difficult to find, in other ecumenical dialogues, such an explicit affirmation by two Churches of common ecclesial roots and heritage so significant for the spirituality, theology and polity of both.

But if Bede stressed the significance of Gregory and of his monks, he also sought to be fair to the Celtic heritage and dedicated many chapters to its saintly monk missionaries. In this way, Bede's *History* constitutes a decisive synthesis of the Celtic, Gregorian and 'Benedictine' heritage, as notes the medieval scholar Mary R. Price:

> Under Bede's eyes, as he toiled away in his cell, the divided peoples of the 'island lying in the sea' were being welded into a nation, and through his eyes and by his pen we can see this happening. We see also the fusion of the free-lance monasticism of the Celtic monks with the more regular discipline of the Benedictine rule, of the Celtic Church with the Roman.[30]

The moment is decisive for the English Church, as notes another Bede Scholar: 'The centuries on which Bede concentrates are a crucial and formative period in our island history, during which the future shape and pattern of the English Church and nation were beginning to emerge.'[31] It is precisely through Bede's interpretative and synthesizing work that these key formative centuries are not only not lost to the English Church, but take on form, life and significance. Bede is fairly rigorous regarding the facts of his narration, as is widely acknowledged,[32] but his approach is obviously not that of positivist historicism. He explicitly offers his own theological interpretation of the history he is treating, and it is clearly a monastic reading in the light of salvation history.[33]

The monk, through an assiduous *lectio divina*, seeks to be shaped by the Word of God to the point that salvation history becomes the key by which he penetrates his own spiritual existence and also human history. The importance of the Word of God for Anglican spirituality, theology and doctrine is also well known.[34] Bede's biblical-patristic-monastic optic renders early English history Christianly significant, and he delivers this meaningful heritage of Celtic, Gregorian and 'Benedictine' monastic Christianity to the later English Church. It is also in this respect that he can be judged, 'that most typically Anglican of all ancient saints'.[35]

Of course, the Anglo-Saxon Church knew other gigantic monastic figures, such as Alcuin, who made a decisive contribution to the Carolingian renaissance, and Dunstan, whose brilliant statesmanship guaranteed the relaunching of the English Church and nation after the onslaught of the Vikings.

But if Anglo-Saxon Christianity can be understood only in the light of the key element of monasticism, William the Conqueror opened up still new avenues of development, and 'with the coming of the Normans monachism went ahead rapidly'.[36] Indeed, the very first Archbishop of Canterbury named by William was the Abbot of Caen, Lanfranc, who embarked on a decisive reorganization of the English Church, including the definitive subordination of the See of York to Canterbury, worked effectively for the renewal of monasticism, and also helped William maintain the fullest possible independence of the English Church from Rome. This is naturally an aspect of his contribution that is noted and appreciated by Anglicans,[37] and that indicates, they argue, that it did not all begin with Henry VIII and Archbishop Cranmer.

Monasteries and monastic schools multiplied,[38] and brilliant monastic Churchmen and theologians such as Anselm continued to emerge. Bishop Moorman notes that the monastic presence was not at all limited to the cloister or school, but often extended to the very heart of the Church diocese: 'Many monks subsequently became bishops, and England developed the curious custom, elsewhere practically unknown, of the "Cathedral priory" where the cathedral of a diocese was manned not by secular clerks but by professed monks. About half of the great cathedral churches in England were monastic, the prior and monks taking the place of the dean and the canon.'[39]

What the medievalist, Friedrich Herr, affirms of monasticism in the Middle Ages generally is thus true in a particular way in England: monasticism constituted 'the heart of the Church'.[40] Thus Anglicanism, in insisting on its continuity with Norman, Anglo-Saxon and Celtic Christianity, all decisively characterized by the monastic experience, realizes that the formative years for the development of its spirituality, liturgy, theology and polity were monastic years.

The flowering of the monastic life continued into the 1100s; and as Bishop Moorman notes, the 'vast number of monastic houses founded in or about the twelfth century shows this type of life was highly valued'.[41] Still, monasticism had reached its peak, and a general decline began. The foundation of the Franciscan, Dominican and other new orders, the new spirit of scholasticism, the Black Death, the monastic decadence linked to excessive wealth and many other complicated causes led to a notable decline in monastic vocations. By the beginning of the sixteenth century, 'the great houses were half empty . . . the shell of English monasticism was too big for its body'.[42] This is the general context of that drastic step of the dissolution of the monasteries. One of the principal authorities on the dissolution writes with vividness:

In April 1536, at the end of the twenty-seventh year of the reign of King Henry VIII, there were, scattered throughout England and Wales, more than eight hundred religious houses, monasteries, nunneries and friaries, and in them there lived close on ten thousand monks, canons, nuns and friars. Four years later, in April 1540, there were none.[43]

Of course, in the post-Reform period monasticism and the dissolution were often topics of controversy between Anglicans and Roman Catholics.[44] All sides seem generally agreed now that, on the one hand, monasticism had seriously declined and, on the other, Henry and Cromwell were quite interested in the financial, and not just the moral and theological, implications of the suppression of the religious houses.[45]

In any case, the fact of the dissolution obviously poses a major difficulty for the thesis of the fundamentally Benedictine spirit of Anglicanism; for if one accepts and defends this thesis, how is one to explain the fact that monasticism was the first thing to go at the moment of the Anglican Reform, and that Anglicanism was able to live on splendidly for centuries without any form of monasticism whatever?

The Book of Common Prayer and Benedictine Spirituality

The first part of the answer that many Anglicans and others propose regarding this objection is that monasticism was not just eliminated by the Reform. Rather, the essentials of the Benedictine spirit were rendered immediately accessible to the entire Church through the key and characteristic work of the Anglican Reform, the Book of Common Prayer. It is extremely important to note this decisive fact about the Anglican Reform: at its centre and guaranteeing its spirit stands not a towering reformer (a Luther, a Calvin), not a theological doctrine or a moral code, but a book of liturgical prayer. In this fundamental respect alone the Anglican Reform has a clearly Benedictine spirit to it.

But quite beyond this, if one examines the basic principles that shape the Book of Common Prayer, note many Anglican writers, one will find that they are specifically Benedictine. Martin Thornton, for instance, argues that the spirituality of the *Rule* is built upon three key moments: the community Eucharist, the divine office, and personal prayer of a biblical-patristic-liturgical cast; these same three elements, and in the same hierarchy of importance, also constitute the substance of the Book of Common Prayer. Thus, notes the same writer, 'from the point of view of ascetical theology, these two documents have a remarkable amount in common, and in a very real sense, Caroline and modern England remains "the land of the Benedictines".'[46]

Monks and Anglicans take these three principles rather for granted and tend to assume that they will constitute the three central moments of any Christian spirituality; but this, of course, is not the case. Indeed, they are so little evident to some Protestant traditions that, as Thornton points out, wars have been fought over them: 'Let it be remembered that the seventeenth-century battles between Puritan and Caroline churchmen were fought over the Prayer Book, especially over "set prayers". They were battles for and against Benedictine principles.'[47]

The Anglican Benedictine monk and spiritual theologian, Bede Thomas Mudge, notes that not only Protestantism deviated from this Anglican-Benedictine model, but also much of Roman Catholic spirituality in its later development, characterized by 'extra-liturgical devotions such as the Rosary and Benediction filling the needs of most lay-people'.[48] Certainly Roman Catholicism, after Trent especially, becomes diversified into a whole series of 'schools of spirituality' which distinguish it from both Anglicanism and Orthodoxy.

The Benedictine spirit is certainly at the root of the Anglican way of prayer, argues Dom Mudge, in a very special and pronounced manner:

> The example and influence of the Benedictine monastery, with its rhythm of divine office and Eucharist, the tradition of learning and 'lectio divina', and the family relationship among Abbot and community were determinative for much of English life, and for the pattern of English devotion. This devotional pattern persevered through the spiritual and theological upheavals of the Reformation. The Book of Common Prayer . . . the primary spiritual source-book for Anglicans . . . continued the basic monastic pattern of the Eucharist and the divine office as the principal public forms of worship, and Anglicanism has been unique in this respect.[49]

Roman Catholic priests and spiritual leaders who have tried to encourage lay groups to pray the psalms as a regular basis for their spiritual life know how arduous that pastoral effort can prove. Thus we should admire the more, 'Cranmer's work of genius in condensing the traditional scheme of hours into the two Prayer Book offices of matins and evensong.'[50] Peter Anson (Roman Catholic) and A. W. Campbell (Anglican), in their classical study of religious communities in the Anglican Communion, note that the Anglican Church is thus a kind of generalized monastic community in that, 'the Book of Common Prayer preserved the foundations of Christian monastic prayer, but simplified it in such a way that ordinary layfolk could share in this type of worship.'[51]

Since Benedictine spirituality was rendered accessible to the Anglican faithful through the Book of Common Prayer, this monastic form of prayer inevitably tended to stimulate a desire for monasticism in its specific form; as Anson and Campbell note: 'The Book of Common Prayer retained the framework of choral worship; a method of prayer which could only find its most perfect development in communities of men and women who were free to give up much of their time to ordered worship in common.'[52]

Indeed, already in the seventeenth century great Anglican spokesmen such as John Bramhall, Archbishop of Armagh, were lamenting the dissolution of the monasteries:

> First, we fear that covetousness had a great oar in the boat, and that sundry of the principal actors had a greater aim at the *goods* of the Church than at the *good* of the Church. . . . Secondly, we examine not whether the abuses which were then brought to light were true or feigned; but this we believe, that foundations, which were good in their original institution ought not to be destroyed for accessory abuses. . . . I do not see why monasteries might not agree well enough with reformed devotion.[53]

And another great seventeenth-century divine wrote even more pointedly that 'seeing that [monastic life] is a perfection to Christianity, it is certainly a blot on the Reformation when we profess that we are without it.'[54]

Anglican divines such as Cosin, Herbert, Laud, Taylor and others produced a whole literature of personal and liturgical prayer that enriched Anglican spirituality even more and recovered additional elements of the monastic heritage.[55] This rich spiritual atmosphere nourished one of the most extraordinary experiences of quasi-monastic life, that of Little Gidding, which we will consider later.

During the rest of the seventeenth, and throughout the eighteenth and first half of the nineteenth centuries, there were regular Anglican proposals for the re-establishment of the monastic life. 'Again and again', note Anson and Campbell, 'we come across instances of writers deploring the lack of monastic institutions in the Church of England.'[56] These two scholars of Anglican monasticism trace these proposals through sixteen pages of their study, and the compendium of authors cited includes some of the most notable figures of Anglicanism in these centuries: John Evelyn, Dean William Sancroft, Bishop Thomas Ken, William Law, Bishop

George Berkeley, Dr Samuel Johnson, and Poet Laureate Robert Southey.[57]

In July of 1833 John Keble preached the famous Oxford sermon that according to Newman and others marked the beginning of the great Anglo-Catholic renewal. In the context of this movement there was a whole explosion of monastic-religious foundations that restored the specifically monastic experience to the Anglican Communion.

There are, of course, specifically Benedictine houses in the Anglican Communion for both monks and nuns. For monks, one thinks of Nashdom Abbey in England, St Gregory's Abbey in the United States, St Mark's Priory in Australia, as well as the Holy Cross houses in the United States, in Canada and in Liberia. For nuns one thinks of St Mary's Abbey and the Priory of our Lady, both in England. But what about the spirituality that characterizes the other numerous Anglican communities, such as the Society of St John the Evangelist, the Community of the Resurrection and the Society of the Sacred Mission?

Dom Bede Thomas Mudge notes that to overcome anti-Catholic suspicions, 'the first communities went out of their way to justify their existence by a great devotion to works of charity: social work with the poor, the operation of "penitentiaries" for wayward women, and nursing were favourite occupations.'[58] Here one could think of certain more actively-oriented Benedictine communities of monks and sisters in the United States, which were invited by bishops into their diocese only on condition that they undertake active apostolates, including parishes, missions, schools, and so forth. These congregations have developed into extremely interesting and fruitful alternative forms of Benedictinism, and recall the variety of ministries the early monks engaged in, before juridical distinctions separated 'active' from 'contemplative' orders.

Dom Mudge makes some interesting points here in connection with the Anglican congregations (and the parallel can be noted with the American Benedictine families):

While the works of the early communities were important and needed, it was the spiritual and communal life which drew applicants, and in this atmosphere the basically monastic pattern of Anglican spirituality, which had survived three centuries after

93

the Reformation, had its inevitable effect. No matter how active the apostolate of the community, the corporate recitation of a full form of the Office was present in all of the communities from the very start. . . . It is an unusual Anglican community which has not had as part of its tradition the singing of the Office to the plainsong melodies, a good deal of corporate silence, and a tradition of the cultivation of an intense devotional life, based on Scriptural and Patristic sources. The traditional emphasis on monastic learning and writing also appeared.[59]

Thus, in the context of a wide variety of foundations and apostolates, 'the pattern has, in fact, remained surprisingly consistent and true to traditional monastic roots'. In the recent wave of religious renewal, which has swept over Anglican communities as it has Roman Catholic, the Anglican tendency has been precisely to intensify the monastic identity, moving beyond certain Victorian forms of religiosity:

Having often begun on an active pattern, the communities have gradually developed a more traditionally monastic life, and this has been done as the result of a consensus of the members of the community . . . few people have entered the communities without some leaning, at least, towards monastic observances. This has caused the outward forms of the recent renewal to appear conservative by Roman Catholic standards. . . . Anglican religious have, for the most part, deliberately chosen the observances of traditional monasticism and are not eager to be rid of them.[60]

The thesis of Mudge is that almost all Anglican religious communities have a basically monastic, Benedictine spirit in them, simply because they are Anglican and thus inheritors of a precise spiritual tradition:

Not infrequently these days, Anglican religious are invited to meetings of Roman Catholic religious, and often asked to describe their community. Normally the reply is that there is no exact counterpart to our life in the Roman Catholic Church. . . . But when asked to describe the life in more detail, more than once the reply has been, 'Oh, you're Benedictine, of course . . . .' It is a pattern that has been inherited from a nation whose monks, scholars, teachers, historians, rulers, missionaries and martyrs were often either Benedictines themselves or under direct Benedictine influence, and the pattern has proved surprisingly stable, through the changes and reforms of many generations.[61]

Some Ecumenical Implications

The thesis of the basically Benedictine spirit of the Anglican Community in general, and of Anglican religious communities specifically, obviously constitutes a healthy challenge for Roman Catholics (and especially for Roman Catholic Benedictines). It means that there is a basic common experience underlying Anglican and Roman Catholic spirituality; since monasticism predates our divisions, it constitutes a kind of 'ecumenical *anamnesis*' that makes present and living a shared heritage, and also opens up fresh horizons for ecumenical hope and commitment.

Certainly Benedictines have played a key role in the development of the Anglican-Roman Catholic dialogue from the very beginning. Dom Leander, President of the English Congregation of Benedictines and Prior of Douai in the seventeenth century, was the first of a series of papal agents sent to England to explore possibilities of dialogue; his intuitive understanding of Anglicanism has received warm praise from Anglican ecumenical scholars.[62]

Closer to our own time, Dom Lambert Beauduin of Chevetogne, founder of the ecumenical review *Irenikon*, opened up new possibilities for the dialogue with his decisive paper, 'The Anglican Church, United not Absorbed', read by Cardinal Mercier at the pioneering Malines Conversations.[63] On the Anglican side, the ecumenist Dom Benedict Ley and the liturgist Dom Gregory Dix, both of Nashdom Abbey, contributed notably to the Anglican-Roman Catholic dialogue.

But beyond specific personalities, Anglicans have noted that the Benedictine commitment to the liturgical renewal and to a more Christ-centred, biblical and patristic approach to Christian life contributed significantly to preparing the way for Vatican II, which has narrowed the gap between Anglicans and Roman Catholics to an extent, 'not even the most sanguine could have foreseen'.[64] Of course, monastic contacts and exchanges have multiplied since the Council, and organizations such as the Fellowship of St Gregory and St Augustine are dedicated to promoting permanent contact at the monastic and also parish levels.[65]

The theological documents published by the Anglican-Roman Catholic International Commission (ARCIC) indicate substantial theological accord regarding many areas of the faith. The Roman Catholic ecumenist, Jean Tillard, has argued that the next step must be, 'a spiritual coming together . . . the reunion of two separated churches . . . is primarily a spiritual matter.[66]

If this 'spiritual coming together' is the key to further progress, what if (as suggested by this chapter) Roman Catholics *already share* a common fundamental spiritual experience not only with Anglican Benedictines, but also with the Anglican family as such? If such were the case, both 'sides' would want to deepen their awareness of this sharing and its important ecumenical implications.

The centrality of the Eucharist and the Word, the importance of praying the Psalms in community, the need to give personal prayer a solid biblical-patristic-liturgical nourishment, all these elements lead to an experience of Christian spirituality for which the emphasis is communitarian and familial, notes Thornton.[67] Dom Bede Thomas Mudge likewise insists on this theme of domestic community:

> There has also been found in traditional Anglican piety a distinct strain of 'homeliness' as it is sometimes called. A warm, tolerant human devotion based on loving persuasion rather than fiery oratory is part of the Anglican temper. Historically, the Anglican clergy . . . have been very much part of the domestic scene in the villages and parishes where they have served, and have often been loved and revered. The Anglican liturgical calendar has more commemorations of faithful pastors, such as George Herbert, than of fiery missionaries, and even Anglican martyrs have commonly been of gentle disposition. Anglicanism has always been more attracted by the image of the Church as family, rather than militia, and the similarity evoked to a community of monks, living as a family, under an abbot who leads them as a father, is not accidental.[68]

It is important to reflect deeply on this shared experience of Christian community, for it might constitute the substance of that Communion, of that *koinonia*, which is the very goal of the ecumenical movement.

The *koinonia* theme has become central for the Anglican-Roman Catholic dialogue. In the recent ARCIC statements on authority, for instance, *koinonia* is one of the key terms which keeps emerging to explain the precise context and scope of Church authority.[69]

The *koinonia* ideal is treasured in a particular way by the Anglican Communion, which has always understood itself to be not primarily a juridical entity or *societas*, bound together by canon law and organs of authority, but rather as a sacramental-liturgical Communion of the faithful. The characteristic designations are revealing in this respect: the Church terms itself the Anglican *Communion*; its key liturgical text that unites the faithful is the Book of *Common* Prayer; and the traditional Anglican designation of the central, unifying sacrament is Holy *Communion*. *Koinonia* does constitute a central *leitmotiv* of the Anglican experience; indeed its whole dogmatic and spiritual theology can be articulated through this theme. One thinks in this context of a classic such as L. S. Thornton's *The Common Life in the Body of Christ*.[70]

But of course Benedictine life is also essentially *koinonia*, an endeavour to live the communion-community ideal as presented in the Acts of the Apostles.[71] Monastic life from the time of St Pachomius has been the affirmation of these values, and indeed Pachomius and his disciples refered to monastic life simply as 'holy koinonia'.[72] This same biblical spirituality flows into Western monasticism and Benedictinism, which also looks to:

> . . . the sustained and total response to the gospel made by the apostles who 'left all to follow Christ', a radical attitude which in the post-resurrection era found expression in the voluntary common life, the *koinonia* of the primitive Church which so impressed St Benedict as it had St Pachomius and St Augustine before him. It is thus the gospel as a whole which should be the ever-present and overriding reality in the mind of the monk. . . .[73]

Later forms of spirituality often brought an individualistic, intimistic approach which worked against the communitarian-sacramental-liturgical approach to Christian life. When the individualistic mentality was coupled with neo-scholastic theology and strongly juridical concerns, difficulties were compounded for understanding the Benedictine experience, or the Anglican approach. Certainly Vatican II has done a great deal to renew the sense of Christian community, centred in Christ and celebrated in liturgy, as the context for Christian spirituality and life:

> It has pleased God to make men holy and save them not merely as individuals without any mutual bonds, but by making them into a single people, a people which acknowledges Him in truth and serves Him in holiness.[74]

> In the liturgy the sanctification of man is manifested . . . in the liturgy full public worship is performed by the Mystical Body of Jesus Christ, that is, by the Head and His members. From this it follows that every liturgical celebration because it is an action of Christ the priest and of His Body, the Church, is a sacred action surpassing all others. No other action of the Church can match its claim to efficacy nor equal the degree of it . . . the liturgy is the summit toward which the activity of the Church is directed; at the same time it is the fountain from which all her power flows . . . devotions should be so drawn up that they harmonize with the liturgical seasons, accord with the sacred liturgy, are in some fashion derived from it, and lead the people to it, since the liturgy by its very nature far surpasses any of them.[75]

If one couples these Conciliar affirmations regarding Christocentric-communitarian-liturgical spirituality with the affirmation of the centrality of the Word of God, 'the soul of sacred theology',[76] then an organic vision of Christian life emerges, which is profound indeed:

> The Church has always venerated the divine Scriptures just as she venerates the body of the Lord, since from the table of both the word of God and of the body of Christ she unceasingly receives and offers to the faithful the bread of life, especially in the sacred liturgy. . . . Therefore, like the Christian religion itself, all the preaching of the Church must be nourished and guided by the sacred Scripture. For in the sacred books, the Father who is in heaven meets His children with great love and speaks with them; and the force and power in the word of God

is so great that it remains the support and energy of the Church, the strength of faith for her children, the food of the soul, the pure and perennial source of spiritual life.[77]

Ecumenists have long been aware of the 'non-dogmatic obstacles' which also separate the Churches; they are much more difficult to discern and to articulate, but often they exercise a significant power in keeping us apart. Our theological dialogues focus on specific, theoretical issues, but often the deeper problems lie elsewhere. It may be, on the other hand, that very significant resources for reunion also lie beyond technical theology. The affirmation of Fr Tillard merits repetition: 'the reunion of two separated churches . . . is primarily a spiritual matter.' One recalls also the affirmation of Vatican II that 'spiritual ecumenism' constitutes 'the soul of the whole ecumenical movement'.[78]

If the thesis of the Benedictine spirit in Anglicanism is true (especially if taken together with the thesis of our next chapter regarding the lay-prophetic component of Anglican spirituality), then clearly the two Churches are drawn much closer together. Benedictine spirituality has not predominated in Roman Catholicism in recent centuries, and particularly not since the Counter-Reform, but remains a most valid current of Roman Catholic spirituality, and recalls its medieval, patristic and biblical roots. To the extent that Roman Catholics focus on that heritage (especially in the light of Vatican II's affirmations about Christocentric biblical-liturgical spirituality), they will be able to understand more clearly the Anglican experience and appreciate the spiritual 'consanguinity' of the two sister Churches.

Notes

1 *La Vita Benedettina: Proposte approvate dal Congresso degli Abbati* (Editrice Anselmiana, Rome, 1968), p. 1.
2 ibid.
3 Martin Thornton, *English Spirituality* (SPCK 1963), p. 76.
4 John Macquarrie, 'What Still Separates Us from the Catholic Church? An Anglican Reply', *Concilium* 6 (1970) 45; to the query posed by the title of the article, Macquarrie replies in true Anglican fashion that nothing whatever separates Anglicans from the Catholic Church, although various issues still separate Anglicans and Roman Catholics.
5 Stephen Neill, *Anglicanism* (Penguin 1960), p. 419.

6 Anthony Hanson, *Church, Sacraments and Ministry* (Mowbrays 1975), p. 15.

7 George Tavard, *The Quest for Catholicity: The Development of High Church Anglicanism* (Herder, New York, 1964), p. 61; to consult primary sources, see the useful anthology *Anglicanism: The Thought and Practice of the Church of England, Illustrated from the Religious Literature of the Seventeenth Century*, ed. Paul Elmer More and Frank Leslie Cross (SPCK 1962), pp. 3–50 *et passim*.

8 See J. W. C. Wand, *Anglicanism in History and Today* (Weidenfeld and Nicolson 1963), pp. 15–18.

9 Certainly the Decree on Ecumenism of Vatican II paved the way for a fuller Roman Catholic recognition of Anglican continuities and the uniqueness of the Anglican Communion when, in treating of the Churches of the Reform, it affirms: '*Inter eas, in quibus traditiones et structurae catholicae ex parte subsistere pergunt, locum specialem tenet communio anglicana.*' *Decree on Ecumenism*, n. 13. Subsequent statements of Paul VI and the ARCIC documents have deepened this awareness.

10 See John R. H. Moorman, *A History of the Church in England* (A. & C. Black 1967), p. 8; and Wand, p. 6.

11 Thomas Gannon and George W. Traub, *The Desert and the City: An Interpretation of the History of Christian Spirituality* (Macmillan 1969), p. 56.

12 ibid.

13 Dorothy Whitelock, *The Beginnings of English Society* (Penguin 1974) p. 258.

14 Stephen Neill, *A History of Christian Missions* (Penguin 1973), p. 67.

15 ibid.

16 It should be remembered that Gregory, 'was the recognized master [of spiritual and mystical theology] throughout Western Europe during the five centuries of the early Middle Ages.' Cuthbert Butler, *Western Mysticism* (Constable 1951), p. 65.

17 Bede, *The Ecclesiastical History of the English People*, Bk 1 ch. 30.

18 See Gregory the Great, *Dialogues*, Bk II ch. 36: '*Nam scripsit monachorum regulam, discretione praecipuam, sermone luculentam.*'

19 Bede, Bk I ch. 27.

20 ibid.

21 A. M. Allchin, 'The Nature of Catholicity: An Anglican Approach' in *Unitatis Redintegratio, 1964–1974: The Impact of the Decree on Ecumenism*, ed. Gerard Békés and Vilmos Vajta (Editrice Anselmiana, Rome, 1977) 114.

22 See Benedetto Calati, 'Aspetti ecclesiali del monachesimo anglo-germanico primitivo', *Vita Monastica* 81 (1965) 54–78; see also Pio Tamburrino 'Il monaco nella Chiesa di Cristo', *Vita Monastica* 89 (1967) 90–4.

23 See Neill, *Anglicanism*, p. 11; also M. W. Patterson, *A History of the Church of England* (Longmans 1937), p. 8.

24 Not only St Augustine but also the four subsequent Archbishops of

Canterbury, the first Archbishop of York, the first Bishop of London, the first Bishop of Rochester and the first Abbot of Canterbury Abbey (all saints) were all monks from the two groups sent by St Gregory from his Rome monastery; thus Gregory and his monks not only set up the basic diocesan structures that have continued up to the present in the Church of England, but also provided the pioneer churchmen who laid the human foundations for that Church.

25 See Kassius Hallinger, 'Papst Gregor der Grosse und der hl. Benedikt' in *Commentationes in Regulam S. Benedicti*, cura Basilii Steidle (Editrice Anselmiana, Rome, 1957), 239–319; for a critical response to Steidle see Olegario M. Porcel, 'San Gregorio Magno y el Monacato, Cuestiones controvertidas' in *Scripta et Documenta, Monastica* (Abadia de Montserrat 1960), pp. 1–95.

26 See Robert Gillet, 'Spiritualité et place du moine dans l'église selon saint Grégoire le Grand' in *Théologie de la Vie Monastique* (Aubier, Paris, 1961), p. 323.

27 Moorman, p. 31; see also Patterson, p. 38: were it not for Bede 'hardly anything would be known of the leaders of our early Church.'

28 Mary Price, *Bede and Dunstan* (Oxford University Press 1968), p. 27.

29 Patterson, op. cit., p. 38. See Bede, Bk 2 ch. 1.

30 Price, p. 27.

31 Leo Sherley-Price, 'Introduction' in Bede, *A History of the English Church and People* (Penguin 1975), p. 21.

32 ibid., pp. 24–6; see also Price, p. 26–9; Moorman, p. 31, etc.

33 See Calati, pp. 57–62; the most significant moments of English Church history for Bede recall and reconstitute the apostolic community life; thus he writes of Augustine's monastic community of Kent: 'As soon as they had occupied the house given them, they began to emulate the life of the apostles and the primitive Church. . .', Bk I ch. 26. Of the community of St Hilda he writes: 'After the example of the primitive Church, no one there was rich, no one was needy, for everything was held in common. . .' etc. Bk 4 ch. 23.

34 See Neill, *Anglicanism*, pp. 89–117; see John Macquarrie, *Paths in Spirituality* (SCM Press 1973), pp. 73–6, 103–11.

35 Neill, *Anglicanism*, p. 419; see also Patterson, p. 38.

36 Moorman, p. 68.

37 See Patterson, pp. 71–2; Moorman, p. 63, etc.

38 See Moorman, p. 68: 'In 1066 there were thirty-five [monastic] houses, but by 1100 this number had grown to fifty independent houses, twenty-nine dependent cells, and forty-five . . . dependencies of foreign monasteries.'

30 ibid., p. 44.

40 Friedrich Herr, *The Medieval World: Europe 1100–1350* (Mentor, New York, 1972), p. 61.

41 Moorman, p. 72.

42 G. W. C. Woodward, *The Dissolution of the Monasteries* (Pitkin 1972), p. 3.

43 ibid., p. 2.

44 See the rather polemical work by the King's Chaplain, Edward Stil-lingfleet, *A Discourse Concerning the Idolatry Practiced in the Church of Rome* (Robert White 1676); the Royal Chaplain criticizes at some length not only later monasticism but also its founders, 'the great Fanaticism of S. Benedict and S. Romualdus: their hatred of Human Learning, and Strange Visions and Revelations', p. 232.

45 See Woodward, pp. 3–19; see below, n. 53.

46 Thornton, p. 57; see also p. 81: 'Benedictinism and Anglicanism have affinities in outlook and temperament.'

47 ibid., p. 79.

48 Bede Thomas Mudge, 'Monastic Spirituality in Anglicanism', *Review for Religious* 37 (1978), 507. His Holy Cross Order has recently de-clared itself formally to be Benedictine in spirit and scope.

49 ibid.

50 Macquarrie, *Paths in Spirituality*, p. 107.

51 Peter Anson, *The Call of the Cloister: Religious Communities and Kindred Bodies in the Anglican Communion*, rev. and ed. A. W. Campbell (SPCK 1964), p. 3.

52 ibid., p. 4.

53 John Bramhall, *Works* (Oxford: Library of Anglo-Catholic Theology 1842) 1. 118–120.

54 Herbert Thorndike, *Works* (Oxford: Library of Anglo-Catholic Theo-logy 1854) 5.571.

55 See John Cosin, *Collection of Private Devotions in the Practice of the Ancient Church, Called the Hours of Prayer in Works* (Oxford: Library of Anglo-Catholic Theology 1845), 2.88–331, which includes liturgies for Matins, Prime, Terce, Sext, None, Vespers and Compline.

56 ibid., p. 19.

57 ibid., pp. 12–28. See also A. M. Allchin, *The Silent Rebellion: Anglican Religious Communities 1845–1900* (London: SCM 1958), pp. 15–35.

58 Mudge, op. cit., p. 509.

59 ibid., p. 510.

60 ibid., pp. 512–13.

61 ibid., p. 514.

62 See Bernard and Margaret Pawley, *Rome and Canterbury through Four Centuries: A Study of the Relations between the Church of Rome and the Anglican Churches, 1530–1973* (Mowbrays 1974), pp. 30–32.

63 See S. A. Quitslund, 'United not absorbed', *Journal of Ecumenical Studies* 8 (1971) 255–285; the entire January 1978 issue of *Unité des Chrétiens* is dedicated to Dom Beauduin.

64 Pawleys, p. 338; after Vatican II, not just the Anglo-Catholic current of Anglicanism but also the 'evangelical' current is very interested in the Anglican Roman Catholic dialogue; the recent statements regarding shared Eucharists by Dr Coggan, who is not considered a 'high church-man', reflect this broad interest in dialogue and reunion.

65 The Fellowship of St Gregory and St Augustine, dedicated to prayer, study and work for the reunion in diversity of the two Churches, is a recently founded international communion already present in some

seven nations. Co-sponsored by the Camaldolese monks and nuns and by the Anglican Order of the Holy Cross and Order of St Helena, the Fellowship numbers among its patrons Cardinal Hume, O.S.B., Archbishop Weakland, O.S.B., the Abbot Primate, Bishop Christopher Butler, O.S.B., and some fifteen Benedictine Abbots and Priors, along with numerous other Roman Catholic and Anglican Churchmen.

66 Jean Tillard, sermon preached at Mass of Reconciliation sponsored by the Order of the Holy Cross, September 18, 1976.

67 See Thornton, p. 50.

68 Mudge, pp. 508–9.

69 See the ARCIC Agreed Statement on Authority in the Church, 1977, pars. 1, 5, 7, 8, 11, 15, 23, etc. See also Agreed Statement on Authority in the Church ii, 1981, par 4, etc.

70 L. S. Thornton, C.R., *The Common Life in the Body of Christ* (Dacre Press 1944).

71 See Sister Augusta Marie, 'Koinonia: Its Biblical Meaning and Use in Monastic Life' in *The American Benedictine Review* 18(1967), pp. 189–212. See also Joel Rippinger, O.S.B., 'The Biblical and Monastic Roots of Poverty in the Rule under the Aspect of Koinonia' in The American Benedictine Review 27(1976), pp. 321–31; see also Robert Hale, O.S.B. Cam., 'La koinonia aperta della vita monastica' in *Comunità Cristiana e Communità Umana* (Quaderni di V.M., Camaldoli, 1976), pp. 128–62.

72 See the *Liber Patris Nostri Orsiesii* in *Pachomiana Latina* (Bibliothèque de la Revue d'Histoire Ecclésiastique, Louvain, 1932), p. 147.

73 Daniel Rees O.S.B. and Other Members of the English Benedictine Congregation, *Consider Your Call: A Theology of Monastic Life Today* (SPCK 1978), pp. 48–49; regarding the koinonia theme, see also pp. 30, 59, 77, 85, 165, 184, 191, 234, etc.

74 Vatican II, Dogmatic Constitution on the Church, n. 9.

75 Vatican II, Constitution on the Sacred Liturgy, nn. 7, 10, 13.

76 Vatican II, Dogmatic Constitution on Divine Revelation, n. 24.

77 ibid., n. 21.

78 Vatican II, Decree on Ecumenism, n. 8. Spiritual ecumenism, if it is truly liturgical, might even significantly illumine theological ecumenism. One thinks of the early Christian principle of 'lex orandi, lex credendi', affirmed by the, 'Roman curia of the era [of Prosper of Aquitaine] . . . the Roman See has always considered it the exact expression of its point of view' (Cipriano Vagaggini, O.S.B., *Il Senso Teologico della Liturgia* (Pauline, Rome, 1965), p. 496): if this principle expresses the pastristic and monastic theological method, it would be interesting to trace its significance for Anglican theology. See, for instance, Stephen W. Sykes, *The Integrity of Anglicanism* (Mowbrays 1978), pp. 46–7: 'The prayers [of liturgy] contain, express and imply particular Christian doctrines and are strongly influenced by the positive doctrinal beliefs of earlier generations . . . the present Anglican church has incorporated a regulated doctrinal structure in the content of its liturgy, and in the rules governing its public performance.' The

Anglican liturgical theologian Massey Shepherd told me that he felt the patristic maxim *'lex orandi, lex credendi'* characterizes Anglican theology at its best. In this context the title of Dr Shepherd's *festschrift*, published in 1981 by Seabury on the fortieth anniversary of his ordination, is certainly significant: *Worship Points the Way: A Celebration of the Life and Work of Massey Hamilton Shepherd, Jr.* The Scottish ARC Consultation has affirmed the significance of this theme specifically for the Anglican/Roman Catholic dialogue, noting their, 'common ground, in that both traditions agree on the continuing application of the principle *"lex orandi, lex credendi"* '. See 'The Ecclesial Nature of the Eucharist: A Report by the Joint Study Group', in *Documents on Anglican/Roman Catholic Relations 3*, op. cit., p. 32.

4

A Second Dimension of Consanguinity: The Lay-Prophetic Current of Anglicanism

We noted above that the first section of a typical Anglican history of the English Church will refer to early monastic figures such as St Ninian, St Germanus, St Patrick, and so on. But it is at least interesting, as these same histories are careful to note, that the first Christian in Britain who is known by name is Alban, a soldier in the Roman army. According to Bede and other early biographers, Alban hid a Christian priest fleeing from persecution, and offered himself up, being tortured and martyred in the place of the priest. The traditional date of his martyrdom is 303 or 304, but recent scholarship indicates that it might have been as early as 209. The site of Alban's martyrdom soon became a shrine, and the strong devotion to him that flourished in the Middle Ages continues into our own time, in both the Anglican and Roman Catholic Churches.[1]

Could our monastic-Benedictine interpretation of the pre-Reform English Church not be questioned by the fact that figures such as Alban illumine the earliest, pre-monastic roots of that Church, roots that are more lay and prophetic in spirit than monastic and Benedictine? What about Queen Bertha and Blessed King Ethelbert of Kent, who welcomed St Augustine and enabled his mission to succeed, who built St Andrew's cathedral in Rochester and were instrumental in the conversion of the East Saxons, in whose territory they built the first cathedral of St Paul in London?[2] And what of King Edwin of Northumbria and his queen Ethelburga, who did so much to favour the mission of Paulinus, ruling their dominions in such peace that, 'a woman could carry her new-born baby across the island from sea to sea and suffer no harm'.[3]

A rich current of Christian witness and ministry can be traced in early British history, a current neither monastic nor Benedictine, which was to continue throughout the Middle Ages. Edward the Confessor, a gentle king dedicated to the poor and infirm, and Thomas Becket, martyred defender of the liberty of the Church, dominated the devotion of the later Middle Ages in England, and neither of these men was a monk. A work such as T. S. Eliot's *Murder in the Cathedral* demonstrates the influence of the non-monastic, prophetic spirit of Becket, which penetrates even contemporary Anglicanism.

If we look at the English Reform itself, so many of the key figures are clearly non-monastic – Henry VIII, Cranmer, Elizabeth, Latimer, Ridley, Tyndale, Edward VI, for example – that it is obvious that the monastic-Benedictine interpretation of Anglicanism is partial at best. It is in need of at least one other complementary interpretive key, if not several others. But any complex of interpretive keys, however varied, will inevitably fall short of the living, mysterious reality of the Anglican spirit; in the words of the Caroline theologian Ralph Cudworth: 'neither are we able to inclose in words and letters the life, soul, and essence of any spiritual truth, and as it were to incorporate it in them.'[4]

Yet, as members of sister Churches we must seek to understand each other if we are to follow the fundamental theological venture of *fides quaerens intellectum*, and such attempt must find expression in words, interpretations, models. We will therefore add the lay-prophetic interpretation to the monastic-Benedictine, believing that it will illuminate other facets of the extraordinary breadth and depth of a beloved sister Church.

The Prophetic Factor

What characterizes the prophetic charism in the life of a Church? How extensive is that charism and what is its centre? Biblical and dogmatic theologians stress that prophecy is not essentially a miraculous foretelling of the future, nor does it require visions or mighty portents; as Rahner notes, 'the prophet does not make predictions in the sense of an oracle or clairvoyant. This would be a very secondary restriction of the concept.'⁵ The prophet, essentially, is the person who can challenge, judge, and read the present in the light of the living Word of God. In the words of the Roman Catholic biblical theologian Norbert Lohfink: 'The only essential characteristic of prophetism is the fact of an immediacy of rapport with God that is rationally unexplainable, which gives rise to a unique, concrete message for a specific, well-determined time and space.'⁶ The prophet's word penetrates the present moment with an explosive force, opening up new possibilities in terms of faithfulness to the Father and to one's fellow humans, especially those most in need of succour. In this sense the prophetic word does radically impinge upon the future, since the prophet:

> . . . creates a new and forward-looking situation in the history of salvation by his criticism of society, and is essentially associated with promises and the future. Furthermore, since the prophet's words are not to be just doctrinal propositions but are to be translated into real action, he will himself nearly always be the leader and organizer of religious and social changes.⁷

Whatever else we might mean when speaking of 'prophetic' Anglicans and Roman Catholics, our primary emphasis must be on the gift to illumine the concrete historical moment with God's Word, and thus to create 'a new and forward-looking situation in the history of salvation'.

Christ himself is the great Prophet, just as he is the great High Priest and King, because he represents the definitive incarnation of God's Word in the concrete moment, in such a way as to open that history up to its salvific hope. Since the ultimate meaning of prophecy is christological, it must also be ecclesial, because the Churches are members of Christ, components of the 'whole Christ'. Thus Vatican II, in its Dogmatic Constitution on the Church, having affirmed that all Christians participate in the Priesthood of Christ, continues: 'The holy People of God shares also in Christ's prophetic office. It spreads abroad a living witness to Him, especially by means of a life of faith and charity and by offering to God a sacrifice of praise, the tribute of lips which give honour to His name' (cf. Heb. 13:15).[8] In the words of the Benedictine biblical scholar N. Füglister, 'All Christians are in principle endowed with prophecy.'[9]

The ecumenical implications of this broader dimension of prophecy are significant: we listen to Christians of other Churches, not simply because they might be repeating some element of Christian tradition which we for the moment had forgotten, but because God is also speaking anew to us *today*, through His prophets, who might well be Christians of other Churches, or entire ecclesial communities. Indeed, it is a particular characteristic of the prophetic spirit that it is hard to confine it to institutional boundaries, not even to those of the Roman Catholic Church.

But if it is true that all Christians, by virtue of their baptism, participate in the prophetic office of Christ, nevertheless (as with universal priesthood of all believers in relation to specific, ministerial priesthood) some are called in a more particular way to exercise a special gift of prophecy.[10] Theologians note that St Paul, in his hierarchy of gifts, lists prophecy in second place, immediately after apostolicity: 'God has given the first place to apostles, the second to prophets. . .' (1 Cor. 12:28). This great ecclesial significance of prophecy also has important ecumenical implications: prophets of other Churches challenge us by an authority that is only superseded by the apostolic charism.

If all Roman Catholics *and* all Anglicans, by virtue of baptism, participate in the prophetic office of Christ, and if the special prophetic charism can fall upon Anglicans and Roman Catholics alike, then this is another significant current of 'consanguinity' which the two sister Churches share. Indeed, it is more primordial than the monastic-Benedictine current. For when we encounter the monastic heritage in the other Church, we can say: 'that spirituality is ours also.' But when someone speaks truly prophetically from either of our Churches, whether that word concern the reform of Christians, social justice or whatever, we cannot claim that utterance as our own spirituality, heritage, or possession, for it is the very Spirit challenging us in a new way, calling us beyond our spiritualities and heritages, with their more limited and human scope.

On the other hand, to the extent that the Benedictine heritage signifies focusing on the Word, especially as proclaimed and invoked in liturgy, in the context of *koinonia*, Christian community, to this extent the prophetic dimension renders the tradition alive and authentic, while at the same time this tradition manifests, discerns and nurtures the prophetic dimension. The Eastern heritage (also profoundly monastic) stresses this organic link between tradition and Spirit:

Tradition is the life of the Holy Spirit in the Church.[11]

Tradition is the witness of the Spirit; the Spirit's unceasing revelation and preaching of good tidings. . . . To accept and understand Tradition . . . we must feel the breath of the Holy Ghost in it. . . Tradition is the constant abiding of the Spirit and not only the memory of words.[12]

The Anglican and the Roman Catholic heritages at their best include this vivifying presence of Spirit in Tradition; the Spirit and the substance of the Tradition are the same, although the two specific histories are distinct. For this reason we are challenged to speak of two *sister* Churches.

Both Churches are very aware of Tradition, as is the great Eastern Church. Archimandrite Kallistos Ware notes some pitfalls here in connection with his own Eastern Church, and surely his words have relevance also for the Western Churches:

Not everything received from the past is of equal value, nor is everything received from the past necessarily true. As one of the bishops remarked at the Council of Carthage in 257: 'The Lord said, I am truth. He did not say, I am custom.' There is a difference between 'Tradition' and 'traditions'. . . . It is necessary to question the past. In Byzantine and post-Byzantine times, Orthodox have not always been sufficiently critical in their attitude to the past, and the result has frequently been stagnation.[13]

To discern the substance of Tradition from the outer layer of ecclesiastical custom, and to vivify our awareness of Tradition is the scope of the prophetic charism. We Roman Catholics need all the help the Spirit will give us, not least when He (She) speaks with an Anglican voice; and *mutatis mutandis* so do our Anglican brethren.

109

Rediscovery of the biblical and early patristic theme of prophecy reintroduces the difficult issue of distinguishing the true prophet from the false, or from the clever or perceptive person. Our two Churches provide precise procedures and rites for training and appointing clergy, religious and official theologians, so that their standing may be easily recognized in a professional structure. But how is a prophet to be recognized? What training is required? What is the minimum age requirement? May one be married? Must one be male?

It is evident from Scripture that prophecy can take a most extraordinary variety of forms, that prophets can be 'the most diverse types of people'.[14] There are ecstatics, but also non-ecstatics, groups as well as individuals, married as well as single, male as well as female, kings and commoners, priests and laity. Lohfink notes that: 'Prophecy is not tied to any condition of life. Amos was a cultivator of sycamore trees, Isaiah was apparently of an aristocratic family, Ezekiel was a priest, and Hulda was a housewife.[15]

This amazing diversity of forms frees us from our narrow stereotypes of Church ministry, and challenges us to be attentive to the possibility of prophetic witness from the most unexpected quarters. Lohfink goes on to reflect:

> Could it not be that many contemporary preachers, as well as journalists and writers should be considered on the same plane as the ancient prophets? Or a pope who knows how to read the signs of the times and has the courage from God to shake the whole Church with a Council?. . . And we do not know what totally new forms of prophetism may present themselves within perhaps two decades, and to our total surprise.[16]

It would be interesting to reflect upon the history of our two Churches in the light of the prophetic charism. We often focus on hierarchical office to understand an ecclesial heritage: Ludwig Pastor's *Lives of the Popes* and Canon Edward Carpenter's recent *Cantuar: The Archbishops in their Office* are two examples of this. A historical reflection upon prophetic witness in the two sister Churches might add a complementary dimension that would enrich the dialogue between them.

Perhaps we are somewhat unaccustomed to this type of perception of the Churches, because we tend to think of prophecy as an Old Testament phenomenon, thereby relegating it conveniently to the pre-Christian era. But Füglister notes that it is precisely in the New Testament that the category flourishes and finds fulfilment:

> It is only with the New Testament that 'prophet' becomes a fundamental theological concept in the strict sense. In fact 'prophet' is a key word above all in the New Testament. This is evident not only from the frequency with which the concept occurs (206 times including derivatives) but above all from the significance that it there comes to encompass: 'prophet' is encountered in the primitive kerygma as an ancient christological title; the faithful who, through the pentecostal outpouring of the spirit constitute the new Israel of the messianic age have a fundamentally prophetic aptitude. Finally, the Church founds itself not only upon the apostolic ministry, but equally upon the prophetic, as upon two functions reciprocally connected and complementary, through which the earthly Jesus extends his mission in space and in time, and the glorified Lord, through his Spirit, remains present and operative on the earth.[17]

If some are empowered in a special way with the prophetic Spirit, and yet at the same time all Christians are called to participate in the prophetic office of Christ, what is the relationship of the former, more restricted group with the prophetic people of God? It might be a temptation of both our Churches, perhaps a bit uncomfortable with the whole notion of 'prophecy', to restrict the charism to a very few, most extraordinary figures (preferably of long ago), so as to defuse any explosive charge from the notion of 'prophetic witness'. Or, on the other hand, the concept might be rendered so abstract and generalized as to eliminate any embarrassingly specific prophetic vocation ('He is challenging, it is true, but after all, we are all of us prophets'). Van Leeuwen notes that the early Christian communities nurtured both of these dimensions, as well as the fruitful interchange between them:

> It is the same Spirit operating in the whole Church and in each of its members, and who summons some persons in a special way to the prophetic office. It is characteristic of the apostolic

111

Church that the special prophetic charism moves forward together with the common prophetism and finds in this its
foundation.[18]

When reflecting, therefore, upon the prophetic dimension of the
Anglican Communion, or of the Roman Catholic Church, we will
want to reflect upon both these dimensions of prophecy and upon
their mutual relationship: To what extent, in the various periods
of their history, are the two ecclesial communities as such
prophetic, and to what extent are their special prophetic vocations
acknowledged, supported and followed. Just as the word of the
prophet penetrates our individual lives and judges us, so the
prophetic vocation judges our ecclesial communities. Sometimes
we are found wanting, and our need of each other is therefore the
more intent, both as individuals and as Churches. We have to
return from the neo-pagan 'go it alone' ideology to the Gospel
concept of mutual support in the Spirit: 'Carry each other's
troubles, and fulfil the law of Christ' (Gal. 6:2).

The prophetic current does not always flourish though; it has its
ebbs and flows. In post-exilic Judaism, for instance, it tends to
disappear totally, but that absence, 'is felt as a tragic loss, and stirs
up the hope for a messianic-eschatological prophetism'.[19] The New
Testament presents the era of Christ in terms of this new and
definitive flourishing of the prophetic charism,[20] which tends to
have a specific identity in the immediate post-apostolic community.[21] But towards the end of the second century, prophetism
as a special, identifiable charism grows increasingly rare: the Roman
Catholic biblical theologian John McKenzie expresses the development with a stark analogy: 'Prophecy does not appear after NT
times; as OT prophecy yielded to the scribe, so NT prophecy was
submerged in the development of the hierarchical office.'[22] Another
Roman Catholic biblical theologian, however, interprets the development in a more nuanced way; it is not that prophecy simply
disappears, being 'submerged' by the hierarchical, but rather that
it flows into other offices, and works through them, 'being
absorbed by other functions (that are not absolutely a-charismatic
or anti-charismatic) and by other offices.'[23] Füglister argues that
this continuance of the charism is theologically necessary, and he
proposes an analogy particularly striking for Roman Catholics: 'If

112

it is noted rightly that the apostolic office of Peter ought to continue as a fundamental function of the post-apostolic Church, this is true also for prophetism, equally fundamental and therefore also essential for the Church.'[24] Thus the prophetic charism, 'must, under some form, continue to exist'.[25] The Jesuit theologian Karl Rahner is in accord here with his Benedictine colleague:

> The Church itself is the permanent presence of the word of *the* prophet, Jesus Christ. It is the Church in which the word effects what it signifies and is therefore a prophetic word. . . . Of their nature, the spontaneous charisms which work in and for the Church are prophetic. They do not cease to be prophetic because they must remain within the 'order' of the Church, though possibly only at the cost of grave conflicts. . . . This charismatic prophecy in the Church helps to make the message of Jesus new, relevant and actual in each changing age.[26]

Rahner laments that, 'in contrast to medieval theology, the present-day theology of the schools pays relatively scant attention to prophetism'.[27] He then sketches an outline of such a theology project, and himself reflects on the forms prophetism might take in contemporary Christianity. He proposes the startling thesis that the Christian priest should be understood primarily as a prophet:

> In the light of the prophetic element in the Church, the official priesthood must be subjected to a re-appraisal. The priest is essentially a preacher of the word, and never a mere administrative officer in a religious society. And his cultic function is not the offering of a new independent sacrifice each time, but the re-presenting of the one sacrifice of Christ through the efficacious words of the Eucharist. Hence the priesthood should be understood rather in the light of the prophetic than the cultic element, a matter perhaps of some practical importance.[28]

This matter is certainly of some ecumenical importance: were we Roman Catholics to consider Anglican clergy in this light, it might open up the possibility of a much fuller appreciation of the contribution they can make to both Churches. Suppose, for example, Roman Catholics were to reflect upon the significance of figures such as Joseph Lightfoot or Brooke Westcott. Both these men were Anglican priests and bishops, towering biblical and patristic scholars, and men committed to a practical form of social justice, convinced that Christian faith must affirm and support serious scholarship as well as solidarity with miners and factory workers. If we Roman Catholics reflect today upon such men as undoubted prophets of their time, we can still receive a great deal from them; but would we have been able to open ourselves to them in such a way one hundred years ago?

Füglister notes that, 'certainly the same danger threatens the Church, as history teaches, as threatened Judaism, that is, that the prophetic element be impeded by the official magisterium.'[29] Rahner puts the matter even more emphatically: 'It may even happen constantly in the Church, without detriment to the ultimate promises to the Church, that true prophecy may be repressed by the holders of office or the indifference of the faithful.'[30] Certainly our Christian divisions tragically reinforce this danger: 'Oh, I needn't pay the slightest heed to him, he isn't even a member of my Church!'

If the priesthood, and the episcopacy and papacy represent some of the forms that prophecy can take in the post-apostolic church, monasticism represents another. Füglister himself notes that, 'the early monks considered themselves to be the descendants or disciples of the biblical prophets', and they called, 'their eminent figures in the monastic life "prophets".'[31] One could trace the whole history of monasticism in terms of this prophetic self-awareness that has characterized it.[32] Thomas Merton, in our own times, explicitly recalls this prophetic function of monasticism.

This point is relevant too in terms of our ecumenical reflection, for if there is in fact a strong monastic-Benedictine current in Anglicanism, then that current will not be unrelated to a prophetic dimension, but rather will call it forth.[33] The *Vita Benedicti* of Gregory the Great offers an image of monasticism that is intrinsically prophetic. Benedict himself possesses 'the spirit of prophecy'[34] and he battles prophetically against the unjust wealthy to help the poor. A series of miraculous interventions by Benedict can be continually paralleled with those of the prophets such as Elijah, Elisha and Habakkuk.[35] The prophet of Scriptures, 'did not tremble before any ruler, nor did anyone bring him into subjugation' (Sirach 48:12). So Benedict reproves the terrible Totila, prophesies his death,[36] and frees a terrorized peasant from the oppressive Zalla.[37]

114

When he defends a poor widow against exploitive noble religious, Benedict calls forth from Gregory the reflection that, 'nobility of birth is a cause of the innobility of spirit for many'.[38] Thus Christopher Dawson has noted that, 'monasticism had ceased to be a helpless spectator of the moral disorder of Christendom, and had become an independent power in Western society'; because '. . . lawless feudal nobles, who cared nothing for morality or law, recognized the presence of something stronger than brute force' in monastic leaders 'regarded as the protector of the poor'.[39] If the prophet proclaims the word with such efficacy as to call forth conversion, Bede, the Father of English history, presents the early monks of his chronicle as, 'having been sent to preach the word to the English'.[40] Whether Celtic monks or of Augustine's monastic community, these prototypes of Bede's Church are presented in very 'charismatic' strokes indeed:

They were constantly at prayer; they fasted and kept vigils, they preached the word of life to whomsoever they could. They regarded worldly things as of little importance, and accepted only the necessities of life from those they taught. They practised what they preached, and were willing to endure any hardship, and even to die for the truth which they proclaimed. Before long a number of heathen, admiring the simplicity of their holy lives and the comfort of their heavenly message, believed and were baptized.[41]

Bede is giving us a theology of the Church as he describes how this prophetic witness of the monks elicits a prophetic wisdom from the King:

At length the king himself, among others, edified by the pure lives of these holy men and their gladdening promises, the truth of which they confirmed by many miracles, believed and was baptized. Thenceforward great numbers gathered each day to hear the word of God, forsaking their heathen rites and entering the unity of Christ's holy Church as believers. While the king was pleased at their faith and conversion, it is said that he would not compel anyone to accept Christianity; for he had learned from his instructors and guides to salvation that the service of Christ must be accepted freely and not under compulsion.[42]

115

As St Paul writes in his letter to the Corinthians: 'Where the Spirit of the Lord is, there is freedom' (2 Cor. 3:17). The early history, and the pre-history of the English Church is thus shaped by currents at once monastic and prophetic, priestly and lay. This spirit of the word that converts the unbeliever in freedom and defends the oppressed in justice will continue to challenge the two sister Churches who strive to offer the same witness in our own age.

Should the endeavour to bring these two Churches into ever deeper dialogue and mutual understanding be considered itself prophetic? One thinks here of the great pioneer ecumenist in this area on the Roman Catholic side, Lambert Beauduin, a Benedictine monk, and of the title of his excellent recent biography: *Beauduin: A Prophet Vindicated*.[43] If prophecy has to do with discerning the 'signs of the times', the Council itself has prophetic office: 'This sacred Synod, therefore, exhorts all the Catholic faithful to recognize the signs of the times and to take an active and intelligent part in the work of ecumenism.'[44]

The Lay Dimension

In the ARCIC Agreed Statement on Ministry and Ordination and their Elucidations it is noted that, 'both our communions have retained and remain faithful to the threefold ministry centred on the episcopacy'.[45] The two Churches are therefore in significant agreement on, 'the nature and purpose of priesthood, ordination, and apostolic succession',[46] as well as the threefold ministry of bishops, priests and deacons.[47] The same Commission significantly noted that both Churches see ordained ministry as situated in the fuller picture of the rich variety of ministries of the people of God: 'Within the Roman Catholic Church and the Anglican Communion there exists a diversity of forms of ministerial service. . . . The ordained ministry can only be rightly understood within this broader context of various ministries, all of which are the work of one and the same Spirit.'[48]

The ecumenical dialogue often seems to be focused on themes that are very institutional, hierarchical and clerical. We should not forget that if both Churches proclaim the threefold ordained ministry, they share a component in some ways much more basic: the

116

lay dimension. The overwhelming majority of the members of both Churches is lay. Indeed, 99.9 per cent of both Churches is lay. The official Anglican statistics in preparation for the Lambeth Conference 1978 point out that for every Anglican priest, there are 1,110 Anglican laity.[49] Official statistics of the Holy See for the same year indicate that for every Roman Catholic priest there are 1,800 Roman Catholic laity.[50] Nor should we think in mere quantitative terms. If every baptized Christian has been given his or her own unique gifts and vocation from the Lord, and if, as Vatican II affirms, 'all are called to sanctity and have received an equal privilege of faith through the justice of God' so that, 'all share a true equality with regard to the dignity and to the activity common to all the faithful for the building up of the Body of Christ',[51] then it is evident that a fundamental task of both Churches will be to encourage and prepare the laity to make that unique contribution to Christian ministry, and ecumenism, that only they can make. The Dominican theologian Yves Congar, in his classic works on the laity in the Church, speaks of the urgent need to encourage 'initiative on the part of the laity',[52] since 'not the walls but the faithful are the Church'.[53] We can apply this Patristic formula to our own theme, noting that if our two sister Churches are going to move into a new relationship which is in fact sisterly, that is going to implicate not primarily buildings but the faithful. The ecumenical movement is fundamentally a lay programme, as is every other mission of the Churches.

Vatican II has explicitly affirmed the dignity and significance of the laity, 'made sharers in the priestly, prophetic and kingly functions of Christ'.[54] Thus, 'pastors know how much the laity contribute to the welfare of the entire Church', and they 'also know that they themselves were not meant by Christ to shoulder alone the entire saving mission of the Church toward the world'.[55] But if the Roman Catholic Church has begun to affirm explicitly the indispensable, invaluable and creative role of the laity in the Church, we must admit that this has not always been so. Ferdinand Klostermann, a Roman Catholic theologian and specialist in the area of the laity, notes that the first draft of the chapter on the laity we have just quoted had to be radically reworked, for it was:

. . . subjected to some harsh criticism: much more should be

117

made of the layman's worth, his witness to the faith, the doctrine of the charismata, lay spirituality, marriage as a principle of the Church's growth, the competence and autonomy of the layman in the world, where he does have something else to do besides carrying out the instructions of the hierarchy.[56]

Although the majority of the Bishops carried the day for a more explicit recognition of the active role of the laity in the Church, Klostermann notes that in the Council itself there were some difficult moments:

> The ideas of what was clearly the majority met with firm opposition from some Fathers – especially in the 49th and 55th general congregations – who seemed to regard the layman as a purely passive element in the Church, at best an instrument of the hierarchy . . . and who were prepared to view the relationship between the hierarchy and the laity . . . in no other terms than those of authority and obedience.[57]

Congar has traced the history of the clerical view of the role of the laity in the Church. The first centuries of esteem declined into something less than full recognition of lay dignity after the peace of Constantine and its favour of authority which, 'took the form, among others, of granting privileges to the clergy . . . a whole series of enactments resulted in distinguishing the priests from the laity'.[58] A whole theological and spiritual understanding of the Church developed in which, 'the clergy thus stood aloof from the ordinary Christians, whose life was considered more carnal'.[59] There was also the development of the invasion of the 'barbarians', the constricting of learning to a small circle, so that, 'culture became a sort of monopoly of the clergy and monks . . . *litteratus* ("one who knows letters", that is, Latin) was synonymous with "cleric" whereas the synonym for "layman" was *illiteratus* or *idiota* (a simple person, one who cannot explain things)'.[60]

The monastic movement itself had been lay in its origins. Thus it is not theologically correct to juxtapose the 'lay' charism with the 'monastic'; many monks today are battling to recover this original lay identity to the movement.[61] But monasticism itself was soon clericalized and its theme of flight from the world, so dominant in the Middle Ages, did a disservice to the role of the laity.

118

The Roman Catholic theologian Ernest Niermann, a specialist in lay themes, notes that: 'Pastoral work in the middle ages paid special attention to the layman . . . to help him to lead a Christian life within the world, though always in terms of a Christian ideal which was monastic in flavour.'[62] Niermann describes how this clericalization and monasticization of the Church found concrete expression in the central moment of worship:

> This dualism within the Church is clearly reflected in the changes which took place in the liturgy during the transition from antiquity to the middle ages. The action is carried on by the clergy, while the ordinary faithful are reduced to a community of 'hearers'. A veil is drawn between them and the mystery – as by the liturgical language, the canon of the Mass pronounced inaudibly, the rood-screen across the chancel, the decrease in the frequency of Holy Communion.[63]

We Roman Catholics must perhaps recognize that many of the efforts of our sister Church at the time of the Reformation were dedicated to removing that unfortunate veil, in order to engage the full participation of the laity in the mysteries and mission of Christianity.

The Lay Dimension and the Anglican Reform

Bishop Stephen Neill, in his classical work on Anglicanism, sums up four of his chapters on the Anglican Reform with a list of things achieved by that Reform. It is of significance that of the first seven developments listed, four have specifically to do with the laity; Bishop Neill argues that the Anglican Reform:

> . . . had *restored* Catholic practice in the provision of worship in a language understanded of the people.
> It had *restored* Catholic practice in the encouragement of Bible-reading by the laity.
> In the Holy Communion, it had *restored* Catholic order by giving the Communion to the laity in both kinds, both the Bread and the Wine, instead of only in one kind, as was the practice of the medieval Church.

It *aimed at* restoring the Catholic practice of regular Communion by all the faithful.[64]

This certainly is an impressive list in terms of re-engaging the laity in the central moment of worship and spirituality. Roman Catholics should note that we have now also affirmed the above reforms, but should acknowledge, however, that it took us more than four hundred years to achieve two of them, and only a little less time to achieve the other two. But do we not want to acknowledge, in all honesty, that it was a *prophetic* programme for the laity that the Anglican reformers initiated, whatever objections we have to other aspects of the Reform, and however much the Anglicans were following initiatives of continental reformers?

The *whole* of the people of God should participate actively in the central moment of the life of the Church, the divine liturgy; but the medieval liturgy had been rendered so complicated that only the clergy and monks (and not all of them) could follow it. As the Preface to the first *Book of Common Prayer* (1549) notes: 'The number and hardness of the Rules called the Pie, and the manifold changings of the service, was the cause, that to turn the Book only, was so hard and intricate a matter, that many times, there was more business to find out what should be read, than to read it when it was found out.' Anglicans note that the *Book of Common Prayer* drew together into one accessible volume the elements of at least seven medieval liturgical tomes: breviary, missal, processional, pontifical, and so on. The Anglican Reform thus made available to the laity the substance of liturgical prayer: Anglican spirituality has been both a liturgical and a lay spirituality ever since. One cannot read the Vatican II Constitution on the sacred Liturgy without recognizing the prophetic force of this central moment of the Anglican Reform, which did not proclaim a series of special 'Anglican doctrines', but rather proposed a way of worship that would actively involve the laity. When asked by what positive bond the Anglican Communion is held together, Dr de Mendieta (a former Roman Catholic Benedictine monk who became an Anglican) responded: 'The answer probably lies in the field of their public and common worship, rather than of explicit and clearly defined dogma.'[65] That bond characterizes the Anglican Reform as 'monastic' and 'Benedictine' in the broader sense of those categories, as we have noted above, but it also characterizes it as lay and prophetic. In all these respects that Reform of Anglicanism continues to challenge the attention of her beloved sister, the Roman Catholic Church.

The Reform could not be focused on liturgy without being at the same time deeply concerned with Scripture. The same Preface to the 1549 *Book of Common Prayer* lamented certain 'abuses' that had crept into the liturgical life of the Church regarding the proclamation of the Word of God at the moment of worship:

> This godly and decent order of the ancient fathers hath been so altered, broken, and neglected, by planting in uncertain stories, Legends, Responds, Verses . . . that commonly when any book of the Bible was begun, before three or four Chapters were read out, all the rest were unread . . . they were only begun, and never read through. . . . And moreover, whereas St Paul would have such language spoken to the people in the Church, as they might understand, and have profit by hearing the same, the Service in the Church of England (these many years) hath been read in Latin to the people, which they understood not; so they have heard with their ears only; and their hearts, spirit and mind, have not been edified thereby.

Bishop Neill stresses with understandable pride this biblical centre of the Anglican Reform, and its explicitly lay dimension. Roman Catholics will read his comments in the light of the recent biblical renewal in our own Church:

> First, then, it is to be noted that Cranmer, like the other Reformers, had fallen in love with the Bible. But his love took a particular form. He believed that the Bible was the living word of God to every man. . . . He was convinced that, if his fellow countrymen could be induced to read the word of God, or, if illiterate, to hear it read, it would in course of time make its way into their hearts and consciences. It was only in the next reign that Cranmer was able to provide his Church with a lectionary; when he was able to do so, he made the Church of England in a day the greatest Bible-reading Church in the world. In no other Church anywhere is the Bible read in public worship so regu-

larly, with such order, and at such length, as in the Anglican fellowship of Churches.[66]

Such an approach demands of the laity something more than a passive, uncomprehending presence. Neill goes on to note proudly the Anglican commitment to this aspect of the Church's life: 'Cranmer was laying heavy demands on his Englishmen, and reposing great confidence in them. But in that too he was the typical Anglican – Anglicanism is a form of the Christian faith that demands and expects a great deal from ordinary people.'[67] If one believes in the living, penetrating efficacy of the Word, then the potential of such a strongly scriptural liturgy in stirring up prophetic ferment and ministry is evident. Bishop John Jewel, 'the oracle of the English Reformation',[68] expresses well this potentiality of the Word which proclaimed and explicated in worship becomes:

> . . . the bush, out of which issueth a flame of fire. The scriptures of God are the mount, from which the Lord of Hosts doth shew himself. In them God speaketh to us: in them we hear the words of everlasting life. We must be sanctified, and wash our garments, and be ready to hear the Lord . . . we must know who it is that speaketh, even God, the maker of Heaven and earth. . . .[69]

The Bishop concludes in terms that specifically encourage the faithful to open themselves to the charismatic and prophetic gifts of the Spirit:

> Let us be of a contrite spirit, and tremble at the words of God: let us, when we know God, glorify him as God. So shall God look upon us; so shall the Spirit of wisdom and understanding, and of counsel, and of knowledge, and of the fear of God, rest upon us; so shall we be made perfect to all good works; so shall we rejoice in his salvation, and with one mouth glorify God even the Father of our Lord Jesus Christ.[70]

It would be fruitful to pursue at length the many prophetic ministries and movements that have enriched the life of the Anglican Communion, and thus of all Christians, during these last four centuries. Space does not allow such a study here, but we wish to indicate at least briefly some of the Anglican movements of prophetic witness, often sustained by great laymen and laywomen.

122

The prophetic charism has to do in a special way with alleviating the suffering of the poor and oppressed. The God of the prophets cries out to Israel:

> Your hands are covered with blood,
> wash, make yourselves clean.
> Take your wrong-doing out of my sight.
> Cease to do evil.
> Learn to do good,
> search for justice,
> help the oppressed,
> be just to the orphan,
> plead for the widow.
> (Isa. 1:16–17; see also Amos 2:6–8; Jer. 22:13–16)

Christ, the fulfilment of prophecy and the prophet, initiates his mission in Luke by reading from the prophet Isaiah:

> The spirit of the Lord . . . has been given to me,
> for he has anointed me
> He has sent me to bring the good news to the poor,
> to proclaim liberty to captives,
> and to the blind new sight,
> to set the downtrodden free,
> to proclaim the Lord's year of favour.
> (Luke 4:18–19)

Then Christ affirmed: ' "This text is being fulfilled today even as you listen" ' (Luke 4:21).

'To set at liberty those who are oppressed.' The slave trade was very lucrative at the beginning of the nineteenth century, and therefore supported by many powerful groups such as merchants, planters and shippers, both in England and throughout Europe and the Americas. Had not humanity always known the institution of slavery, from the beginning of history? Indeed, St Paul himself exhorted slaves to, 'submit voluntarily to their masters in a spirit of humble obedience' (1 Tim. 6:1; Eph. 6:6–7). In the Roman Catholic tradition theologians such as Albert the Great, Thomas Aquinas, and Duns Scotus defended slavery on theological grounds. At the end of the seventeenth century some theologians were still insisting that, 'It is certainly a matter of faith (*de fide*) that the institution of slavery in which a man serves his master as his slave is altogether lawful . . . all theologians are unanimous on this.'[71] In fact not all theologians, not even all Roman Catholic ones, were unanimous;[72] but the fight against the institution of slavery was certainly an uphill one, against the odds of economic interest as well as religious and theological conviction.

The prophetic battle that William Wilberforce and his Anglican Evangelical friends waged against that 'venerable institution' is the more astonishing, given this context of near unanimous support for the trade. Wilberforce, Thomas Fowell Buxton, John Venn and Zachary Macaulay – the 'Clapham Sect' – 'spared no effort to arouse public opinion against the slave trade. They spoke in Parliament, organized public meetings, collected subscriptions, and issued pamphlets.'[73] Wilberforce had decided against the priesthood in order to dedicate himself to a Christian lay career, and carried this witness into the heart of Parliament. He is a particularly eloquent example of the tremendous contribution that the laity can make to the Churches and indeed to all humanity:

> Victory came on February 23, 1807, when, as the result of many years of unremitting labour, Wilberforce carried the House with him and persuaded them, by 283 votes to 16, to declare the Slave Trade illegal. In 1833 all slavery was abolished throughout the British dominions.[74]

As the industrial revolution spawned new social problems, innumerable groups of Anglican clergy and laity formed to battle against one aspect or another of social injustice and hardship. Outstanding theologians also, such as Charles Gore and F. D. Maurice, dedicated much of their time and energies to the social and political dimension. The Jesuit exegete McKenzie notes that the biblical prophets were 'politically active' and this 'in the external and internal politics of Israel'.[75] The particular choices and evaluations that one has to make on the political plane cannot but be controversial, and no one claims infallibility at such a level. But to simply float above the hard decisions of history so as not to 'dirty one's hands' is to witness to a disincarnate Christianity, and invite the condemnation of Christ: 'I was hungry, and you never gave me

food; I was thirsty, and you never gave me anything to drink'
(Matt. 25:42). So individuals such as Stewart Headlam and Henry
Scott Holland, Percy Widdrington and Conrad Noel, and organizations such as the Guild of St Matthew, the Christian Social
Union, as well as groups of clergy and sisters working in the slum
areas of English cities, struggled to improvise programmes at a
whole variety of levels. They used an amazing variety of political
instruments in their biblical aim of witnessing Christ to the poor,
oppressed, captives, widows and orphans of the modern centuries.

Through Archbishops of Canterbury such as William Temple,
and through the commitment of early Lambeth Conferences, this
social concern entered into the very institutional structures of the
Anglican Communion. Documents such as *Christianity and Industrial Problems*, the Report of the Archbishops' Fifth Committee
of Enquiry (1918)[76] still merit study, and reflect an early consciousness of the Church as such, as does a study such as John Oliver's
*The Church and Social Order: Social Thought in the Church of
England 1918–1939*.[77] The attention that the last Lambeth Conference dedicated to questions such as human rights and justice evi-
dences the consciousness of the Anglican Communion regarding
the urgency of such problems.[78] The energy crisis, economic
depression, the threat of nuclear disaster – the world's problems
do not permit us too much time to enjoy the luxury of our differences and our separation. In this critical period, the Spirit is calling
the two Churches to collaborate, so that Christ's mission may be
experienced by all humanity.

The Prophetic Call to Knowledge of the Lord

If the prophet challenges Israel to turn to the poor, he also, in the
same saving word, insists that Israel open itself again to the Lord:

> Let us set ourselves to know Yahweh;
> that he will come is as certain as the dawn . . .
> he will come to us as showers come,
> like spring rains watering the earth.
> (Hosea 6:3; *see also* Isa. 29:22; 37:20)

A Church needs its moments of spiritual renewal, and so needs the prophetic voices to call people to that renewal. The history of our sister Church can also be read as the sequence of such remarkable voices, the series of waves of a new interior and missionary commitment.

There was, for example, the holy layman Nicholas Ferrar and his family witness:

> In 1626 he and his household, consisting of his mother, his brother and sister-in-law with their three children and his sister with her husband and sixteen children, together with a number of servants, left London and settled in the manor house at Little Gidding in Huntingdonshire. Here they restored the church and devoted themselves to a life of religious seclusion and devotion. The chief purpose of their life was a regular round of prayer which, says Isaak Walton, 'was done as constantly as the sun runs his circle every day about the world'.[79]

What Ferrar was witnessing to was the possibility of a lay and familial counterpart to the monastic community of prayer and work; certainly there was nothing lax about the Christian commitment of the Ferrar household. One wonders how many Roman Catholic households, or monastic communities, surpass its dedication or sanctity of life:

> The family rose at 4 a.m. and the first office was said at 6. From then until 9 p.m. offices were said at frequent intervals, and much of the night was spent by one or more of the community in the 'Night Watch' when the whole Psalter was said kneeling. In addition to the offices, which formed the framework of the day's activity, much time was devoted to the making of Gospel Harmonies, to study and discussion (the so-called 'Little Academy') to educating the children of the household and those of the district, and to good works among the sick and poor. This regular routine was kept up from 1626 to 1637 when Nicholas died . . . [the Community] survived until 1646 when Little Gidding was sacked [by the Puritans].[80]

Among the close friends of the Ferrar household was the brilliant and saintly George Herbert, whose *A Priest to the Temple* provides a model of pastoral dedication that can instruct all parish priests of whatever Church or age. His religious poetry is theologically pro-

126

found and spiritually sublime, and is capable of nourishing the religious life of any Church. His pastoral ministry in a humble rural corner, after the promise of a brilliant ecclesiastical career, is a particularly moving witness to Christian fidelity to vocation:

> In humility and simplicity he showed what the life of an Anglican country parson can be. Daily he read the Morning and Evening Prayers of the Church 'at the canonical hours of ten and four', and had to pray with him 'most of his parishioners and many gentlemen in the neighbourhood, while some of the meaner sort would let their plough rest, whenever Mr Herbert's saint's-bell rang to prayers'.[81]

Isaac Walton, his friend, summed up George Herbert in these terms: 'Thus he liv'd, and thus he dy'd like a Saint, unspotted of the World, full of Alms-deeds, full of Humility, and all the examples of a vertuous life.'[82] In his preface to Herbert's *The Temple*, Nicholas Ferrar describes his friend as 'a companion to the primitive saints'.[83] Ecumenism seems a much less difficult task when we look at this level of Christianity lived and prayed; surely the Roman Catholic will see in figures such as Herbert a witness and a light that strengthens us all? For Herbert is not some sort of curious marginal figure; Bishop Neill, in his work on Anglicanism, argues that this seventeenth-century parson and poet is at the very heart of the life of his Church: 'One who wishes to know what Anglicanism is and has not much time for study cannot do better than to pay attention to the life, the poems, and the prose of George Herbert.'[84] Whether the Roman Catholic has more or less time available, he needs to meditate on poems from the Herbert corpus such as 'The Call', 'Dialogue', 'Christmas', 'Mattens', 'The Temper', 'Prayer (1)' and 'Prayer (2)', to understand more fully the spirit of that Church which he would embrace as sister. Certainly after such a reading, it becomes impossible to reject that Church as stranger or enemy.

We have taken the Ferrar household and George Herbert simply as two examples of a whole series of individuals, groups and movements witnessing to spiritual renewal in the Anglican Communion during the last four hundred years. It is also important to study at length figures such as William Law and his *Serious Call to a Devout and Holy Life* (1728), as well as his profoundly mystical writings.

John and Charles Wesley, both of whom remained faithful to the Church of England, provided dynamic pastoral ideas, from the organizing of conferences of lay preachers, to hymnology to outdoor missions, which still challenge both our Churches. Other examples include the 'Clapham Sect', as committed to personal sanctity and the missionary proclaiming of the Word as to the abolition of slavery, and numerous other groups and organizations that expressed the life of witness of the Anglican Church, including the Church Missionary Society, the Society for the Promotion of Christian Knowledge, the Religious Tract Society, the British and Foreign Bible Society, and so on. The Oxford Movement carried with it such a spiritual and theological dynamism that both Churches are still enjoying the fruits of its fecund efforts. Richard Meux Benson, founder of the Society of St John the Evangelist in 1866, initiated the movement of religious orders which, in both England and America, and throughout the Anglican Communion, were to make such a contribution to the spirituality of the Church, as well as to its theology, liturgy and scholarship. A Roman Catholic layman, Peter F. Anson, has done much to document the richness of this movement of religious life in the Anglican Communion.[85] The Anglican/Roman Catholic Consultation on Religious Life has just begun, at the international as well as national levels, to probe the significant ecumenical implications of the fact that there are, for example, Anglican as well as Roman Catholic Benedictines and Franciscans, and that there are Anglican orders that bring a new contribution to religious life. The US A/RC Consultation on Religious Life dedicated its conference in 1981 to the theme of 'The Ecumenical Vocation of Religious in Sister Churches', and in their final document affirmed, among other things, 'that we mutually recognize the authenticity of our vows as religious of sister Churches'.[86]

Spiritual renewal is inevitably ecumenical, because it is the one Spirit who enlivens Christ's Churches. We have just noted a few examples of Anglican spiritual ferment, so we must now make reference to the unique Anglican ecumenical vocation itself.

We have noted that Vatican II challenges Roman Catholics, and hopefully all Christians, to acknowledge the ecumenical movement as prophetic and providential:

> The Lord of Ages wisely and patiently follows out the plan of grace on our behalf, sinners that we are. In recent times, more than ever before, He has been rousing divided Christians to remorse over their divisions and to a longing for unity. Everywhere, large numbers have felt the impulse of this grace, and among our separated brethren also there increases from day to day a movement, fostered by the grace of the Holy Spirit, for the restoration of unity among all Christians. . . .
>
> This sacred Synod, therefore, exhorts all the Catholic faithful to recognize the signs of the times and to take an active and intelligent part in the work of ecumenism.[87]

If the Roman Catholic Church is now officially committed to the ecumenical venture, we must acknowledge that this was not always so. Yet the movement was able to go forward without us, 'fostered by the grace of the Holy Spirit'. God does not intervene magically, but works through the co-operation and efforts of believers. We Roman Catholics should recognize that we, and all Christians, owe a debt of gratitude to the Anglican Communion for shouldering an altogether disproportionate amount of the weight in the great ecumenical task that challenges all of us. And Roman Catholics especially should recognize that, in the words of the Roman Catholic ecumenist George Tavard, 'the great contribution of Anglicanism to the formation of ecumenical thought has been to propose the question of Catholic unity.'[88] Father Tavard explains this key point further:

> Protestantism properly speaking, that of the Calvinist and Lutheran Churches, is primarily directed towards Protestant unity. . . . Anglicanism has clearly considered the problem of Catholic unity . . . this contribution has been irreplaceable. It has made possible an ecumenism that will not be a Protestant imperialism. It has opened the way to a dialogue with the Catholic Church.[89]

One should always be concerned for one's sister and defend her to others even when she, for one reason or another, is not able to reciprocate in kind. We should recognize that Canterbury has been pointing out to the Protestant and Orthodox participants of the ecumenical dialogue for many decades the significance of the Roman Catholic Church for any real Christian reconciliation. Lambeth Conferences have been officially affirming the same thing since 1908, as Archbishop McAdoo, Anglican Co-Chairman of ARCIC, has pointed out:

> We recall the statement made in the Lambeth Conference of 1908, and repeated in 1920 and 1930 'that there can be no fulfilment of the Divine purpose in any scheme of reunion which does not ultimately include the great Latin Church of the West, with which our history has been so closely associated in the past, and to which we are still bound by many ties of common faith and tradition.' We recognize the Papacy as a historic reality whose developing role requires deep reflection and joint study by all concerned for the unity of the whole Body of Christ.[90]

The second Lambeth Conference, in 1878, was already committed to ecumenism, 'but it was the third Conference of 1888 which marked the great watershed in this matter and saw the course of Anglican affairs firmly beginning to be guided towards the notion of the reunion of Christendom.'[91] It was that Conference that adopted the famous 'Lambeth Quadrilateral' which was to constitute a foundation document for the Anglican ecumenical commitment. The Pawleys note that the principles articulated were already opening the door towards Rome, however much prophetic foresight this opening required to justify itself:

> The visionaries who framed the Quadrilateral certainly had the possibility of Rome in mind, at a time when it would have been hard to commend it as a possibility to the majority of Anglican people, and when the answer of Rome to the practical problems involved was clear enough to everyone except Lord Halifax and his friends.[92]

It was certainly a difficult period for the Anglican/Roman Catholic dialogue, and 'the gap was to get wider before it showed signs of narrowing'.[93]

The Lambeth Quadrilateral was not the product of some committee, nor did it occur spontaneously to the Lambeth bishops. William Reed Huntington, an American Anglican priest and sixth rector of Grace Church, New York, dedicated his life to Christian unity. In his book, *The Church Idea* (1870), he articulated the essentials of Christian unity as he saw them. The United States House of Bishops affirmed them in Chicago in 1866, and with only slight modifications they were adopted by Lambeth in 1888. Father Huntington is yet another example of how much one dedicated Christian can achieve in the area of ecumenism.

Lord Halifax is another startling case in point: 'Since the age of nineteen [1858] Halifax had dreamed of the union of Christendom.'[94] His profound friendship with one Roman Catholic priest, the Lazarist Abbé Fernand Portal, led eventually to the pioneering Malines Conversations. If one person can accomplish an extraordinary amount, two friends with prophetic charism can open new horizons: 'They both had the idealism which leaps over practical difficulties towards a distant vision.'[95] Of course too much zeal and not enough awareness of the slowness and complexities of history can lead to setbacks, and the efforts of Halifax and Portal, of Beauduin and Cardinal Mercier have been variously evaluated. No one pretends that their record is of unqualified success. But as Professor Owen Chadwick has observed, Malines established a very important precedent: 'Until Malines Roman and Anglican divines had not sat together round a table since the day of Archbishop Laud, and had never sat together in this way.'[96] The Pawleys agree: 'An evaluation of the Malines Conversations reveals above all a dimension which had been absent too long in relations between separated Christians: a spirit of charity and fellowship.'[97] The Conversations had also challenged Beauduin to compose his famous paper proposing that the Anglican Church should be united rather than absorbed.[98] The official reaction on both sides was less than enthusiastic. But when Pope Paul VI greeted Archbishop Coggan in 1977 he affirmed, 'these words of hope, "The Anglican Church united not absorbed", are no longer a mere dream.'[99] Quitslund speaks of 'the lasting merit of Beauduin's Proposal', and of 'the momentum generated by these pioneers' which has now 'reached a crucial point'.[100]

In the meantime, the Anglican Communion as such was continuing to follow out its ecumenical vocation. The Lambeth Conference of 1920 published the famous 'Appeal to all Christian People', which, as Bishop Neill has justly noted, should be considered as 'inspired', as 'a noble and prophetic utterance on Christian unity'.[101] It is interesting how the Appeal echoes the key phrase of Beauduin: 'We do not ask that any one Communion should consent to be absorbed in another. We do ask that all should unite in a new and great endeavour to secure and to manifest to the world the unity of the Body of Christ for which He prayed.'[102] The Appeal, 'in attempting tactfully to commend the Episcopate',[103] added 'a significant rider to show how the historic episcopate in particular might be adapted to the future needs of uniting churches in bringing into being a ministry universally recognized.'[104] The proposal indicates how far the Anglican Communion as a whole was willing to go in order to serve ecumenism; it reminds us that ecclesial institutions need not always be self-sufficient and self-serving:

> If the authorities of other Communions should so desire, we are persuaded that, if terms of union have been otherwise satisfactorily adjusted, Bishops and clergy of our Communion would willingly accept from these authorities a form of commission or recognition which would commend our ministry to their congregations, as having its place in the one family life.[105]

The Pawleys note the evident significance of this document specifically for the still-hoped-for dialogue with Rome: 'The effect of this document was to confirm Anglican bona fides in the sphere of ecumenical relations, and was a further indication of her intention to keep eventual union involving Rome in the centre of her picture.'[106] *Apostolicae Curae* (1896) with its negative judgement on Anglican orders had greeted Lord Halifax's early efforts at dialogue, and on the other hand the Edinburgh Conference of 1910 raised real hopes regarding the generous commitment of the Churches of the Reformation to ecumenism. One wonders, frankly, why the Anglican Communion kept struggling, quite alone, to keep a door open towards Rome, without the slightest encouragement from the eternal city. The only possible answer was that she had intuited that deep kinship which, whatever the appearance to the contrary, had still to be there, and had to be revitalized between the two Churches. Apart from individual Anglican prophets in the area of ecumenism, and there have been many, one must acknowledge a prophetic charism within the Communion as such, and particularly in terms of the role of Rome in the reunion of Christians.

Of course Canterbury was also actively pursuing the dialogue with the Reformation Churches and with Orthodoxy, as well as with the Old Catholic Churches, as indeed the Roman Catholic Church itself is now, many decades later. The point is important, in order to situate the dialogue between the two Churches in its fuller, very complicated context. There are not just two sisters in the remarkable family of Communions established by the Spirit of Christ, and their relationship can never be a closed, exclusivistic one and indeed it never has been. Things are always more lively and involved in a large family than a small one; and just as sister 'a' thinks her friendship with sister 'b' is going splendidly, 'b' feels she has to give more time to 'c', who is having some problems with 'a', and so it goes on. But one sister can never demand a monopoly of the attention of another; and to the extent that the relationship is healthy, each will hope for a bond of love that will open and nourish other relationships, however challenging. Roman Catholics will want to rejoice that their Anglican brethren have been so active in the dialogue with the other Churches, preparing the way for their own entry into a series of bilateral dialogues with these Churches. The World Council of Churches, besides doing its own significant work, has also been the nurturing ground for these series of bilateral relationships. It is good for us Roman Catholics to remember that our Anglican brethren have not only participated from the beginning in the broader ecumenical movement, but have played such a predominant role and offered such a generous contribution to its continuing momentum. Bishop Neill, who himself has worked with the World Council and is co-editor of *The History of the Ecumenical Movement 1517–1948*,[107] has noted with understandable pride the Anglican, and not just the English Anglican, contribution:

For seventeen years Faith and Order was almost exclusively an Anglican, and an American Anglican venture. The inspirer of the movement, Bishop Brent, the Secretary, Robert H. Gardiner, and the Treasurer, George Zabriskie, were all American Episcopalians. The faith and the money that kept the movement going through long and discouraging periods came mainly from the same source. When at last the first World Conference on Faith and Order met at Lausanne in 1927, the Anglican Churches were well and truly represented. By the time of the second Conference, Edinburgh 1937, William Temple (1882–1944), then Archbishop of York, had revealed himself as the greatest ecumenical personality of this age. . . . At last in 1948 the World Council of Churches was formed. . . . It fell to Temple's successor, Geoffrey Francis Fisher, to declare the World Council of Churches duly and formally constituted, and to lead the great assembly in prayer. The first Chairman of the Central and Executive Committees was Dr G. K. A. Bell, Bishop of Chichester.[108]

We leave the quotation at this point, not because Bishop Neill has concluded his list of Anglican ecumenical leaders, but because the general picture should be more than clear. Among the consolations which Rome may draw from her younger sister's outstanding record in the ecumenical area is the thought that Canterbury's deep commitment to dialogue with Rome does not arise from a lack of other partners, nor can it be thought that Canterbury does not really understand all that inter-Church dialogue entails. Canterbury is dedicated to Rome because of Rome: that is what a true sister's dedication is all about.

One of the Anglican Communion's bilateral dialogues which has borne special fruit, and which might have much to contribute to her dialogue with Rome, is that which took place with the Old Catholic Churches. These consist of a group of small national Churches of quite varied histories, ranging from the Church of Utrecht, which separated from Rome in 1724, to German, Austrian and Swiss Churches which refused to receive the dogma of the infallibility of the Pope as defined by Vatican I, to small groups of Slav origin. This Communion of Churches finds its doctrinal basis in the 'Declaration of Utrecht' agreed upon in 1889.[109] Christopher Wordsworth, Bishop of Lincoln from 1869, followed with great interest the first Old Catholic Congress at Munich in 1871, and brought to the attention of the English Church Congress the deliberations of the Old Catholics. He accepted an invitation to the second Old Catholic Congress the next year, with the approval of the Archbishop of Canterbury, and played an important part in the public sessions and private meetings in the establishment of a bond between the two Communions. From that time exchanges multiplied, the Society of St Willibrord was established for fostering closer relations, and a series of theological meetings led to the Agreement of Bonn in 1931, which established inter-communion between the Church of England and the Old Catholic Churches. The terms of the Agreement are sufficiently brief to be cited here in full:

1. Each Communion recognizes the catholicity and independence of the other, and maintains its own.
2. Each Communion agrees to admit members of the other Communion to participate in the sacraments.
3. Intercommunion does not require from either Communion the acceptance of all doctrinal opinion, sacramental devotion, or liturgical practice characteristic of the other, but implies that each believes the other to hold all the essentials of the Christian faith.[110]

The Agreement, made with the Church of England, was subsequently accepted by all other parts of the Anglican Communion. E. W. Kemp (then Canon of Lincoln, now Bishop of Chichester) notes the importance of the agreement for Anglican bonds with other sister Churches: 'Its terms have served as the model for agreements between the Church of England and the Philippine Independent Church, the Spanish Reformed Church, and the Lusitanian Church.'[111] The Bishop notes an interesting fact regarding the agreement: 'There is perhaps significance in that it has been applied only in the case of relations with Churches which possess the historic episcopal ministry.'[112]

This aspect has implications for Anglican relations with Rome; for, as Bishop Neill has noted, the Roman Catholic Church:

. . . recognizes the Old Catholic succession of episcopal consecrations as valid but irregular. Old Catholic and Polish National Catholic bishops have often taken part in Anglican consecrations. Considerably more than half the Anglican episcopate has now the Old Catholic as well as the Anglican succession, and before long this is likely to be true of the whole episcopate. If at any time the Roman Catholic Church wished to move nearer to the Anglican Churches, this might clear the way to happier relations. No Anglican imagines that anything is added to his consecration or ordination by Old Catholic participation; but from the Roman Catholic point of view such orders might be held to have regained something of that regularity and validity which the Pope's Bull of 1896 denied to them.[113]

Fr Edward Yarnold, a Jesuit theologian and ecumenist who is a member of ARCIC as well as being Senior Tutor at Campion Hall, Oxford, has written an illuminating little paper entitled 'Anglican Orders – A Way Forward?'[114] In it he suggests that more recent theological work concerning the concepts of 'apostolic succession' and 'the concept of ministry' might encourage the Roman Catholic Church to 'presume validity' in the case of present Anglican orders, 'while trying to ensure Catholic, as well as Orthodox or Old Catholic participation' in future Anglican ordinations.[115] Fr Yarnold's paper was published some two years before ARCIC's Elucidations which, as we have seen, 'calls for a reappraisal of the verdict on Anglican Orders' in the light of the remarkable 'agreement on the essentials of eucharistic faith . . . and on the nature and purpose of priesthood, ordination and apostolic succession.'[116] Fr Yarnold feels that any solution through the participation of Old Catholic bishops in Anglican ordinations would not be helpful on the Anglican side, because 'although the number of such [Anglican] clergy must be quite high, it is still well short of one hundred per cent', so that such a solution would in effect seem to be 'dividing the Anglican Communion'.[117] However, he notes of the Old Catholics that their 'orders are of indisputable validity',[118] and with their participation in the ordination of Anglican bishops, such lineage then quickly multiplies geometrically. In the US, for example, Bishop Arthur Lichtenberger's ordination included the Old Catholic succession. He was elected Presiding Bishop in 1958; and since Presiding Bishops try to take part in all Episcopal ordinations, he himself extended that lineage to dozens of other US Anglican bishops, including the present Presiding Bishop, John Allin. He in his turn has participated in dozens of Episcopal ordinations, and so have his colleagues; so that the Old Catholic lineage, 'of indisputable validity', extends like an opening fan into Anglican episcopal, and therefore sacerdotal and diaconal, orders. Many who are aware of more recent theological developments will object that these considerations imply an excessively traditionalist and 'tactile-mechanistic' understanding of succession. But in the thorny and painful tangle of the issue of Anglican orders, surely at this point painful to both sides, these considerations at least establish this minimalistic, but for many Roman Catholics perhaps startling, conclusion: that the validity of the great majority of Anglican deacons, priests and bishops must now be assumed, according to a most traditionalist criterion, and with no recourse to contemporary theological developments which would validate those orders also on other grounds. As time passes, that validity is rapidly extending geometrically and will soon include all Anglican bishops, priests and deacons. This is a development entirely subsequent to the Vatican Bull *Apostolicae Curae* (1896) and so, as Bishop Neill has observed from the Anglican side, facilitates the new conclusion without having to reintroduce old controversial questions, or even having recourse to more recent theological developments.

We feel most ill at ease even raising this painful subject, but the dialogue between the two Churches is now at such an advanced point that we are called to deal with substantive matters, as the Archbishop of Canterbury has noted, and not be satisfied with courtesies. A general consensus among Roman Catholic theologians often develops, and this then extends to the informed laity. The Roman Catholic journal, *The Tablet*, has commented in a recent editorial:

> It would be an immense relief, therefore, were Rome to express willingness to reopen the question [of Anglican orders] by means of a joint commission. . . . An immediate statement by the Pope to the effect that the whole matter was *sub judice* once more and was by no means closed would mark the end of the beginning. It would be a big step towards unity without a hint of absorption.[119]

Whatever Rome does or does not do, the Anglican Communion will certainly continue to be there, throughout the world, proclaiming and celebrating the mystery of Christ, witnessing and ministering in a contemporary world beset by staggering problems. And Anglicanism, it can be safely predicted, will remain loyal to its ecumenical vocation. For that is the charism not simply of individual Anglicans, lay and clergy, but of the Anglican Communion as a whole. Dr Stephen Sykes of Durham University has observed:

> Anglicans are, by the very terms of their own self-understanding, committed to labour for the restoration of [Christian] unity, and to offer the whole of the life and witness of their own Communion in the service of the larger body of Christ's church which has existed from the dawn of humanity and will be consummated in the life and joy of the united worship of God in heaven.[120]

The American Jesuit theologian Herbert J. Ryan, member of ARCIC and also of ARC-USA, notes that Roman Catholic theology holds that all catholic elements, all the 'gifts of the Holy Spirit' can be found in the Roman Catholic Church; but this doesn't mean necessarily, '. . . that the Roman Catholic Church has developed all the elements fully. Another Christian church may possess some of the catholic elements and may have developed these elements more fully than has the Roman Catholic Church.'[121] What service might the See of Peter eventually offer to these other Churches which might have developed several of the gifts of the Spirit to a remarkable extent? Fr Ryan argues that these Churches themselves should be invited to offer their response, since 'no Roman Catholic theologian can properly essay this task'.[122] He notes the indispensable role Anglicanism can play here:

> Broadening how Rome's service of love is exercised will enable the whole Church to be truly united.
> Anglican theology is richly equipped for this required theological reflection and mutual collaboration with the Roman Catholic tradition. No Christian theological tradition surpasses the depth with which the *Ecclesia Anglicana* has analysed the task of the Church and the role of its members, has been more creative in polity or more sensitive to the imperatives of Christian conscience.[123]

The Anglican Communion not only encourages individual laypersons to offer their unique contribution, but it has introduced the lay dimension into its very structure, and at every level, from the parish, diocesan, and national to the international expressions of the Communion, such as the Anglican endeavour to open up in-

138

stitutions to the full range of charisms, whether lay or sacerdotal, so that the manifold gifts of Christ's Spirit might be more explicitly witnessed to.[124] Fr Ryan notes:

> The Anglican ethos sees that organizational authority in the Church varies directly with the role which the communicant member is prepared to undertake to advance the tasks of the Church. From vestry to Lambeth Conference the forms of organizational authority in the Anglican Communion are perceived ideally to be functions of evangelization.[125]

We may conclude this study of the lay-prophetic current in our sister Church with the concluding sentence of Fr Ryan's article, which notes Roman Catholic gratitude for Anglican gifts:

> In this area the Roman Catholic Church will gratefully and gladly learn from her 'beloved sister Church', whose missionary efforts have brought the Gospel to tens of millions who in turn have created a polity suited to evangelize each different culture in which the Anglican communion thrives.[126]

Notes

1 See Donald Attwater, *A Dictionary of Saints* (Penguin 1979), p. 37; see also *The Proper for the Lesser Feasts and Fasts together with the Fixed Holy Days* (Church Hymnal, New York, 1980), p. 252.
2 Attwater, ibid., p. 118.
3 Cited in Attwater, ibid., p. 271.
4 Quoted in Paul Elmer More, 'The Spirit of Anglicanism' in *Anglicanism*, op. cit., p. xxxvii.
5 Karl Rahner, S.J., 'Prophetism' in *Sacramentum Mundi: An Encyclopedia of Theology*, op. cit., vol. v, p. 111.
6 Norbert Lohfink, S.J., *I profeti ieri e oggi* (Queriniana, Brescia, 1973), p. 85.
7 Rahner, 'Prophetism', op. cit., p. 111.
8 Vatican II, Dogmatic Constitution on the Church, n. 12.
9 Füglister, O.S.B., 'Profeta' in *Dizionario Teologico* (Queriniana, Brescia, 1967), vol. ii, p. 730.
10 See N. Füglister, ibid., p. 730; see also Bertulf Van Leeuwen, 'La partecipazione comune del popolo di Dio all'ufficio profetico di Cristo' in *La Chiesa del Vaticano II* (Vallecchi, Florence, 1965), p. 768.
11 Vladimir Lossky, quoted in Timothy Ware, *The Orthodox Church* (Penguin 1978), p. 203.
12 Georges Florovsky, quoted in Ware, ibid., pp. 206–7.

13 Ware, ibid., p. 205.
14 Lohfink, op. cit., p. 16.
15 ibid., pp. 87–8. See also Füglister, op. cit., p. 728.
16 Lohfink, ibid., p. 88.
17 Füglister, op. cit., p. 725.
18 Van Leeuwen, op. cit., p. 476.
19 Füglister, op. cit., p. 725.
20 Füglister, ibid., p. 729; see also Van Leeuwen, op. cit., pp. 467, 471.
21 See Füglister, ibid., p. 731. See also Irenaeus, *Adversus Haereses*, V,
   6, 1, quoted also in Eusebius, *Ecclesiastical History*, V, 7, 6: 'As we
   have heard, many of the brethren in the Church have the prophetic
   gifts, and through the Spirit speak in all tongues and bring to light the
   hidden things of men for their benefit and expound the mysteries of
   God.'
22 John L. McKenzie, S.J., *Dictionary of the Bible* (Bruce, Milwaukee,
   1965), p. 699.
23 Füglister, op. cit., p. 731.
24 ibid., p. 730.
25 ibid., p. 731.
26 Rahner, 'Prophetism', op. cit., p. 113.
27 Rahner, ibid., p. 112.
28 ibid., p. 113.
29 Füglister, op. cit., p. 745.
30 Rahner, op. cit., p. 113.
31 Füglister, op. cit., p. 725.
32 See R. Hale, O.S.B., Cam., 'Dimensione profetica della vita monastica' in *Dimensione Profetica della Comunità Cristiana* (Quaderni di
   Vita Monastica, Camaldoli, 1975), pp. 40–74.
33 St Gregory the Great, *Dialogorum libri quattuor*, II, xxi.
34 ibid.
35 ibid., xxvii, xxxii, xxii, etc.
36 ibid., xv.
37 ibid., xxxi.
38 ibid., xxiii.
39 Christopher Dawson, *Religion and the Rise of Western Culture* (Sheed
   and Ward, New York, 1950), pp. 149–50.
40 Bede, *A History of the English Church and People*, Bk IV ch. 4.
41 ibid.
42 ibid., Bk I ch. 26.
43 Sonya A. Quitslund, *Beauduin: A Prophet Vindicated* (Newman,
   New York, 1973); the work contains a careful treatment of the Malines
   Conversations and their significance for the Anglican/Roman Catholic
   dialogue (pp. 56–79 and notes), and also an extensive bibliography
   (pp. 335–58).
44 Vatican II, Decree on Ecumenism, n. 4.
45 Anglican/Roman Catholic International Commission, Elucidations,
   n. 14. See also the Agreed Statement on Ministry and Ordination, nn.
   8–10.

46 Elucidations, ibid., n. 16. ARCIC notes that this remarkable agreement, along with 'our agreement on the essentials of eucharistic faith with regard to the sacramental presence of Christ and the sacrificial dimensions of the eucharist' constitute 'the new context' in which the question of Anglican Orders should now be considered, and 'calls for a reappraisal of the verdict on Anglican Orders in *Apostolicae Curae* (1896)', n. 16.

47 Agreed Statement on Ministry and Ordination, n. 2.

48 ibid.

49 *The Lambeth Conference 1978: Preparatory Information* (CIO Publishing 1978), p. 30.

50 *Annuarium Statisticum Ecclesiae* (Typis Polyglottis Vaticanis, Rome, 1978), p. 103. The 1,800 figure is, of course, a world average; in Central America the average is 1 priest to 6,862 laity.

51 Vatican II, Dogmatic Constitution on the Church, n. 32.

52 Yves Congar, O.P., *Christians Active in the World* (Herder and Herder, New York, 1968), p. 3.

53 ibid., p. 29; the phrase is originally Clement's of Alexandria.

54 Vatican II, Dogmatic Constitution on the Church, n. 31.

55 ibid., n. 30.

56 Ferdinand Klostermann, 'The Laity' in *Commentary on the Documents of Vatican II* (Herder and Herder, New York, 1967), vol. i p. 231.

57 ibid., p. 231.

58 Congar, op. cit., p. 4.

59 ibid.

60 ibid., p. 5.

61 See for example A. Nuij, O.S.B., 'Waren alle monniken ook priester?' in *Benediktijns Tijdschrift* 21(1960), pp. 58–65. One thinks, in this context, of the great Franciscan movement, whose origins were also distinctly lay in spirit; scholars have noted striking parallels between the charism of Francis, and that of early Syrian monks. The *Liber Graduum*, an anonymous fifth-century Syria work, describes thus the 'perfect Spirit-filled monk': A life of absolute propertyless wandering, continuous prayer and fasting, preaching and peace making, with humble and kind love for all, especially for sinners and enemies or persecutors, ever celebrating a silent liturgy of praise in the church of the heart. The whole theme of Franciscanism is of significance for our topic both because of the influence of the friars in England prior to the reform and because of the vitality of the Anglican Franciscans today.

62 Ernst Niermann, 'Laity' in *Sacramentum Mundi: An Encyclopedia of Theology*, op. cit., vol. iii, p. 260.

63 ibid.

64 Stephen Neill, *Anglicanism*, op. cit., p. 131.

65 Quoted in Stephen W. Sykes, *The Integrity of Anglicanism*, op. cit., p. 48.

66 Neill, op. cit., p. 54.

67 ibid.

68 John Booty, *Three Anglican Divines on Prayer: Jewel, Andrewes, and Hooker* (Society of St John the Evangelist, Massachusetts, 1978), p. 3.

69 John Jewel, *Works* (Cambridge University Press 1850), vol. iv p. 1188; cited in Booty, ibid., pp. 3–4.

70 ibid.; Booty, p. 4.

71 P. Leander, *Quaestiones Morales Theologicae* (Lyons 1668–1692), Tome VIII, De quarto Decalogi Praecepto, Tract. IV, Disp. I, Q. 3.

72 The Dominican missionary Bartholomew de las Casas opposed slavery in the sixteenth century, but was silenced. For a fuller treatment of this tragic theme, see J. Kahl, 'The Church as Slave-owner' in *The Misery of Christianity* (Penguin 1971), pp. 28–33.

73 J. R. H. Moorman, *A History of the Church in England*, op. cit., p. 320.

74 ibid. It is interesting that the Evangelical Wilberforce was an early supporter of Roman Catholic emancipation in the 1780s.

75 McKenzie, op. cit., p. 695.

76 *Christianity and Industrial Problems, the Report of the Archbishops' Fifth Committee of Enquiry*, SPCK 1918.

77 John Oliver, *The Church and Social Order: Social Thought in the Church of England, 1918–1939*, (Mowbray 1968), the study has a very extensive bibliography, pp. 207–20.

78 Perhaps the most remarkable was Resolution n. 002 concerning human rights in politically oppressive contexts; see *The Report of the Lambeth Conference 1978* (CIO Publishing 1978), p. 37. See Robert Hale, O.S.B. Cam., 'La sfida di Lambeth XI' in *La Comunione Anglicana: Chiesa ponte, Chiesa sorella* (Quaderni di Vita Monastica, Camaldoli, 1978), pp. 36–74. The title of this booklet of essays is interesting in terms of our topic: *The Anglican Communion: Bridge Church, Sister Church*.

79 Moorman, op. cit., p. 236.

80 ibid.

81 Neill, op. cit., p. 149.

82 Izaak Walton, *The Life of Mr George Herbert* (1670) in *Lives* (World's Classics edn. n.d.), p. 319.

83 Nicholas Ferrar, 'The Printers to the Reader' preface to George Herbert, *The Temple: Sacred Poems and Private Ejaculations*, (Thom. Buck 1633).

84 Neill, op. cit., p. 149.

85 It is interesting how many pioneering figures and founders of the Anglican religious orders were themselves actively committed to social justice. One thinks of Fr William Sirr and his work with the English dock workers; or, in America, of Fr James Huntington, founder of the Order of the Holy Cross, and his early work as co-founder of the Church Association for the Advancement of the Interests of Labor, as member of the Knights of Labor. Surely Fr Huntington is a towering figure in the area of social concern as well as spirituality, and his life deserves further study. See Robert William Adamson, *Father*

Huntington's Formative Years (1854–1892): Monasticism and Social Christianity, Doctoral Thesis, Columbia University, New York, 1971). See also Geoffrey Curtis, C.R., *William of Glasshampton: Friar, Monk, Solitary* (SPCK 1978), pp. 13–30.

86 Anglican/Roman Catholic Consultation on the Religious Life, 'The Ecumenical Vocation of Religious in Sister Churches' (March 30–31, New York, 1981), p. 1.

87 Vatican II, Decree on Ecumenism, nn. 1, 4.

88 George H. Tavard, *Two Centuries of Ecumenism* (Fides, Notre Dame, 1960), p. 53.

89 ibid. In connection with Fr Tavard's reference to Protestant ecumenism, this book was written more than twenty years ago. Several of the principal Protestant Churches are now engaged in very fruitful bilateral dialogues with Rome, and Fr Tavard as a professional ecumenist is participating in those dialogues. All this reinforces the weight of his central point: it was Anglicanism that opened the door of the ecumenical movement as such to the significance of Roman Catholicism, quite before Vatican II. And insofar as that movement had a real influence on Roman Catholic theologians and clergy, it indirectly influenced Vatican II itself, in its considerations not only regarding ecumenism, but also concerning the Church, the liturgy, etc. The Pawley's have noted that the general syllabus of the Council, 'couldn't have been more satisfactory, from an Anglican point of view, if it had been drawn up at Lambeth'. Bernard and Margaret Pawley, *Rome and Canterbury*, op. cit., p. 341. They go on to note how many of the affirmations of the Council bring the two Churches remarkably closer; pp. 341–52.

90 Henry R. McAdoo, *Being an Anglican* (SPCK 1977), p. 41.

91 ibid.

92 Bernard and Margaret Pawley, op. cit., p. 274.

93 ibid.

94 Owen Chadwick, 'The Church of England and the Church of Rome, from the beginning of the nineteenth century to the present day', op. cit., p. 87.

95 ibid., p. 88.

96 ibid., p. 94.

97 Bernard and Margaret Pawley, op. cit., p. 297.

98 See Sonya A. Quitslund, op. cit., pp. 56–79.

99 Paul VI, Welcoming Address to the Archbishop of Canterbury, April 28, 1977; see *L'Osservatore Romano* (April 29 1977), p. 1.

100 Sonya A. Quitslund, op. cit., p. 77.

101 Stephen Neill, op. cit., p. 367.

102 'An Appeal to All Christian People from the Bishops Assembled in the Lambeth Conference of 1920', n. ix; in *The Lambeth Conferences (1867–1930)* (SPCK 1948), p. 121.

103 Stephen Neill, op. cit., p. 368.

104 Bernard and Margaret Pawley, op. cit., p. 280.

105 'An Appeal', op. cit., n. viii; in *The Lambeth Conferences*, p. 121.

106 Bernard and Margaret Pawley, op. cit., p. 280.
107 Stephen Neill and Ruth Rouse, ed., *A History of the Ecumenical Movement*, 1517–1948, SPCK 1954.
108 Stephen Neill, *Anglicanism*, op. cit., p. 385.
109 See E. W. Kemp, 'The Church of England and the Old Catholic Churches' in *Anglican Initiatives in Christian Unity*, op. cit., pp. 145–62.
110 See Stephen Neill, *Anglicanism*, p. 373; see E. W. Kemp, op. cit., p. 159.
111 E. W. Kemp, *idem.*, p. 160.
112 ibid.
113 Stephen Neill, op. cit., pp. 373–4. It must be noted that the seventeenth-century Archbishop M. A. de Dominis, a convert from Roman Catholicism, had taken part in consecrations during his stay in England.
114 Edward Yarnold, S.J., 'Anglican Orders – A Way Forward?' (Catholic Truth Society 1977).
115 ibid., pp. 13, 14.
116 Elucidations, n. 16.
117 Edward Yarnold, S.J., op. cit., p. 9.
118 ibid.
119 'A church united not absorbed' in *The Tablet* 235(21 March 1981), p. 275.
120 Stephen W. Sykes, op. cit., pp. 99–100.
121 Herbert J. Ryan, S.J., 'The Roman Catholic Vision of Visible Unity', in *A Communion of Communions: One Eucharistic Fellowship* (Seabury, New York, 1979), p. 123.
122 ibid., p. 127.
123 ibid., p. 127.
124 See Henry R. McAdoo, *Being an Anglican*, op. cit., pp. 29–31: 'Lay-Participation'.
125 Herbert J. Ryan, S.J., op. cit., p. 128.
126 ibid.

5

What Then are We to Do? Some Practical Ways to Live the Model of Sister Churches

The joint statements and agreements at the official level and the theologies that accompany them have quite out-distanced the practice of the members of both Churches. One Jesuit rector of an American theological college recently affirmed that we don't so much need more documents as more doing. We recall Bishop Clark's comment, quoted above, to the Anglican Synod: 'Mere intellectual acceptance of our consensus has a way of being of little avail. No real commitment is involved, no real movement of persons towards one another need take place.'[1]

Bishop Charles Henry Brent, the great American pioneer in Anglican ecumenism, affirmed, 'Unity, visible and invisible, is not an accident of the Gospel; it is the Gospel.'[2] The thought is startling in its simplicity, and one's first reaction may be to suspect the hyperbolic. But if one recalls Christ's last prayer, 'that they may be one', and thinks of his Gospel of redemptive love as precisely reconciling love, then surely the work for the unity of Christians is deeply rooted in the Gospel itself. The problem with the Gospel is that listening to it is not enough; Christ requires that we *live* it:

Still happier are those who hear the word of God and keep it. (Luke 11:28).

Why do you call me 'Lord, Lord' and not do what I say? Everyone who comes to me and listens to my words and acts on them, I will show you what he is like. He is like the man who

when he built his house, dug deep, and laid the foundations on rock. . . . But the one who listens and does nothing is like the man who built a house on soil, with no foundations.
(Luke 6:46–9).

The Eastern Church honours St John as *'the* Theologian', but no writings insist more than the Johannine literature on this practical living out of the Gospel of reconciliation: 'Little children, let us not love in word or speech but in deed and in truth' (1 John 3:18). Biblical theologians note that the semitic notion of 'word' (*dabar*) includes the notion of deed, of event, because our God is a God of the Word, and his Word effects what it proclaims. It is unfortunately we, in our disobedience, who effect the tragic disjunction. The first expression of real conversion is in the utterance of the question 'What must we do then?' (Luke 3:10). It was the question of the multitudes to John the Baptist who was preaching repentance. His response was notably practical and concrete: 'If anyone has two tunics, he must share with the man who has none, and the man who has something to eat, let him do the same'. To the tax collectors, he said, 'Exact no more than your rate', and to the soldiers, 'No intimidation! No extortion! Be content with your pay' (Luke 3:14). What can all this mean to us, who in the twentieth century wish to live the Gospel, including its implications of reconciliation and love between Christians?

At the Personal and Interpersonal Level

Surely the Gospel of Luke is suggesting that each of us, within our own specific place and vocation in life, will be able to find ways on the most concrete of levels to advance love, to further Christian reconciliation. Concerning the relations of the two Churches, I probably already know some members of my sister Church, perhaps in the neighbourhood, perhaps among friends, perhaps even in the family. I can certainly work on bettering my rapport with them; that is ecumenism at the grass roots level, and is its very substance. Christ came to establish fellowship, *koinonia*; and the sacraments, the proclamation of the Gospels, the institutions – all have as their scope the furthering of this salvific *koinonia*: 'What we have seen and heard we are telling you, so that you too may be in union [*koinonia*] with us; as we are in union [*koinonia*] with the Father and with his Son Jesus Christ' (1 John 1:3). Thus to the extent that I *live* Christian *koinonia* with members of my sister Church, I am living out the very substance of the Gospels and ecumenism.[3] One sometimes hears the question: 'What is my Church doing about ecumenism?' There is a very clericalistic presupposition in the use of the term 'Church' in such a question, as though my 'Church' is constituted exclusively by the officials at the top, and only they can 'do' anything for ecumenism, or any other of the pressing issues confronting the 'Church'. But if the 'Church' is the people of God, then I also am the Church, whether I am a layperson or Archbishop, specialized theologian or barely literate. A Camaldolese Doctor of the Church, St Peter Damian, noted that just as each one of us is a member of the one mystical body, so the whole Church is somehow mysteriously present in each one of us:

> Indeed the Church of Christ is united in all her parts by such a bond of love that her several members form a single body, and in each one the whole Church is mystically present; so that the whole Church universal may rightly be called the one bride of Christ, and on the other hand every single soul can, because of the mystical effect of this bond, be regarded as the whole Church.[4]

It is a difficult notion to grasp. And yet when Pope Paul VI and Archbishop Ramsey embraced, the moment was particularly moving because we somehow intuited that not only were two men expressing their friendship, but two Christian Communions were embracing. So, in an analogous way, when any one of us establishes a deep bond with a member of the sister Church, that *koinonia* is a small 'summing up' of the hope of the two Churches; it is a 'sacrament' in the broader sense of a sign that also efficaciously realizes, even if on a small scale, what it points to – the reconciliation of the Roman and Anglican Communions.

Ecumenical groups talk about 'covenants', friendship pacts between parishes, dioceses or seminaries of two Churches. But there is no reason that two individuals might not establish an ecumenical covenant between themselves. At a conference on Anglicanism at the Monastery of Camaldoli in Italy, an Anglican monk, Fr Brian

McHugh of the Order of the Holy Cross, proposed this idea in his presentation. After the discussion period a Roman Catholic sister approached Fr Brian and said she wished to establish such a covenant with him. He was soon to return to the United States; she would be remaining in Italy. But they could pray for each other, and for their respective Churches every day, and seek through their daily ministry to live out this inter-personal covenant. They agreed to it, and it remains a continuing pledge for each. Although only a commitment of two individuals, it has certainly changed their lives, and is an example of the very substance of the *koinonia* our two sister Churches are seeking. Were such inter-personal bonds multiplied thousands of times over, they would constitute a network of fellowship that could play a decisive role in the relations of the two Churches. And in fact, are there not thousands, indeed, hundreds of thousands of such friendships even now? So many of the Church leaders and ecumenists who have had the opportunity to meet their brethren over any length of time have witnessed to this phenomenon (certainly of the Spirit) of the development of real friendship between Anglicans and Roman Catholics. Even the very first encounters were marked by this perennial Christian sign; one thinks of Lord Halifax and l'Abbé Ferdinand Portal. But the same Spirit came to animate the other participants at Malines, as the Pawleys note:

> An evaluation of the Malines Conversations reveals above all a dimension which had been absent too long in relations between separated Christians: a spirit of charity and fellowship. Inspired initially by Cardinal Mercier, it so permeated the whole group that there are constant references to it in the correspondence between its members. On hearing of the Cardinal's illness, the Dean of Wells wrote that the Belgian Archbishop was daily in his prayers. 'I am bold enough to write, for hearts have been drawn very close together at Malines': strong words from an Englishman.[5]

The first thing that each of us can 'do', then, is to reach out personally to a member of the other Church, and cultivate that relationship as a 'sacramental sign' of the reunion in diversity we seek. Should that relationship grow into Christian friendship, we

148

will treasure that bond as the very essence of the *koinonia* Christ has bestowed on us:

> This is my commandment: love one another, as I have loved you. A man can have no greater love than to lay down his life for his friends. I shall not call you servants any more, because a servant does not know what his master's business is; I call you friends, because I have made known to you everything I have learnt from my Father. (John 15:12–15)

Christian friendship is no mere human comradeship: it attains a profundity that can only be termed prophetic and mystical (one thinks here of the deep bond between Baron von Hügel and Evelyn Underhill). If I open myself to Anglicans on this inter-personal level, if I commit myself loyally to them and accept also the gift of friendship, I shall already be doing a great deal for ecumenism, and indeed for my own communion with God. The great British medieval theologian Aelred of Rievaulx wrote a marvellous tract entitled *Spiritual Friendship*. In it he discusses the origin of Christian friendship, essentially a gift of the Spirit, and friendship's fruition and excellence. His conclusion is that true friendship is the privileged context for living out one's Christian life; he offers this startling paraphrase of St John: 'What is true of charity, I surely do not hesitate to grant to friendship, since "he that abides in friendship, abides in God and God in him".'[6]

Christian love and friendship, of course, are not just matters of emotion and sentimentalism. They involve the *heart*, which in the biblical perspective also involves the mind, the intelligence, in short, the full, illumined commitment of a person. And so the second thing one can do at a very personal level is simply to keep informed, be intelligently aware of what has happened and is happening in the area of the dialogue between the two sister Churches. How many Anglicans or Roman Catholics, clergy or lay, have actually read through the ARCIC agreed statements, even though they are brief documents, yet remarkably exciting and enriching? How many have read through the joint statements issued by the Popes and Archbishops of Canterbury in recent years, again brief, but certainly challenging to their faithful? The person who has taken to heart this dialogue will certainly dedicate the little time necessary to be conversant with these basic documents. To those

149

attracted to studying and reading, there is an extensive list of books and articles that probe every particular area and issue of the dialogue. Without heroic effort one can become something of a specialist in one facet or another of the Canterbury-Rome rapport, and make one's own contribution in helping others to become more informed, whether simply through conversations with family, friends and parishioners, or whether eventually through speaking or writing for larger groups.

If one is drawn towards more practical forms of service and ministry, the opportunities for ecumenical work will certainly be there, once one starts searching. I know Anglican laity who help out in a Roman Catholic social centre, run by Franciscans, in the poor section of San Francisco; they work in the kitchen that prepares free lunches, and they also serve the poor at tables. The Franciscans of course are delighted by the help, and have discovered a great deal about their sister Church from this concrete, lived ecumenism. On the other side, I know of a Roman Catholic priest who helps out in an Anglican centre for recovering alcoholics, the centre itself ministering to Roman Catholics as well as Anglicans and others. In such a profoundly human and suffered context, the issues which divide us appear in another light, and the urgency of common ministry becomes much clearer. And so the examples might be multiplied; but, in any event, ways of dedicating most fruitfully one's time and energy will be discovered, once the decision to serve Christian reconciliation in deed as well as word is made.

The Work of Prayer

The most important thing is to pray. Prayer is an activity open to everyone including the elderly and invalids and it is essential in ecumenical work. The Dominican theologian and experienced ecumenist, Fr Jean Tillard, member of ARCIC, preached the sermon at a liturgy of reconciliation sponsored by the Anglican Order of the Holy Cross; and he described the relationship of the two sister Churches in these terms:

> Our two churches are, now, discovering that in spite of our separation the Spirit of God kept in each one the same essential

150

features. Objectively they remained sister Churches and we may recognize in one of them the characters, the face of the other. This is a marvellous grace, coming from God. For us, reconciliation does not imply a long and difficult building up of common attitudes and common beliefs. They are already there, preserved by the Spirit of Christ. We have to thank God for this privilege.[7]

Thus, the first duty of the Anglican and Roman Catholic is that of thanksgiving: expressing in prayer our profound gratitude for all the Father has done for our two sister Churches through the one Spirit of our one Lord.

On the other hand, both Churches must still travel a great distance to reach their common goal of full reconciliation, for, 'centuries and centuries of division, sometimes full of arrogance or resentment, cannot be superseded in a few years, and only by the decision of the supreme authorities.'[8] It is not a matter of total union now or nothing, as we have noted above, but of steadily moving forward. So what is the very first step to be taken now?

The Malta Report, which initiated the official discussion for unity between the Anglican Communion and the Roman Communion, rightly spoke of a unity by stages. Yet, looking at the actual situation, I become more and more convinced that our first stage must be what I shall call a spiritual coming together.[9]

We have made real progress at other levels, and that gives the two sister Churches a new confidence in viewing their bond of fellowship; but now we must get to the heart of the matter:

Now that we have become sure of our common will for unity, sure of our basic doctrinal positions, sure of our profound similitude based on a common faith and a common understanding of the main elements of the Church, sure of our common mission, we have to start seriously this first stage. It is a necessity.

Why such a necessity? Precisely as a consequence of the importance of reconciliation in the heart of the Christian mystery. The reunion of two separated churches is not a mechanical process. And it cannot be the result only of theological discussions and official authoritative decisions. It is primarily a spiritual matter.[10]

Fr Tillard then uses a rather exalted phrase to describe what is,

151

after all, a rather sublime event: the rediscovery by two Churches, themselves Body of Christ, themselves Mystery, of their one source, the ineffable Spirit: 'Our reconciliation will be a true one and our unity a full one only if they are spiritually prepared and spiritually received. In other words, reunion has a mystical dimension.'[11]

There is a theological consensus now that all baptized Christians, in virtue of the inhabitation of the Holy Spirit, are called to mystical prayer; the language rather frightens us, but it simply means opening ourselves up to participate in our full destiny as members of Christ.[12] As St John exclaims with astonishment: 'My dear people, we are already the children of God but what we are to be in the future has not yet been revealed; all we know, is that when it is revealed, we shall be like him because we shall see him as he really is' (1 John 3:2). Prayer is anticipation of our glorified condition, for it is the substance of the Kingdom: communion with God and with his children. And so Fr Tillard insists on this key dimension of ecumenism, this chief task to be 'done' by each of us:

During the last years, we probably did not care sufficiently about this profound dimension of our reunification. We had a theological, doctrinal, official ecumenism. Did we have a real spiritual one?. . . Give me the permission to use a word that, perhaps, some of you dislike; and let me apologize for this boldness. We need, more and more, a contemplative dimension in our search for unity. Unity is a gift of God so profoundly linked with the mystery of the Cross and Resurrection of Christ that it can be received only by a people whose heart and eyes are captivated by the glory of God which is shining in the face of Christ.[13]

This passage from Fr Tillard seems to describe prayer in its more joyful and lightsome moment, when experience of the glorified Christ predominates. But all of us also know moments more characterized by aridity and darkness, and we know that this prayer experience is also valid. Indeed, spiritual guides stress that such periods can represent real growth in the journey of prayer, as we move from the phase of spiritual 'consolations' to that of pure faith struggling forward, so that our love develops from a kind of religious eros to purer Christian agape, as we cleave to God not because of what we can get out of it, but because of God.

This dimension of dark prayer will also have its great ecumenical significance, for it will carry us deeper into the mystery of the crucified Christ who gained our reconciliation and who unites us, and it will render us more mature, more robust Christians, with greater perseverence and staying power through difficult periods. Cardinal Hume has suggested that the ecumenical movement seems to be entering 'a phase which is characterized in the spiritual life – the dark night of the soul.'[14] The analogy is most telling, because the dark night, 'follows on an initial period of fervour and enthusiasm and, when it happens, the soul runs the risk of giving way to frustration and impatience. It can sometimes have the impression of having been abandoned by God.'[15] Anyone acquainted with the contemporary ecumenical situation will recognize the aptness of the Cardinal's image. We have come a very great distance, in a few years, from that visit of Archbishop Ramsey to Pope Paul VI in 1966, and the progress has been measured in joint statements and common documents. There has been enthusiasm, and a sense of great momentum. But now? So many doubts can rise up and torment us. Are we moving as quickly? Have not things stalled? As Rome dedicates more time to the Orthodox, and the Anglicans are drawn in the direction of the Protestant Churches, apparently much more available for concrete dialogue and decisions, does not any further progress specifically in the area of the Anglican/Roman Catholic relationship seem to be postponed indefinitely? Will not Rome, with the Orthodox, be drawn away into ever remoter areas of stagnation? Will not Anglicanism and Protestantism, certainly more directly engaged in concrete history and the real human condition, nevertheless be sucked away from their catholic fonts and substance? The gloomy projections can go on and on: will not the converging Anglican-Protestant bloc splinter, as Anglo-Catholics, strict Lutherans and strict Calvinists go their separate ways, perturbed by the vague ecclesial conglomerate that is so doctrinally fuzzy? On the other hand, will not 'liberal' Roman Catholics pull away from a Rome-Constantinople alliance that seems so stultifying and appears to imply such a betrayal of Vatican II and all renewal hopes? And will not the rigorously anti-ecumenical currents in Orthodoxy pull away in another direction, forming still other groups analogous to the Old Calendarists? What possible interest will any of these angry, doctrinaire splinter groups have in any other? And what possible interest will the two much larger blocs have in each other, as they career away in opposite directions? And so, after all the ecumenical hullabaloo of recent decades, what will be the final result? Is it not very possible that our last state will be much worse than our first?

Predictions of disaster such as these can trouble the individual dedicated to ecumenism, can indeed trouble the movement itself, as the 'letters to the editor' column of the religious press bears frequent witness. They plague the ecclesial consciousness in the same way that innumerable fears, temptations and demons plagued St Anthony in Athanasius' classic biography of the first Christian hermit. But Anthony won through, simply by facing up to the fact of the tormenting forces, and coming to terms with them through faith in Christ; he repeated with the psalmist: 'The Lord is my help, I look down on my enemies.'[16] So we can exorcize our fears and doubts by drawing them out of their dark recesses, holding them at arm's length and coming to terms with them explicitly. Often just the light of day relativizes such phobias, robs them of their force; and also a bit of humour is effective; things are often not quite as tragic as they might seem in our dark nights. And for the rest? Well, we can always work mightily, and pray mightily. We have mentioned the prayer of thanksgiving, for all that God has wrought for the two sister Churches in these years; Fr Tillard's sermon alluded to the prayer of adoration, 'captivated by the glory of God which is shining in the face of Christ'. Cardinal Hume's comments remind us of that prayer of naked faith which struggles doggedly, in an almost inarticulate form, through the dark night. But there is also the simple prayer of petition and intercession as splendid resource, as primary task for each of us to 'do' in our ecumenical commitment. We sometimes feel a certain disdain for this form of prayer, and see it as too humble and 'primitive' for such sophisticated and advanced Christians as we. If we are always asking things of God, instead of abandoning ourselves to His wisdom and love, surely we have not advanced too far. Madame Guyon, a leader of the Quietist movement, felt herself to be so splendidly beyond the stage of mere prayer of petition or intercession that she would not ask of God anything, even deliverance for herself and others from eternal separation from God; far better to accept sublimely 'the eternal decree that He would pronounce', even if it were a 'decree of eternal damnation.'[17] Clearly this doesn't leave much space for petition or intercession. How different the approach of another Frenchwoman some two hundred years later, Thérèse of Lisieux, whose startling 'little way' consisted of recognizing that she had nothing of the sublime, and was less of a soaring eagle in the heavens than a wet chick foolishly distracted on earth, and that she needed to ask for and to receive everything from Christ.[18] Moreover, she hoped to dedicate her earthly life and even her eternity to intercessory prayer.[19]

Whichever side of this ancient dispute we favour, it should at least be remembered that the Our Father is simply a series of petitions; and, in the words of yet another Frenchwoman, Simone Weil, the mystic and our near contemporary, 'the Our Father contains all possible petitions . . . it is to prayer what Christ is to humanity'.[20] As the Word assumed our human condition, and in some mysterious way 'God made the sinless one into sin' (2 Cor. 5:21), so also the Our Father assumes our human condition, and certainly our human fragility and need. The Anglican spiritual theologian Kenneth Leech has noted:

> As in the human community, to ask is an essential element in the relationship of prayer. We ask as members of a family, not in the spirit of selfish individualism. The Lord's Prayer in fact is entirely a prayer of petition – asking that God's name be hallowed, that his Kingdom may come, that we may be nourished, forgiven, preserved from temptation, and delivered from evil. The teaching on prayer in the Gospels centres around petition. 'Ask and it shall be given you; seek and you shall find; knock, and it shall be opened to you' (Matt. 7:7). Jesus' own prayer included a core of petition – for forgiveness of his murderers, for the increase of Peter's faith, for the sanctifying of his disciples, for the unity of the Church, and for his own faithfulness to God's will.'[21]

It is interesting that petition and intercession also constituted the core of the earliest Christian contemplative tradition. Cassian, for instance, proposes to the very advanced contemplative the constant repetition of the verse from the Psalms: 'Oh God make speed to save me: O Lord make haste to help me.'[22] This profound prayer is an 'important stage'[23] towards the emergence of the Prayer of

Jesus in Sinite and Athonite Hesychasm.[24] 'Lord Jesus Christ, Son of God, have mercy on me,' is not the only formula used, but the prayer almost always has the character of a petition.[25]

In the English spiritual tradition, the author of the *Cloud* suggests that when persons advanced in prayer formulate in words their deepest urgings, 'their words are few. . . . A short prayer pierces the heavens.'[26] And what should this briefest prayer be?

> Let me try to illustrate what I mean with an example from real life. A man or woman terrified by sudden disaster is forced by the circumstances to the limits of his personal resources, and marshals all his energy into one great cry for help . . . summoning all his strength, he expresses his desperate need in one loud cry: 'Help!'[27]

It seems that as we grow in prayer, we become more aware that all is grace; we can, like Thérèse become more childlike, more like the insistent widow in Christ's parable, and thus 'storm heaven' with our expression of need. The fathers speak of the prayerful person as a Jacob who must frequently wrestle with God. George Herbert's striking poem entitled 'Prayer' reinvokes this more urgent and dramatic function of prayer:

> Engine against th'Almightie, sinners towre
> Reversed thunder, Christ-side-piercing spear.[28]

We need a little of this violent urgency when praying about reunion, for if we do nothing, probably our habitual solution, burying our talent fearfully in the ground, our condemnation might be the worse (see Matt. 25:14–30). What are we then to do? Ecumenical theologians are unanimous in insisting that we are not going to be able to get out of this one trusting merely in our own skills. Authentic reunion in diversity will be primarily a *gift* of the Spirit who draws together, quickens and raises up the sundered body of Christ. But we must pray for this miracle; Christ's Spirit is not going to force it on us.

Some might find the lovely seventeenth-century Anglican prayer helpful, abbreviated in the eighteenth century to the following:

> O God the Father of our Lord Jesus Christ, our only Saviour, the Prince of Peace: Give us grace seriously to lay to heart the

great dangers we are in by our unhappy divisions; take away all hatred and prejudice, and whatever else may hinder us from godly union and concord; that, as there is but one Body and one Spirit, one hope of our calling, one Lord, one Faith, one Baptism, one God and Father of us all, so we may be all of one heart and of one soul, united in one holy bond of truth and peace, of faith and charity, and may with one mind and one mouth glorify thee; through Jesus Christ our Lord. Amen.

The Fellowship of St Gregory and St Augustine, dedicated 'to the reunion in diversity of the Anglican Communion and the Roman Catholic Church'[29] offers its members and associates this prayer formula which is of assistance to many:

> Enable and fulfill, O heavenly Father
> the unity in diversity of Anglicans and Roman Catholics,
> that we may ever more profoundly experience
> your eternal communion with Christ the Lord
> in the unity of the Holy Spirit
> one God, for ever and ever. Amen.

Soee might, with Cassian and the *Cloud*, prefer a shorter formula, repeated frequently, and with much insistence. Shifting the formula of Cassian and the psalmist into the plural, we can beg, 'O Lord, make speed to help us!' Or maybe we will just cry out with the author of the *Cloud*: 'Help!'

The ecumenist has his vision of sister Churches reconciled in love, each enabling the other to live and share the uniqueness of her own heritage. The person of prayer also has a vision: a glimpse of that Communion which binds the Son to the Father in the one Spirit. Such prayer needs the human flesh of our sister Churches and of the intentions of ecumenism, while ecumenism needs the spiritual depth that can only come from such prayer. What then are we to do for the reunion of the two Churches? The primary thing is to pray.

At the Community Level

If one can contribute a great deal to the dialogue by working and praying by oneself or with a friend, clearly those efforts will be more fruitful if they can be related to a larger community effort, 'for where two or three meet in my name, I shall be there with them' (Matt. 18:20). One should therefore explore what can be done at the parish and inter-parish level, at the diocesan level, and with national and international ecumenical groups. Many dioceses now, both Anglican and Roman Catholic, have an 'ecumenical officer' who can be contacted through the Chancery Office or the Diocesan Office, and who will know of the ecumenical groups and resources available. Some religious orders, both Roman Catholic and Anglican, have a special ecumenical ministry. For example, the Franciscan Friars of the Atonement who have houses in London, New York and San Francisco, as well as Japan and Jamaica. They publish informative ecumenical newsletters (in the US *Ecumenical Trends*) and operate fine ecumenical libraries, as in London. The Benedictine monks and nuns of Cockfosters publish from London *One in Christ*, an outstanding ecumenical journal which contains significant articles and documents, and reviews books and events of significance. Other Benedictine houses throughout the world have a special ecumenical interest and can serve as points of reference. These include:

In Great Britain: St Michael's, Farnborough; Downside; Nashdom (Anglican); Quarr; Ramsgate; Pluscarden.

In the United States: St John's, Collegeville (with its Ecumenical Institute); St Meinrad's; St Gregory's; Three Rivers (Anglican); Pecos (especially interested in the charismatic renewal area); Incarnation Priory (Anglican/Roman Catholic ecumenical); Valyermo;

In Canada: the Benedictine Priory, Montreal (Roman Catholic, but hosting an Anglican Bishop, The Rt Rev Henry Hill); Westminster Abbey, British Columbia.

In Australia, St Mark's (Anglican) Benedictine Priory at Camperdown; the Trappist Abbey of Tarrawarra.

Monks of the Benedictine tradition have no monopoly of course on ecumenical commitment, and often Franciscan Friaries or Jesuit houses or Dominican communities are centres of ecumenical commitment. Anglican religious houses of whatever order will very likely have ecumenical interests and contacts.

Often one can find in one's own diocese, or in a neighbouring one, an ecumenical group already formed; in the Berkeley area of America, for instance, parishioners of a Roman Catholic parish have been meeting with those of an Anglican parish once a month for many years, to discuss spiritual themes that bind the two Churches. In San Francisco 'BAY-ARC' has gathered the Anglican/Roman Catholic dialogue at a more theological level. In several countries there are also local groups affiliated to the Fellowship of St Gregory and St Augustine, which, with its newsletters, conferences and other activities and especially with the prayers of its members and friends, advances the dialogue between the two Churches.[30]

It may be that there is no such group in one's area. Perhaps that absence could itself challenge one to create such a group. Many are interested in the dialogue, and it is often not difficult to find four or five, or more who would be willing to meet every other month or so to discuss and pray about the relation of the two Churches.

Suppose such a group does in fact exist, or can be organized; what does it then do and where does it direct its energies? The possibilities are numerous, and the group itself can choose its own path according to its own particular interests and local needs. Booklets are available that offer a suggested structure for such meetings as well as possible themes (such as history of Anglican-Roman Catholic ecumenism, the ARCIC agreed statements; etc.).[31] Some groups discuss specialized issues, such as mixed marriages and the pastoral and human challenges they pose. Some groups move on to reflect on Scripture or key liturgical feasts, or on the many saints whom both Churches celebrate, often on the same day and who constitute a common heritage.[32] Spiritual classics can be studied together as well as recent books on spirituality or theology.

The group itself might sponsor conferences, social activities or joint retreats, for the larger community. It might also encourage parish, seminary or diocesan covenants, actively support the Week of Prayer for Christian Unity (celebrating in 1983 its 75th anniversary), gather the nucleus of an ecumenical library, and in other ways encourage a broader commitment to the dialogue.[33] The possibilities are innumerable, and the Malta Report lists some recommendations simply as examples of what can be done both at the official and at the more informal levels:

In every region where each Communion has a hierarchy, we

159

propose an annual joint meeting of either the whole or some considerable representation of the two hierarchies.

In the same circumstances we further recommend:

a) Constant consultation between committees concerned with pastoral and evangelistic problems including, where appropriate, the appointment of joint committees.

b) Agreements for joint use of churches and other ecclesiastical buildings, both existing and to be built, wherever such use is helpful for one or other of the two Communions.

c) Agreements to share facilities for theological education, with the hope that all future priests of each Comr union should have attended some course taught by a professor of the other Communion. Arrangements should also be made where possible for temporary exchange of students.

d) Collaboration in projects and institutions of theological scholarship is to be warmly encouraged.[34]

The above are only some of the recommendations made by the Malta Report in 1968 and indicate how frequently the positions of our most informed experts go quite beyond our current practice. The primary point, again, is not to project more proposals but to begin to put into practice those that have been formulated for us for some time. ARC-USA drew up another list of recommendations in 1970 that also still challenge us today. Some of the recommendations were as follows:

The projected meeting of bishops, combining a day of recollection with a day of discussion of pastoral concerns and problems. . .

Joint clergy conferences should be encouraged, and our ecumenical officers and diocesan ecumenical contacts should become resources for subjects and speakers (perhaps as 'travelling teams') to assure successful programs that would move our two Churches toward the common goal.

Co-operation should be fostered between our program resource persons, especially in the areas of adult education, professional leadership development and missions. Steps should be taken toward unifying our basic approaches toward religious education of the young.

The religious orders should be made aware of the desirability of closer relationships between orders of similar inspiration as recommended in the Malta Report and approved by authority.

Participation of the laity in joint retreats and conferences, in living-room dialogues, and in the week of prayer for Christian unity, should be systematically encouraged.[35]

Dealing specifically with the contribution that religious can make to the dialogue, the fourth Ecumenical Consultation on the Religious Life was an important event which took place in Rome in May of 1981. Nine Roman Catholic and six Anglican superiors heard the honorary president of the Consultation, Fr Pedro Arrupe, S. J., Superior General of the Jesuits, stress that 'as religious, we have special means available to us to bridge gaps within the church and to be instruments of reconciliation both among Christians and in the world at large.'[36] In their US meeting the previous year major superiors of Anglican and Roman Catholic religious communities 'described a number of ecumenical experiments in which their members were already engaged, including covenants of prayer and fellowship, reciprocal personnel arrangements, and economic strategies.'[37] Specific cases of ecumenical joint communities, between Anglican and Roman Catholic religious who 'share everything but the eucharist'[38] were mentioned. In the Caribbean, Roman Catholic Friars 'are embarking upon an exchange programme with Anglican Franciscans'.[39] But it is our third world communities, which are also the most thriving for both Churches, that are advancing the quickest: 'More dramatic ecumenical progress was reported overseas, where people are thrown together out of need and close personal relationships develop.'[40] The report goes on to describe quite startling ecumenical developments among Anglican and Roman Catholic religious in South America and Africa. It is precisely in England, America, Canada and Australia 'first world Christian countries' that, 'despite increasing ecumenical involvement, contacts between Anglican and Roman Catholic communities are still largely social and individual.'[41] So there is much work that still must be done: 'Our future actions should make us a people who can't stay apart.'[42]

What is remarkable about these meetings of religious is that they are not clandestine, slightly subversive gatherings of restless novices in some corner of the 'underground church'. They represent, rather, the formally established Ecumenical Consultation, brought into being by the two Unions of Roman Catholic Superiors General and by the Religious Advisory Boards of the Anglican Church" and the participants themselves are 'Religious Superiors General'.[43]

The international Consultation has its national counterparts, and the US gathering of major superiors in March 1981 proposed a series of concrete programmes, including the following:

This official ecumenical consultation affirms . . . that religious life itself, predating and in certain ways transcending our divisions, is especially suited to serve the People of God in this ecumenical vocation, and through a variety of concrete ways, such as:
  a) study of the ARCIC's joint documents, ARC-USA documents, and other ecumenical studies.
  b) Week of Prayer for Christian Unity.
  c) Thursday Unity Prayer.
  d) covenants – of orders, communities, individual religious.
  e) joint houses.
  f) joint retreats.
  g) ecumenical hospitality.
  h) Bible study.
  i) study of our common spiritual heritage.
  j) the Fellowship of St Gregory and St Augustine.[44]

That same meeting of the US Consultation affirmed, as we have seen, the clear implications for religious solidarity of the ecclesiology of sister Churches: 'We mutually recognize the authenticity of our vows as religious of sister Churches.'[45]

The religious life is simply a modality of the Christian life and call to perfection; thus the various concrete suggestions of these Consultations will be relevant and challenging to all of us in one way or other, whatever our specific vocation in the two sister Churches. Certainly these Consultations' fundamental affirmation of the significance of the commitment touches us all: 'We are called to the Gospel priority, injunction, and urgency of ecumenism, "that the world may believe" (John 17:21).'[46]

The US Consultation list above of concrete ways to promote ecumenism refers to 'e. joint houses'. There are now several ecumenical monasteries throughout the world, the most famous of which is Taizé. Tens of thousands of pilgrims of every age and religious affiliation are drawn to the monastery for the conferences, but most especially for the prayer, silence, and lived experience of Christian community found there. The monastery itself is not denominational, but seeks to unite more than seventy monks of many Church affiliations into a new ecumenical, Christian experience that can be seen as a parable of the unity the various Churches are seeking.[47]

Incarnation Priory in California represents a rather different model and conception of the same ideal of ecumenical religious community. This small, urban Priory, 'a joint monastic venture in which monks of the Order of the Holy Cross (Anglican) and of the Benedictine Camaldolese Order (Roman Catholic) participate',[48] is made up of Anglican and Roman Catholic monks only, who remain members of their own religious order, each with its own heritage and history. The Priory is thus a 'joint community' and, 'the Camalodolese and Holy Cross monks remain juridically distinct (each group with its own constitutions, superiors, etc.) but are spiritually united at many levels.'[49] The basic statement enumerates some of these important points of unity:

> Key moments of monastic common life – joint meetings, meals, recreations, etc. are shared, and the Divine Office according to the Holy Cross Breviary is alternated with that of a Camaldolese Office Book. The monks naturally observe the disciplines and authorities of their respective Churches.[50]

Although everything is shared except the Eucharist, there has been no attempt to shape a new amalgam whether of liturgy or of the hours; the endeavour has been, rather, to realize a 'communion in diversity, safeguarding the distinctiveness of each heritage in the substance of unity we already share.'[51] The joint community thus seeks to witness to the unity-in-diversity which the two sister Churches are committed to.

A splendid moment for the Priory came in July 1981 when the Archbishop of Canterbury and the Roman Catholic Archbishop of San Francisco bestowed a joint blessing on the community in Grace Cathedral, before a large congregation attending the solemn Evensong service.[52]

This basic model of 'unity in diversity' can be applied in various ways to small ecumenical study and prayer groups, to parishes, to theological schools in an ecumenical consortium, to joint ventures in the area of social action, and so on. Our bond is already such that, without muddying distinctions or rushing ahead before the moment is mature, many areas of Christian life can be shared in a dialectical way that witnesses to this unity-in-diversity.

What is true of joint study groups, theological ventures and mission is of course true for the key moment in the life of both Churches: prayer. We have already reflected on the urgency and significance of personal prayer; community ecumenical prayer is of equal importance. The Malta Report had already noted in 1968 (before the remarkable conclusions of accord of the agreed statements):

> Prayer in common has been recommended by the Decree on Ecumenism and provisions for this common worship are to be found in the *Directory* (para. 56). We urge that they be implemented.
>
> Our similar liturgical and spiritual traditions make extensive sharing possible and desirable; for example, in non-eucharistic services, the exploration of new forms of worship, and retreats in common. Religious orders of similar inspiration in the two Communions are urged to develop a special relationship.
>
> Our closeness in the field of sacramental belief leads us further to recommend that on occasion the exchange of preachers for the homily during the celebration of the Eucharist also be permitted, without prejudice to the more general regulations contained in the *Directory*.
>
> Since our liturgies are closely related by reason of their common source, the ferment of liturgical renewal and reform now engaging both our Communions provides an unprecedented opportunity for collaboration. We should co-operate, and not take unilateral action, in any significant changes in the seasons and major holy days of the Christian year.[53]

This long text indicates how our two liturgical-spiritual traditions are in such accord as to 'make extensive sharing possible and desirable'. It is difficult to imagine that our people will feel any real impetus to move closer if we do not pray regularly together; for this reason the obstacles to shared Eucharistic celebration and com-

164

munion are a cause of real sorrow for all. The official positions of the two Churches are not identical here, but the Roman Catholic stance that Eucharistic celebration expresses a unity between Churches, and thus could not be shared by communities still unhappily divided in areas of faith and order, is well known. Many ecumenists regard our inability to share in the central Christian moment as their basic motive to work all the harder to overcome the remaining obstacles. They fear that shared celebration too facilely anticipated would paper over difficulties that, with sufficient commitment, could be overcome in the foreseeable future, given our ecumenical momentum now. And that would pave the way for a real union-in-diversity between the two sister Churches, and thus for a Eucharistic sharing that would be fully celebrative of the unity expressed. Whatever the various positions of Anglican and Roman Catholic theologians regarding this issue are, there certainly remains a disaccord which must be frankly acknowledged. Ecumenical dialogue is not all light and roses. Bishop Clark, in discussing the issue with the Anglican Synod, could only conclude: 'Perhaps it is best to say, at this particular moment, that our way to unity is not only a great grace but that it is also the way of the Cross.'[54]

The one point that should be added is that the Eucharist, for all its centrality, does not exhaust the forms or expressions of liturgical prayer. Sometimes members of both Churches feel that if we do not celebrate the Eucharist together, we simply cannot pray together, other than perhaps for a brief recitation of the Our Father. The monastic tradition of praying the psalms, which has continued into the Anglican Morning Prayer and Evening Prayer liturgies, and into the Roman Catholic office, has nourished Christians for centuries in a very fundamental way. Many of the early monks celebrated the Eucharist only infrequently, but they would gather for psalmody, and this profound and classical form of Christian community prayer would bind them together. Of course the liturgy of the hours cannot substitute for the Eucharist, cannot remove the experience of the Cross that our separation at that central moment implies. But if, as we celebrate the Eucharist in our own Church, we unite ourselves spiritually not just with all members of our own Communion, living and dead, but also with all members of our sister Church, and if from this centre we participate regularly in other forms of common worship with brethren of the other Communion, then we are celebrating Christian *koinonia* to a very great extent. We might well find that a shared office that involves hymns, prayers and the psalms nourishes very profoundly our achieved union, and gives us increased impetus to live our Christian ecumenical commitment towards full reunion. The Anglican and Roman Catholic co-priors of Incarnation Priory have written of their community's lived experience of sharing the divine office for over two years:

> While present Church regulations do not yet permit Eucharistic sharing, what we experience in the celebration of the Office is, in fact, a eucharistic liturgy in one of its essential biblical dimensions – the sacrifice of praise and thanksgiving, the *opus Dei* of singing which uniquely serves to bring one's whole being into the presence of God and to transform consciousness. Regular and frequent experience of this sort tends, we have found, to transcend ecclesiastical boundaries and was important in setting the stage for the initial covenant between the two Orders.[55]

All of us could certainly give more time and energy to a deeper praying of the psalms. As ecumenical worship they are most appropriate, for they recall our deepest roots in the prayer of Israel, in Christ the fulfilment of the psalms, who prayed them with his own disciples, as well as in the psalm worship of the earliest apostolic communities, the Churches of the patristic period, and the entire medieval heritage. The Benedictine centuries in England particularly stressed psalmody as a form of Christian prayer, and according to the Holy Rule, which cites the psalms more than any other book of the Bible, praying the psalms is the 'Work of God', and 'nothing, therefore, is to be put before the Work of God'.[56]

Psalmody is particularly indicated for ecumenical worship because it enables us to discover now our common centre who is Christ; as the Rule joyfully observes, 'What can be sweeter to us, dear brethren, than this voice of the Lord inviting us? Behold, in His loving kindness the Lord shows us the way of life.'[57]

Psalmody points us to the future, too. It opens for us prophetically that communion of the Kingdom which we shall forever celebrate. Claude Peifer, an American Roman Catholic Benedictine, has noted in this respect:

The psalms are not only a witness to the religious history of the past, but also a prophecy of the future, a prophecy of Christ, of the Church, and of all the mysteries of salvation which have now been realized. The Fathers saw Christ everywhere in the psalms: for them the value of the Psalter was principally prophetic. In this they were only following the example of Christ himself, who told the disciples on the road to Emmaus: 'All things must be fulfilled that are written in the Law of Moses and the Prophets and the Psalms concerning me' (Luke 24:24).[58]

We have noted above the centrality of praying the psalms for the Anglican liturgical tradition, and we have also noted the prophetic thrust which characterizes Anglicanism at its best. It would be fascinating to discover to what extent that prophetic dimension is triggered and nourished by the daily meditating upon and praying of the psalms and canticles that has characterized the spirituality of so many Anglicans. Fr Geoffrey Curtis, Anglican religious of the Community of the Resurrection, quotes, in his excellent biography, this moving passage from a sermon of William of Glasshampton:

The great message of the Incarnation is that God came down. He humbled Himself and made Himself of no reputation. He took upon Himself the form of a servant. He was in our midst. . . . He came to our side to help us. He shared our sorrows and our shame. . . . The Church is the perpetual expression of all this. Her members have to be true to the spirit of the Incarnation. . . . If you mean to be a Christian, then it must be a real equality. You must come down. You must be in the midst [of the poor] ready to share. If need be everything must go. You must be willing to part with all for Love's sake.[59]

Fr William was at the time in the midst of the unemployed and the striking dock workers in the difficult year of 1906, so what was the source of his prophetic strength? Fr Curtis notes that, 'this sacrificial aspect of his pastoral work in Plaistow had as its background the life of austere recollection and prayer at Stanford-le-Hope to which he returned at regular intervals.'[60]

What then can we *do* for ecumenism? The possibilities are almost limitless, at the personal, the parish and the diocesan levels. But in case our *doing* becomes simply a frenetic activism, a 'spinning of

167

the wheels', we will need to be faithful to our fundamental task of personal prayer and common worship. To the extent that we open ourselves to God's Word, for 'The Word of God is something alive and active' (Heb. 4:12), and to the extent that we pray that Word, united in Spirit to our beloved sister Church, to that extent our *doing* can take on prophetic power, 'through the Gospel coming not only in word, but also in power and in the Holy Spirit and as utter conviction' (1 Thess. 1:5).

Notes

1 Bishop Alan Clark, 'Where Anglicans and Roman Catholics Agree, op. cit., p. 68.
2 Quoted in 'The Ecumenical Vocation of Religious in Sister Churches: Agreed Statement of the Anglican/Roman Catholic Consultation on the Religious Life,' op. cit., p. 3 n. 5.
3 See Robert Hale, 'La koinonia aperta della vita monastica', op. cit., pp. 128–162.
4 St Peter Damian, 'The Book of "The Lord Be With You" ', ch. 5; in Peter Damian, *Selected Writings* (Faber and Faber 1959), p. 57.
5 Bernard and Margaret Pawley, op. cit., p. 297.
6 Aelred of Rievaulx, *Spiritual Friendship*, n. 70; in the Cistercian Fathers edition (Cistercian Publications, Michigan, 1977), p. 66.
7 Fr Jean Tillard, O.P., Sermon Text, September 18, 1976, manuscript distributed by the Order of the Holy Cross, West Park, New York.
8 ibid.
9 ibid.
10 ibid.
11 ibid.
12 For a classically neo-Thomist formulation of the thesis of the 'general call to contemplation or to the mystical life' see R. Garrigou-Lagrange, O.P., *Christian Perfection and Contemplation according to St Thomas Aquinas and St John of the Cross* (Herder 1958), pp. 337–73. For an Anglican affirmation of the same thesis, but utilizing an entirely different method and language, see Evelyn Underhill, *The Mystic Way: A Psychological Study in Christian Origins* (J. M. Dent 1929), pp. 56–7 *et passim*.
13 Fr Jean Tillard, O.P., op. cit.
14 Cardinal Hume, cited in the *Catholic Herald* (July 6, 1978), p. 3.
15 ibid.
16 Ps. 117:7; quoted in Athanasius, *Vita Antonii*, 6; P.G., XXXVII, col. 849.
17 Quoted in Pierre Pourrat, S.S., *Christian Spirituality: From Jansenism to Modern Times* (Newman, Maryland, 1955), p. 197.
18 Thérèse insists that she is just a 'weak little bird' that can only 'raise

its little wings; to fly is not within its little power', yet she notes that she has 'an eagle's *eyes and heart*', and with great theological and spiritual acumen she notes who is the one eagle who carries the rest of us: 'O Divine Word! You are the Adored Eagle whom I love and who alone attracts me' lifting up all 'to the bosom of the Eternal Fire of the Blessed Trinity'. Thérèse of Lisieux, *Story of a Soul: A New Translation from the Original Manuscripts* (Institute of Carmelite Studies, Washington, 1976), pp. 198–9; see also her powerful image of Christ not as the ladder, upon whom we climb to the Father, but rather as the escalator who lifts us up; Thérèse has a radical, Augustinian experience of human fragility and the requirement of grace, and in this way is close to central insights of the reformation fathers. See pp. 207–8. See Ruth Burrows, *Guidelines for Mystical Prayer* (Sheed and Ward 1976), p. 68: 'Thérèse rejected utterly the cash-in-hand mentality, good works and merit, "heroism". . . . There was no limit to what God could do in Thérèse once she held out her empty hands, abandoning forever any thought of earning or achievement.' For the convergence of mystical experience and reformation insight, see Bengt R. Hoffman, *Luther and the Mystics: A Re-examination of Luther's Spiritual Experience and His Relationship to the Mystics* (Augsburg, Minnesota, 1976).

19 Thérèse of Lisieux, *Story of a Soul*, ibid., pp. 196–7.

20 Simone Weil, *Waiting for God* (Putnam's, New York, 1951), pp. 226–7.

21 Kenneth Leech, *True Prayer: An Invitation to Christian Spirituality* (Harper and Row 1980), p. 24. See also pp. 25–6.

22 John Cassian, Conferences, X, 10, 2; in *Sources Chrétiennes* (Paris: Editions du Cerf, Paris, 1958), LIV, p. 88.

23 O. Chadwick, *John Cassian* (Cambridge University Press 1968), p. 106.

24 See A Monk of the Eastern Church, *The Prayer of Jesus* (Desclee, New York, 1967), pp. 29–58.

25 ibid., pp. 65f.

26 *The Cloud of Unknowing and The Book of Privy Counseling* (Image Books, New York, 1973), pp. 95–6.

27 ibid., p. 95.

28 George Herbert, 'Prayer (1)'; in *The English Poems of George Herbert* (Dent 1974), p. 70.

29 Fellowship of St Gregory and St Augustine, basic statement; see *Documents on Anglican/Roman Catholic Relations*, IV, pp. 113–4 for the full text.

30 On the Fellowship, see *Documents on Anglican/Roman Catholic Relations*, IV, op. cit., pp. 113–4; see also *Ecumenical Trends* 6(1977), pp. 164–5. For further information on national and local chapters, write: Incarnation Priory, 2451 Ridge Road, Berkeley, California 94709, USA. See above, chapter 3, note 65.

31 For a structured programme of dialogue see Lawrence Mullaly and John Osgood, ed., *A Call to Communion: Documents of the International Anglican-Roman Catholic Dialogue, 1966–1977 with Study*

169

Guides and Anglican-Roman Catholic Inter-Parish Dialogue: Participant's Guide (The Graymoor Ecumenical Institute, New York, 1979).

32 Some of the saints whom we both celebrate in our common liturgical calendars who might be studied by an ecumenical group are: Sts Anselm, Bede, Boniface, Benedict, Aidan, Theodore, Francis of Assisi Ambrose, Augustine, Bernard, Clement, etc.

33 For covenants, see 'Covenants, Covenant Relationship' in *Documents on Anglican/Roman Catholic Relations*, III, op. cit., pp. 36–55. Often two parishes or dioceses enter into covenant, but the bond is quite as appropriate for religious communities and orders. The Camaldolese-Holy Cross experience has been particularly positive; see Bede Thomas Mudge, O.H.C., 'Anglican Roman Catholic Religious Communities Make Covenant' in *Ecumenical Trends* 6(1977), pp. 161–4. Theological colleges, such as Nashotah House and Sacred Heart School of Theology in the US, can also bind themselves in covenant; see 'Covenant Agreement Signed' in *The Living Church* 182(June 7, 1981), p. 6.

34 The Malta Report in *Anglican/Roman Catholic Dialogue*, op. cit., p. 110.

35 'ARC VII Statement' in *Documents on Anglican/Roman Catholic Relations*, I, op. cit., pp. 18–19.

36 Cited in 'Religious of Three Traditions Consult in Rome' in *The Living Church* 183(July 5, 1981), p. 5.

37 Cited in 'Anglican and Roman Catholic Major Superiors hold Historic First Meeting' in CMSM National Secretariat Press Release (Conference of Major Superiors of Men, Washington, May 3, 1980), p. 1.

38 ibid., p. 2.

39 ibid.

40 ibid.

41 ibid.

42 The affirmation was made by the Rev Connor Lynn, O.H.C., then Superior of the Order of the Holy Cross, and one of the strongest promoters of Anglican/Roman Catholic religious dialogue.

43 Cited in 'Permanent Ecumenical Consultation of Religious', an explanatory sheet issued from Rome, Centro Pro Unione, 1981.

44 'The Ecumenical Vocation of Religious in Sister Churches' (Anglican/Roman Catholic Consultation on the Religious Life, New York, 1981), p. 1.

45 ibid.

46 ibid.

47 See Jean Marie Paupert, *Taizé et l'Eglise de demain* (Fayard, Paris, 1967).

48 See Robert Hale, O.S.B., 'Incarnation Priory: A Venture in Ecumenical Community Life' in *Holy Cross* 3 (Winter 1981) p.2. The article is to be reprinted in *Encounter and Exchange* and *Ecumenical Bulletin*.

49 ibid. See also 'Incarnation Priory' in *One in Christ* 18 (1981) pp. 181–182.

50 ibid.

51 ibid.

52 See *The Living Church* 183 (July 5, 1981), p. 7.
53 The Malta Report, op. cit., p. 110.
54 Bishop Alan Clark, 'Where Anglicans and Roman Catholics Agree', op. cit., p. 69.
55 Robert Hale, O.S.B. and Roy Parker, O.H.C., 'Praying the Psalms: an Ecumenical Experience', in *Modern Liturgy*, 9 (Feb. 1982) pp. 28–29.
56 St Benedict, *Holy Rule*, ch. 43.
57 ibid., prologue.
58 Claude J. Peifer, O.S.B., *Monastic Spirituality* (Sheed and Ward, New York, 1966), p. 414. See the entire section, pp. 405–17.
59 Fr William Sirr, 'The Love of Man', sermon preached for the Guild of St Matthew, cited in Geoffrey Curtis, C.R., *William of Glasshampton*, op. cit., pp. 29–30.
60 ibid., p. 30. Fr Curtis, who died in 1981 at the age of 79, was himself an outstanding ecumenical pioneer and a very holy priest.

Conclusion

Remarkable progress has been made in the dialogue between the Roman Catholic Church and the Anglican Communion in recent years, especially since Vatican II and the visit of Archbishop Ramsey to Pope Paul VI in 1966. All Roman Catholics and Anglicans are now faced with a fundamental option: are they going to continue to look at each other according to a human logic of hostility, suspicion, and aloofness, or in a Christian spirit of solidarity and love? The exhortation of Pope and Archbishop is that we should employ this latter spirit. But we will need the Spirit of Christ to achieve this.

The challenge faces us on the local level, between parishes of the same town, as well as on the diocesan, national, and indeed international levels. The issue facing us is ecclesial, not just individual: it is not merely what I think of one Anglican person which is the issue, but how I view the Anglican Communion as a whole. The matter is of great urgency in terms of evangelizing our secularist, 'post-Christian' western nations as well as the third world; for how can divided and hostile Christians witness in a convincing way to the compassionate and reconciling Christ? The matter is of equal urgency for our own spiritual, and human welfare; for one 'who does not love the brother that he can see cannot love God, whom he has never seen' (1 John 4:20).

We are called to reflect upon the great challenge of the full reconciliation of the two Churches perhaps not primarily in juridical or neo-scholastic terms, but in the light of the Gospel, of the Fathers and of our worship experience ('*lex orandi, lex credendi*').

This 'monastic theology' approach is also characteristic of the Anglican theological method. As we discover our common roots, we discover our common language.

Our reflection upon the relationship between the two Churches does not, fortunately, occur in a vacuum. The splendid joint declarations of Popes and Archbishops of Canterbury, the very significant and carefully articulated agreed statements of ARCIC and of the national ARCs, the work of ecumenical theologians engaged in this dialogue for many years – this is all heartening material that offers a solid foundation, context and language for further reflection and dialogue.

Our goal must be *reunion* and nothing less, for Christian love urges us always beyond hostility and separation. Yet our goal must also be to safeguard authentic *diversity* – in liturgy, theology, spirituality and polity. For Christian love must acknowledge 'everything that is true, everything that is noble, everything that is good and pure, everything that we love and honour' (Phil. 4:8). In a true rapport of Churches, as in any authentic inter-personal relationship, 'union differentiates'. These recent years assure us, as Pope Paul VI affirmed to Archbishop Coggan, that, 'these words of hope, "The Anglican Church united not absorbed" are no longer a mere dream'.

We need to give a focus and more concrete element to our somewhat abstract formula of unity in diversity. Most of the Scriptural, patristic and monastic writings deal in *concrete models* taken from the interpersonal realm: these include God as Father, Christ as Son, Christ as brother, Christ as bridegroom and Christ as friend. Such images penetrate deeper, resonate more richly and engage us more fully than abstract categories, and we need such a concrete model to express the Anglican-Roman Catholic relationship. Again it is Paul VI who encourages us with his famous affirmation in 1970: 'There will be no seeking to lessen the legitimate prestige and the worthy patrimony of piety and usage proper to the Anglican Communion when the Roman Catholic Church . . . is able to embrace *her ever beloved sister* in the one authentic communion of *the family* of Christ.' The gift of his episcopal ring to the Archbishop of Canterbury, his invitation to the Archbishop to bestow a joint blessing on the faithful and the statements of Cardinal Hume in Westminster Abbey, the ARC-USA Twelve Year

173

Report are among many significant re-affirmations of the 'sister Churches' model applied to Anglican-Roman Catholic relations. This model is particularly rich, for it is rooted deeply in the first Christian ecclesial experiences: affirmed explicitly in 2 John 13, it underlies the ecclesiology of Paul, of *Acts*, and so forth. The Apostolic Fathers, such as Clement of Rome and Ignatius of Antioch, presuppose the same family model in their writings to the Churches, as do later Fathers such as Irenaeus, Tertullian and Cyprian. Gregory the Great, of particular significance to both Rome and Canterbury, insists particularly on the theme of diversity in unity in his important letters to his 'most reverend and holy brother and fellow-bishop Augustine'.

When we think and speak of 'the Church', we often tend to dwell exclusively on the one, universal Church; we sometimes simply identify our own specific Church with it, to the exclusion, explicitly or implicitly, of other Christian Churches. But the biblical-patristic heritage helps us to complement the key theme of the one, universal Church with the other, equally important, affirmation of the plurality of specific Churches; for it is these which open up to us rich possibilities for theological and spiritual pluralism, as well as opening the way finally to the urgently needed reconciliation of the Christian Communions.

If we begin again to affirm the theology of Church*es*, in the plural, and more especially if we are able to live and to experience this theology in our Christian lives, then we will break out of the constricting limits of ecclesiological unitarianism into the full, richly varied reality of the People of God. We will begin to breathe more deeply the divine, Triune Life, where Christian unity-in-diversity is ultimately rooted: 'May they all be one. Father, may they be one in us, as you are in me and I am in You. . . .' (John 17:21).

But such newness of life and perspective presupposes basic conversion and full commitment. We must, with Pope Paul VI and Archbishop Ramsey, 'leave in the hands of the God of mercy all that in the past has been opposed to this precept of charity.' We must personally come to terms with the affirmation of the other Church as beloved sister, not as an interesting theological idea, but as a basic challenge to our full, Christian commitment. Our conversion must be, among other things, a conversion *to* the *other*

174

Church in her concreteness, so that we are finally rejoicing again with her in her joys and grieving with her in her sorrows precisely because she is not our enemy or rival, but our beloved sister.

As we turn to face our companion Church openly and sympathetically, for the first time really in four centuries, we are going to be able to discover in her qualities that we share, but have lost sight of and dimensions of consanguinity. One such dimension would be the Benedictine spirit, which Anglicans have noted as characteristic of their own religious approach. Anglicans have always stressed that their own particular Reform was not so much a cutting off the head of the *Ecclesia Anglicana* as a thorough washing of her face. This Anglican commitment to ecclesial continuity opens up the wealth of the Catholic experience, and particularly in its Anglo-Saxon and Norman expression in Britain. This includes the heritage of St Patrick, St Columba, St Augustine, St Cuthbert, St Bede, St Anselm and a line of monastic saints and Church leaders that extends through the middle ages. It means stress on the Word of God, and on liturgy as its living context and initial fulfilment; it means community, and in its Benedictine development, *moderatio*, the key elements in the Anglican Reform itself. At the centre of that Reform we find, not a charismatic leader or a series of doctrines, but a liturgical book which makes accessible to the full community the centre of the Benedictine life: Eucharist and *Opus Dei*. Thus Anglican spiritual theologians note the 'Benedictine' character of Anglicanism, and the point is decisive for deeper, 'spiritual ecumenism'. To the extent that Roman Catholicism, through Vatican II and through her own Benedictine heritage, rediscovers the central moment of liturgy and the Word, and the significance of local community, to that extent she can discover her own consanguinity with the Anglican Communion. Ecumenism means discovery of the other, but also self-discovery, when sister Churches are again dialoguing. The Churches live their real, day to day lives not at the level of fine theological points, but of liturgy and spirituality and ministry. As Fr Tillard affirms, 'the reunion of two separated Churches is primarily a spiritual matter'. Perhaps no two other principal Churches of Christendom are so in tune at this deepest level of lived spirituality.

The spirituality of an entire Christian Communion, however, can never be expressed in merely one-dimensional terms. To inter-

175

pret the global Anglican experience in merely monastic-Benedictine categories would clearly be forced and simplistic, and Anglicanism will not lie on that procrustean bed. Other complementary (or perhaps dialectical) categories of interpretation are needed for a fuller rendering of the rich, lived experience of the Anglican heritage.

The Anglican Reform, which rendered the liturgy and the Word of God into a glorious form of the language of the people, created social movements which outlawed slavery and ministered to the poor in the darkest hours of the industrial revolution, the rich currents of Anglican mysticism, the pioneering work of Anglicans and of Lambeth in the area of ecumenism, the shaping of a polity which expresses episcopal collegiality and also extensively involves the laity – all these ferments and others express the prophetic-lay dimension of Christianity, so present in Anglicanism. It would be simplistic to juxtapose such a prophetic-lay pole with the monastic-Benedictine one, which in its origins and most authentic moments is itself a prophetic and lay movement. But later monasticism did experience a process of clericalization, an institutionalization which tended to isolate it from missionary and social commitments it had previously been engaged in. So the prophetic-lay dimension can, for functional and 'phenomenological' purposes, be distinguished from the monastic-Benedictine one, and their dialectic can suggest something of the richness and vitality of the Anglican experience. It can also spark and nourish true Christian *sanctity*, in figures as diverse as George Herbert, Nicholas Ferrar, William Wilberforce, Florence Nightingale, John Keble, William Reed Huntington, James Huntington and Evelyn Underhill, to mention but a few. Such figures enrich both Churches and bind us the closer in Christ's Spirit, the one source of all sanctification.

If both Churches share the monastic-Benedictine heritage, their mutual participation in the prophetic-lay dimension of Christianity is also of fundamental importance. It is often noted that both Communions affirm the threefold ministry of bishops, priests and deacons which is in itself significant. But both Churches – and this is less frequently noted – share the wider reality of Christian laity who are full members of Christ's body, and called also to sanctity and a fruitful ministry of their own. If 99.9 per cent of both

176

Churches is lay, we share an immense reservoir of creative Christian life that can serve to enrich us both. As Roman Catholics discover more and more of this lay dimension within their own Church, its needs and gifts, they will better understand their sister Anglican Communion, which has already engaged the laity in fuller partici-pation at many levels of ecclesial life. If the laity are the body of Christ, the prophetic dimension recalls Christ's Spirit, which vi-vifies and enlivens that body in all its members. Institution can sometimes smother the prophetic voice, and such a smothering occurs in both Churches. Both have traditions which are somewhat less than divinely inspired, and both have less edifying moments in their long histories. One priest, whose denominational and national affiliations will remain unspecified here, told me his own diocese was apparently trying to combine the worst of both Church heri-tages. The idea makes the mind boggle.

Ecumenical dialogue between the two sisters aims to bring to-gether not the worst but the best in each heritage. And it is precisely the prophetic voices which permit the best to re-emerge, which cut through mere form and appearance, and even revitalize our insti-tutions: this is the chief proof of their divine origin and of their blood kinship in the one family of Christ. The words and actions of our prophets are eruptions of the Spirit into contemporary Christian life and both Churches can only rejoice in this dynamism and sanctity enriching both, and strengthening their common bond.

But if the two Churches are in fact sisters, it is not enough just to derive consolation from this fact, just to contemplate the affir-mation passively. St Paul's letters, exegetes point out, characterist-ically have a twofold part, and this structure reflects that of the Gospel itself. First, the apostle announces what Christ, through His cross and resurrection, has made us and what we now are; but the apostle then insists on what we must therefore *do* to be what we fundamentally *are*. We are now children of God, therefore we must in our thoughts, words and actions *be* children of God. Christ has given birth through his Paschal Sacrifice to the Churches, which are sister Churches in the redeemed family of His Father; but now we must behave as sister Churches. It is interesting that 'sister' has a substantive form, expressing what two persons or groups are, but also a verbal form, 'to sister', expressing a way of being. Theo-logians have suggested that in the light of Scriptures we should think of God more as a verb than as a substantive; certainly we should think of our Churches as verbs, and their interrelations would best be expressed by the verb 'to sister'.

How can each of us participate in this call from our Churches, and favour and advance their bond of unity in diversity? The range of possibilities is now much greater than it has been these last four centuries and indeed is now limited principally by our own tepidity in committing time, energy and imagination. Among present possibilities, nurturing interpersonal contacts between Anglicans and Roman Catholics is of fundamental importance. The web of relationships will expand and acquaintanceships grow into that friendship and love which is the very stuff of the *koinonia* to which our two Churches are committed. On a more organized level, parish and ministries, and national and international movements dedicated to the dialogue all offer opportunities to relate personal commitment to broader Church efforts. And prayer is always possible, always decisive, for as we pray for one another, we enter into the mind and heart of Christ, our one high priest; and in his prayer to the Father in the Spirit we are already one. Ecumenical prayer is necessarily Christological and Trinitarian confession.

I had lunch recently with an American Anglican priest who had a remarkable story to tell. After university studies in engineering he had gone on to the priesthood, but then lapsed from active ministry for many years. He developed a successful engineering career, and one day, while working on a structural problem relating to a hospital, he encountered the supervisor, a Roman Catholic sister and a very emphatic person. She quickly intuited that he was a 'lapsed priest', and urged him, in no uncertain terms, to return to active ministry. He explained that his priesthood was Anglican, but that did not matter. She also wanted money, engineering advice, and prayers from him for a special project of hers: a clinic she wanted to establish in a very poor *barrio* of a South American city. He insisted that in exchange for all these things he was being compelled to pledge her, she had to promise him at least her prayers. She promised. He gave her the engineering advice she wanted, and the substance of his savings, some $90,000, and his prayers. He returned to active ministry, which he has been engaged in ever since, while she now runs her South American clinic.

The story is true, but it really doesn't make sense, in the light of four hundred years of reciprocal acrimony. Why should a Roman Catholic sister want a man to return to the Anglican priesthood? And why would an Anglican give $90,000 to a Roman Catholic sister for a mission in a Roman Catholic country? Why should each even want the support of the other's prayers? There is no answer whatever except one, which makes all the difference. The affirmation that two Christian Communions are sister Churches is ultimately a Christological confession: that the Son of Man, through His cross and resurrection, is able to reconcile even us, to turn our hostility into love. It is ultimately a Trinitarian confession, for God is love, and we who abide in love abide in God, and He in us.

Afterword

This book leaves us with a striking instance of the way in which our two sister Churches need each other, complement each other and can rediscover themselves through discovering one another. The experience of finding Christ anew through finding him in those from whom we have been estranged is one of the characteristic Christian experiences of our century. Meeting someone who at first we had thought of simply in terms of all the things which divide us from them, we suddenly find that we are members of one family, are united by deep but hidden bonds of faith and by a whole world of unsuspected shared experience. In this way we can gain a new and much larger vision of the Lordship of Christ and the Communion of the Holy Spirit. Those whom we had excommunicated have not fallen outside the action of God's healing grace. The interrupted circulation of life and love, of sympathy and understanding is restored between us. We discover anew something of the creative power of God's forgiveness.

These are themes which Father Hale presents to us in this attractive and encouraging book. It is a work which itself bears witness to this kind of creative interaction, this co-inherence between our two traditions. It reflects much coming and going between the traditions of Rome and Canterbury, of England and Italy. But it does this with a freshness and originality which owes something to the particular genius of California, and to the common life and prayer of Incarnation Priory to which the author belongs. It embodies in itself a remarkable blending of the old and the new, the traditional and the innovative. Thomas Merton, the foremost monastic writer of the English-speaking world in our century, speaks of the way in which men or women of prayer are called to unite within themselves the differing traditions of Christian East and West, of Spain and Russia, of England and Scandinavia, of Catholic and Evangelical. Dom Robert, we feel instinctively, is one who has done this very thing. In this book he helps us to allow that work of renewal and reconciliation to go on inside us and between us. From the inner work of reconciliation and unity, the outward reconciliation of our sister Churches can grow. And this rediscovery of unity will not be something which touches Anglicans and Roman Catholics alone. It is a part of a larger work of renewal and rebirth which will allow the whole Christian family to be in our age the sign and sacrament of a healed humanity. For opening this vision to us, and encouraging us to move towards it, we must be deeply grateful for the pages of this book

A. M. Allchin
Canon Residentiary of Canterbury Cathedral

Select Bibliography

(Except where otherwise indicated, place of publication is London)

Anglican Initiatives in Christian Unity: Lectures Delivered in Lambeth Palace Library 1966. SPCK, 1967.

Békés, Gerard, Vilmos Vajta, ed., *Unitatis Redintegratio 1964–1974: The Impact of the Decree on Ecumenism.* Rome Editrice Anselmiana, 1977.

Booty, John, *Three Anglican Divines on Prayer; Jewel, Andrewes and Hooker.* Massachusetts, Society of St. John the Evangelist, 1978.

Carpenter, Edward, *Cantuar: The Archbishops in their Office.* Cassell, 1971.

Clark, Alan C., Colin Davey, ed., *Anglican/Roman Catholic Dialogue: The Work of the Preparatory Commission.* Oxford University Press, 1974.

Curtis, Geoffrey, C. R., *William of Glasshampton: Friar, Monk, Solitary.* SPCK, 1978.

Documents on Anglican/Roman Catholic Relations. Washington, United States Catholic Conference Publications Office, 1972–1979.

Lambeth Essays on Unity: Essays Written for the Lambeth Conference 1968. SPCK, 1969.

Leeming, Bernard, S. J., *The Vatican Council and Christian Unity.* Darton, Longman & Todd, 1966.

Macquarrie, John, *Christian Unity and Christian Diversity.* Philadelphia, Westminster Press, 1975.

McAdoo, H. R., *The Spirit of Anglicanism: A Survey of Anglican Theological Method in the Seventeenth Century*. New York, Scribner's, 1965.

Moorman, J. R. H., *A History of the Church in England*. A & C Black, 1976.

More, Paul Elmer and Frank Leslie Cross, *Anglicanism: The Thought and Practice of the Church of England, Illustrated from the Religious Literature of the Seventeenth Century*. London, SPCK, 1962.

Neill, Stephen, *Anglicanism*. Mowbrays, 1977.

Pawley, Bernard and Margaret, *Rome and Canterbury through Four Centuries: A Study of the Relations between the Church of Rome and the Anglican Churches 1530–1973*. Mowbrays, 1974.

Quitslund, Sonya A., *Beauduin: A Prophet Vindicated*. New York, Newman, 1973.

Ramsey, Ian T., *Religious Language: An Empirical Placing of Theological Phrases*. New York, Macmillan, 1967.

The Report of the Lambeth Conference 1978. London, CIO Publishing, 1978.

Sykes, Stephen W., *The Integrity of Anglicanism*. Mowbrays, 1978.

Tavard, George, *The Quest for Catholicity: The Development of High Church Anglicanism*. New york, Herder, 1964.

Tavard, George, *Two Centuries of Ecumenism*. Indiana, Fides, 1960.

Thornton, L. S., C. R., *The Common Life in the Body of Christ*. Westminster, Dacre, 1944.

Thornton, Martin, *English Spirituality*. SPCK, 1963.

Wand, J. W. C., *Anglicanism in History and Today*. Weidenfeld and Nicholson, 1963.

Wright, J. Robert, ed., *A Communion of Communions: One Eucharistic Fellowship*. New York, Seabury, 1979.

Index

Aelred, Saint, of Rievaulx 149, 168n
Agreed Statements on Authority 31, 52n, 97, 103n
Agreed Statement on Ministry and Ordination 31, 116, 140n, 141n
Agreed Statement on Eucharistic Doctrine 7, 11nn, 31–2, 50n
Agreement of Bonn 135, 144nn
Aidan, Saint 82, 170n
Alban, Saint 105, 139n
Albert, Saint 124
Alcuin, Saint 88
Alexander, Neil 34–5, 51nn
Allchin, Canon Arthur Macdonald 8, 11n, 28, 30–1, 43, 50n, 54, 100n
Allin, Presiding Bishop John 33–4, 136
Anglican Orders 25, 135–7, 141n, 144nn
Anselm, Saint of Canterbury 46, 52n, 86, 170n, 175
Anson, Peter 91, 102n, 128
Anthony, Saint 154, 168n
Apostolicae Curae 132, 137
Appeal to All Christian People 101n, 132
ARC Consultation on the Religious Life 33, 50n, 128, 143n, 161–2, 168n, 170nn
ARC-USA 31–3, 50nn, 54, 63, 64, 160–1, 170n, 172, 173–4
ARCIC Consultations 7, 9, 31, 34, 50nn, 63–5, 70, 76–7, 140n, 141n, 150, 158, 162
Arrupe, Pedro 161
Athanasius, Saint 154, 168n
Augusta Marie, Sister 103n

Augustine, Saint, of Canterbury 21, 40–1, 45–6, 53n, 82, 84–6, 97, 115, 174–5
Auxerre, Monastery of 83

Banks, Robert 38, 51nn
BAY-ARC 159
Bea, Cardinal Augustin 11n, 23, 49n
Beauduin, Lambert 9, 11n
Becket, Saint Thomas, of Canterbury 106
Bede, Saint 49nn, 53n, 82, 86, 100nn, 101nn, 115, 170n, 175
Bell, Bishop George 11n, 12–13, 134, 144n
Benedict, Saint 49n, 53n, 114–15, 140n, 166, 170, 171n
Benedictine Spirit 25–6, 81, 86–7, 90–7, 108, 166, 172, 175–6
Benson, Richard M. 128
Berkeley, Bishop George 93
Bertha, Queen 105
Biscop, Saint Benedict 106
Black Death 89
Book of Common Prayer 59, 78n, 90–1, 120, 156–7, 175
Bouyer, Louis 40, 52n, 77n
Bramhall, Archbishop John 29, 50n, 92, 102n
Brent, Bishop Charles Henry 11n, 133, 145
British and Foreign Bible Society 128
Bultmann, Rudolph 34–5, 51n
Butler, Bishop Christopher 67–8, 78n
Butler, Bishop Joseph 55
Buxton, Thomas Fowell 124, 142n

Calati, Abbot Benedict 100n, 101n
Calvin, John 90
Camaldolese 103n, 147, 163, 166, 170n
Campbell, A. W. 91, 92, 102nn
Carolingian Reform 86
Carpenter, Canon Edward 53n, 110
Cassian, Abbot John 41, 157, 169n
Celestine, Pope 83
Celtic Christianity 41, 82–4, 115
Cerfaux, Lucien 35–7, 39, 51n, 52n
Chadwick, Owen 12–13, 47n, 48n, 169n
Christian Social Union 125
Christianity and Industrial Problems, Archbishops' Committee Report 125
Church Missionary Society 128
Civiltà Cattolica, La 19–20, 23, 49n
Clapham Sect 124, 128
Clark, Bishop Alan C. 11n, 49n, 63–4, 73, 76, 78nn, 79nn, 171n
Clement, Saint, of Rome 44, 53nn, 170n, 174
Cloud of Unknowing 59–60, 78nn, 156–7, 169nn
Coggan, Archbishop Donald 11n, 18, 23–4, 28, 131, 143n, 173
Columba, Saint 84, 86, 175
Common Declaration of Pope Paul VI and Archbishop Ramsey 7, 20, 22, 49nn, 57, 78n
Community of the Resurrection 93, 167, 171nn
Conference of Episcopal and Roman Catholic Leaders in the U.S. 33, 50n, 51nn
Congar, Yves 77n, 117–18, 141nn
Consider Your Call: A Theology of Monastic Life Today 103n
Cosin, Bishop John 92
Cousins, Ewert 11n
Couturier, Paul 77
Covenants 147–8, 170n
Cranmer, Archbishop Thomas 88, 91, 106, 121–2
Cromwell, Thomas 89
Cross and Dove 50n
Cudworth, Ralph 106
Curtis, Geoffrey 167, 171nn
Cuthbert, Saint 82
Cyprian, Saint 29, 174

Damian, Saint Peter 147, 168n
Dante 41, 52n
Dawson, Christopher 115, 140n

Declaration of Utrecht 134
Decree on Ecumenism, Vatican II 14, 42, 50n, 52n, 60, 62–6, 71, 72, 77n, 78nn, 129, 143n
de Mendieta, Emmanuel A. 120, 141n
Dissolution of the Monasteries 89, 101nn
Dix, Gregory 12, 95
Dodd, Charles H. 34
Dogmatic Constitution on the Church, Vatican II 42, 46, 49n, 51n, 98, 103n
Dominican Order 89, 150, 158
Downside Abbey 158
Dulles, Avery 9n
Duns Scotus, John 123
Dunstan, Saint, of Canterbury 86, 88

Ecumenical Trends 158, 169n
Ecumenical Vocation of Religious in Sister Churches 128, 143n
Edinburgh, Conference of 132
Edward, Saint 106
Edward VI, King 106
Edwin, King of Northumbria 105
Ekklesia 35–7, 39, 46
Eliot, Thomas Stearns 106
Elizabeth I, Queen, 15, 27
Elizabeth II, Queen 15, 48n
Elucidations of ARCIC 116, 140n
Ethelbert, Saint, of Kent 105
Ethelburga, Queen 105–6
Evelyn, John 92
Exsultet 59, 78n

Fellowship of St. Gregory and St. Augustine 95, 102n, 103n, 157, 159, 162, 169nn
Ferrar, Nicholas 126, 176
Fisher, Archbishop Geoffrey 12, 23–4, 28, 55, 77n, 134
Fitzmyer, Joseph A. 35–6, 51nn
Forty Martyrs of England and Wales, Canonization of 14–15, 48n
Franciscan Order 34, 89, 128, 141n, 142n, 143n, 150, 158, 161, 170n
Füglister, Notker 111–14, 139nn, 140nn

Gardiner, Robert H. 133
Garrett, Samuel 50n
Germanus, Saint 83, 105
Gore, Bishop Charles 124
Gregory I, Saint of Rome 16–17, 40–1,

43, 45–6, 49nn, 53n, 60, 82, 84–7,
100nn, 114, 174
Guild of St. Matthew 125
Guyon, Madame 154

Hale, Robert W. 10n, 103n, 140n,
142n, 168n, 170n, 171n
Halifax, Viscount, Charles Lindley
Wood 131–2, 148
Hanson, Professor Anthony 82, 100n
Headlam, Stewart 125
Henry VIII, King 81, 83, 88
Herbert, George 2–3, 92, 96, 126–7,
142nn, 169n, 176
Herr, Friedrich 89, 101n
Hill, Bishop Henry 158
Holy Cross, (Anglican) Order of 150,
163, 166, 168n, 170nn
Hooker, Richard 69, 142n
Hume, Cardinal Basil 4, 10n, 24–8, 31,
43, 50nn, 61, 72, 78n, 153–4, 168nn,
173
Huntington, James Otis 142n, 176
Huntington, William Reed 131, 176

Ignatius, Saint, of Antioch 44, 53nn,
174
Incarnation Priory 158, 163, 166,
169n, 170nn
Infallibility, Papal 65
Irenaeus, Saint 41, 45, 174

Jesuits 19, 158, 161
Jewel, Bishop John 122, 142nn
John XXIII, Pope 19, 23, 29, 67, 70,
76, 79n
John Paul II, Pope 15
Joint Blessing 20–3, 163, 171n
Johnson, Dr. Samuel 93

Kaufman, Gordon 11n
Keble, John 30, 50n, 176
Kemp, Bishop Eric W. 135, 144nn
Ken, Bishop Thomas 92
Klostermann, Ferdinand 117–18, 141nn
Koinonia 33, 97, 103nn, 146–9, 165,
168n, 178

Lambeth Conferences 19, 21, 70, 79n,
117, 125, 130, 143n, 176
Lambeth Quadrilateral 28, 130–1, 143n
Lanfranc, Archbishop of Canterbury
88
Latimer, Bishop Hugh 106

Laud, Archbishop William 28, 50n, 92
Law, William 127
Leander, Dom 95
Leclercq, Jean 5–6, 10n
Leech, Kenneth 155, 169n
Lefebvre, Archbishop Marcel 67
Lessard, Bishop Raymond W. 33
Ley, Benedict 95
Lichtenberger, Presiding Bishop
Arthur 136
Lightfoot, Bishop Joseph 113
Little Gidding 126
Liturgical Prayer 26, 165–7, 175–6
Lohfink, Norbert 107, 110, 139n
Lusitanian Church 135
Luther, Martin 90, 169n

McAdoo, Archbishop Henry Robert
70, 78n, 79nn, 130, 143n
Macaulay, Zachary 124
McHugh, J. Brian 147–8
McKenzie, John 112, 124, 140n, 142n
Macquarrie, Professor John 9, 11n, 40,
52n, 74, 79n, 82, 91, 99n, 102n
Malines Conversation 25, 95, 131,
140n, 148
Malta Report 50n, 66, 68, 72, 78nn,
79n, 151, 158–9, 164, 170n, 171n
Marian doctrines 65
Maurice, Frederick Denison 124
Mercier, Cardinal Désiré Joseph 11n,
95, 131, 148
Merton, Thomas 114
Metanoia 56–8
Meyvaert, Paul 16, 46, 49nn, 53n
Monastic Spirituality 81, 84, 90–1,
93–4, 96–7
Montini, Cardinal Giovanni-Battista
see Paul VI, Pope
Moorman, Bishop John R. H. 48n,
52n, 88–9, 100n, 101nn
More, Paul Elmer 8, 11n, 50n, 79n,
139n
More, Saint Thomas 58
Mortalium animos 13
Mother, Christ as 52n
Mother Church Model 38–42, 52n
Mudge, Bede Thomas 91, 93–5, 102nn,
103n, 170n
Mullaly, Lawrence 169n, 170
Mystery 8–9, 11n, 71–4

Nashdom Abbey 12, 26, 81, 95, 158
Neill, Bishop Stephen 41, 52n, 82, 84,

99n, 100n, 101nn, 119, 121–2,
132–6, 141nn, 142nn, 143nn, 144nn
Newman, Cardinal John Henry 70
Niermann, Ernst 119, 141nn
Ninian, Saint 82–3, 105
Noel, Conrad 125

Old Catholic Churches 133–6
Oliver, John 125, 142n
One in Christ 20, 49nn, 78n, 158,
170nn
Orthodox Churches 16–17, 30–1, 47,
153
Osgood, John 169n, 170n
Osservatore Romano, L' 11n, 20, 24,
49n, 143n

Pachomius, Saint 97, 103n
Pastor, Ludwig 110
*Pastoral Constitution on the Church in
the Modern World, Vatican II* 72
Patterson, Melville W. 87, 100n, 101nn
Patrick, Saint 83, 105
Paul VI, Pope 7, 9, 10n, 11n, 12–24,
26, 28, 31, 43, 48nn, 49n, 56–7, 77n,
78n, 131, 143, 147, 153, 172–4
Paulinus, Saint of York 106
Pawley, Archdeacon Bernard, and
Margaret 13, 47nn, 48n, 49n, 57,
77nn, 78n, 130–2, 143nn, 144n, 148,
168n
Pearson, Bishop John 37, 51n
Philippine Independent Church 135
Pluralism 41–2, 46–7, 49, 53n, 69–74
Pluscarden Abbey 158
Polish National Catholic Church 135
Portal, Ferdinand 131
Prestige, Leonard 12–13
Price, Mary R. 87, 101nn
Primacy of Pope 16–17
Prinknash Abbey 81
Priory of Our Lady 93
Prophetic Charism 106–39, 174, 177

Quitslund, Sonya A. 11n, 102n, 116,
131, 140n, 143n

Rahner, Karl 71–2, 79n, 107, 113,
139nn, 140nn
Ramsey, Archbishop Arthur Michael
6–7, 10n, 18–22, 28, 48n, 49n, 78n,
82, 147, 153, 172, 174
Ramsey, Bishop Ian T. 8, 10n, 11nn,
18, 55, 57, 77nn

Ramsgate Abbey 157
Rees, Daniel 97, 103n
Religious Tract Society 128
Reunion by Stages 64–9, 78nn
Richardson, Cyril C. 44, 53n
Ridley, Bishop Nicholas 106
Roach, Archbishop John 33
Runcie, Robert, Archbishop of
Canterbury 68, 78n, 79n, 137, 163
Ryan, Herbert J. 11n, 34, 52n, 138–9,
144n

St. Gregory's Abbey 93, 158
St. John's Abbey, Minnesota 158
St. Mark's Priory, Australia 93, 158
St. Mary's Abbey 93
St. Michael's Abbey 158
St. Paul's Episcopal Church, Rome 24,
42, 49
Sancroft, Archbishop William 92
Scarlett, Sir Peter 23
Schnackenburg, Fr. Rudolf 39, 51n,
52n
Shepherd, Massey H. 104n
Sister Churches 16–54, 61, 65, 68–9,
74–7, 85, 87, 99, 106–10, 116,
133–5, 139, 149, 151, 157, 165, 168,
170n, 173–4, 177–9
Slave Trade 123–4, 142n
Smythe, Harry 4, 10n, 14
Society for the Promotion of Christian
Knowledge 128
Society of St. John the Evangelist 93,
128
Society of St. Willibrord 135
Society of the Sacred Mission 93
Southey, Robert 93
Spanish Reformed Church 135
Spiritual Ecumenism 22, 150–8, 175–6
Staniforth, Maxwell 44, 53n
Suenens, Cardinal Léon-Joseph 68,
78n
Sykes, Stephen 138, 141n, 144n

Tablet, The 50n, 137, 144n
Taizé 163, 170n
Tardini, Cardinal Domenico 23
Tavard, George H. 82, 100n, 129,
143nn
Taylor, Bishop Jeremy 92
Temple, Archbishop William 28, 125,
134
Tertullian 41, 45, 53n, 174

Thérèse, Saint, of Lisieux 155–6, 168n, 169nn
Thomas Aquinas, Saint 123
Thorndike, Herbert 92, 102n
Thornton, Lionel S. 97, 103n
Thornton, Martin 81, 90, 96, 99n, 102
Tillard, Jean M. R. 65–78n, 96, 99, 103n, 150–2, 168nn, 175
Tyndale, William 106

Underhill, Evelyn 149, 168n, 176
Urban II, Pope 46
Utrecht, Church of 134, 144n

Vagaggini, Cipriano 5–6, 10n, 53n, 103n
Van Leeuwen, Bertulf 111, 139n, 140n
Vatican II 9n, 10n, 16, 25, 29–30, 37, 42–3, 46, 49n, 50nn, 51n, 52n, 53n, 57, 62–7, 71–3, 77nn, 78nn, 79nn, 98, 100n, 103n, 107, 139n, 140n, 141n, 143n, 153, 172, 175
Venn, John 124
Vita Monastica 100n, 103n, 140n, 142n, 168n
Vogel, Bishop Arthur A. 34

von Hügel, Baron Friedrich 149

Walton, Isaac 127, 142n
Ware, Archimandrite Kallistos 109, 139nn, 140n
Weil, Simone 51n, 155, 169n
Wesley, Charles 128
Wesley, John 128
Westcott, Bishop Brooke Foss 113
Whiteley, Denys Edward 37, 51nn
Whitelock, Dorothy 84, 100n
Widdrington, Percy 125
Wilberforce, William 124, 176
William I, King 88
William of Glasshampton (William Sirr) 142n, 143n, 167, 171n
Williams, Bishop Ronald Ralph 34, 51n
Willibrands, Cardinal Jan 24
Wordsworth, Bishop Christopher 134
World Conference on Faith and Order at Lausanne 134
World Council of Churches 133–4
Wright, J. Robert 34, 52n

Yarnold, Edward 136, 144n

Zabriskie, George 133